Hiding in the Open

The Library of Holocaust Testimonies

Hiding in
the Open

A Young Fugitive in
Nazi-Occupied Poland

ZENON NEUMARK

*To Barbara – a dear friend,
and in memory of Fred
– a friend and a co-worker
in KAWĘNCZYN, 1943.
With best wishes*

Zenon

VALLENTINE MITCHELL
LONDON • PORTLAND, OR

First published in 2006 by
VALLENTINE MITCHELL

920 NE 58th Avenue, Suite 300
Portland, Oregon 97213-3786

Suite 314, Premier House
Edgware, Middlesex HA8 7BJ

reprinted 2008

www.vmbooks.com

Copyright © 2006 Zenon Neumark

British Library Cataloguing in Publication Data

Neumark, Zenon
   Hiding in the open : a young fugitive in Nazi-occupied
   Poland. – (The library of Holocaust testimonies)
   1. Neumark, Zenon 2. Holocaust, Jewish (1939–1945) –
   Personal narratives 3. Jews – Poland – Biography 4. Poland
   – History – Occupation, 1939–1945
   I. Title
   940.5'318'092

ISBN 978 0 85303 633 3
ISSN 1363 3759

Library of Congress Cataloging-in-Publication Data

A catalog record has been applied for

Printed by Edwards Brothers Inc., Ann Arbor, MI

To the memory of my parents

Contents

List of Plates

The Library of Holocaust Testimonies

Ten years have passed since Frank Cass launched his Library of Holocaust Testimonies. It was greatly to his credit that this was done, and even more remarkable that it has continued and flourished. The memoirs of each survivor throw new light and cast new perspectives on the fate of the Jews of Europe during the Holocaust. No voice is too small or humble to be heard, no story so familiar that it fails to tell the reader something new, something hitherto unnoticed, something previously unknown.

Each new memoir adds to our knowledge not only of the Holocaust, but also of many aspects of the human condition that are universal and timeless: the power of evil and the courage of the oppressed; the cruelty of the bystanders and the heroism of those who sought to help, despite the risks; the part played by family and community; the question of who knew what and when; the responsibility of the wider world for the destructive behaviour of tyrants and their henchmen.

Fifty memoirs are already in print in the Library of Holocaust Testimonies, and several more are being published each year. In this way anyone interested in the Holocaust will be able to draw upon a rich seam of eyewitness accounts. They can also use another Vallentine Mitchell publication, the multi-volume *Holocaust Memoir Digest*, edited by Esther Goldberg, to explore the contents of survivor memoirs in a way that makes them particularly accessible to teachers and students alike.

Sir Martin Gilbert
London, April 2005

Acknowledgments

In the preparation of this manuscript I received much encouragement, advice and assistance from many: from my wife Irene and daughters Arianne and Kitty, from friends, and from professionals. Their help was much needed and is greatly appreciated.

A work colleague, Ray McCormack urged me for years to write down my wartime stories; a friend from my bridge club, Debra Stern, encouraged me to actually sit down and start writing; my daughter Kitty helped with my computer problems. I owe special gratitude to my old friend Jerome Janger for his wise counsel and continuous support. I also wish to thank those who were kind enough to review the manuscript and offer valuable critiques and comments.

Several provided professional editorial services. Charlotte Hildebrand edited my early drafts and put me on the right path, Linda Schubert provided copyediting, and Stephanie Chasin integrated and edited late rewrites. I also wish to thank Mark Anstee of Vallentine Mitchell Publishers for all his assistance in preparing the manuscript for publication. These editors, each at a different stage, contributed their skills to make my story more readable and grammatically correct.

I would like to acknowledge the help I have received from all the above and to all of them I extend a heartfelt THANK YOU!

Foreword

Zenon Neumark's book joins the many stories that have been told in recent years by younger survivors who used their youth as a weapon of survival and escaped into the 'Aryan' world.

These stories were told later than most Holocaust narratives, in part because their tellers had not yet reached the stage of their lives where there are few tomorrows and so many yesterdays; the time in life when one must look back with urgency, not knowing how long they will have the vigor required to write a book. But there is a deeper reason. For a long time the younger survivors of the Holocaust had their stories denigrated. Children survivors had their recollections dismissed. 'How much can you remember, you were but a child,' they were told. And those who survived in hiding had their recollections devalued for they had not lived through the Holocaust; they had escaped it by masquerading as someone else. Their stories were considered less instructive for they revealed less about life inside the extermination camps, less about the killers and more about ordinary life lived by ordinary people while extraordinary events were occurring elsewhere.

Still, these stories tell us what we need to know. They provide us the perspective of one who was both inside and outside and they give us all-important information about the civilian populations that lived their own lives throughout the war working, loving, enduring, and surviving. They didn't imagine the outside; they experienced it. They didn't project unto the native populations; they encountered them day in and day out, and their ability to 'read' the people they encountered was essential to their survival. They experienced those who were good, majestically good and those who were evil, demonically and irredeemably evil – and all those in between, who had moments of decency and weakness, and who were indifferent or cowardly or both.

Zenon Neumark writes with a unique sense of empowerment not often found in Holocaust literature; his story is profoundly unlike the stories told by other survivors. He took his fate into his own hands and he acted: escaping the ghetto, escaping the work camps, masquerading and working, holding on until the war ended. He knew that he had some major advantages. He was young and unburdened by old parents or young children; also unburdened by love for a woman. He was at that stage of life where he had the freedom to be concerned solely with his own survival.

He could pass. His appearance was not overtly Jewish. His Polish was fluent and without the mannerisms associated with Jewish culture and ethnicity. His parents spoke Polish at home. He had been friendly with Polish youngsters. He also had the daring of youth and the courage of youth. His daring and courage must be seen in a larger context. When the famed pediatrician, writer and radio personality Janusz Korczak marched with his orphanage to the Umschlagplatz, the deportation point in the Warsaw Ghetto, and refused entreaties that he escape the ghetto alone and seek sanctuary among Polish friends, his refusal to abandon the children was an act of courage no less great and no less admirable than the courage of the fighters who resisted. His ethics were so seamless – he was so much the teacher and doctor – that there was no decision to make. It took courage for fathers to stay with their children in the ghetto and for mothers to accompany their infants to the camps; it took no less courage for rabbis to continue teaching Torah, for the devout to pray, for physicians to continue to see patients. Courage took many forms and the courage to escape was one such form, a privileged form. Zenon did meet the test: he had the courage to endure the uncertainty of life in hiding.

Life was uncertain for all, but life on the outside was uncertain moment by moment, hour by hour, day by day. Meeting someone who once knew you, seeing someone familiar, could spell doom. Letting down your guard for a moment could mean a sentence of death. One had to have the skill to manage so many uncertainties and to deal with anxiety without betraying one's inner feeling. Zenon handled that anxiety well. Some retreated from that tension; they found it unbearable. He had to be daring and disciplined; cautious and yet reckless. He had to work to the limits of his ability and beyond those limits. And, like all survivors, he needed luck, which too came in so many forms. He recounts the machine that he fixed without knowing how to fix it; had it not started his lack of training would have been revealed. Zenon is grateful for that luck.

But survival depended on more than daring, courage or luck; it also depended on people. Some dissented from Nazism. Others merely wanted to make some money. Some valued friendship more than racist ideology; others were just decent men and women. Some in hiding were helped by those who did not notice that they were different; others assisted because they shrewdly wanted to position themselves for the post-war world where German defeat was all but certain. We meet all of these people in Zenon's memoir. His ability to understand them, their gifts and their limitations, was essential to his survival. Zenon rightfully resists the temptation to gloat over his decision to escape, or that he took his future into his own hands or that he risked his life to help others survive. And he does not judge the situation or the limitations of those left behind.

From reading this book we get a sense of the world before. We enter the ghetto and the work camp; we experience the Polish countryside and city; we go to Warsaw and Vienna. We live through the years 1941–45 and then experience the aftermath of survival, the journey home, the search for lost relatives, the realization that those whom one did not find were actually dead and the long journey toward freedom and life.

Zenon makes that journey interesting and unforgettable. He does not resort to fantasy or tales of fortune and daring. He reads himself and others cautiously though insightfully. So too, we should read his book.

Michael Berenbaum
Professor of Theology, University of Judaism
Los Angeles, California
June 2005

Introduction

For the past decade or so, stories relating to the Holocaust have been brought to prominence through numerous museums and memorial sites; through films, plays and other performance media; and through thousands of books. Historians have written about the horrors of the period; about acts of armed resistance, such as the heroic Warsaw Ghetto Uprising and the Jewish partisans; and about the decent and courageous Christian rescuers who saved thousands of Jewish lives. Survivors, meanwhile, have written memoirs about their suffering, their miraculous survival, and their successes in starting anew. While each survivor's story differs in its events and setting, most share a common denominator: their survival was due to forces and circumstances beyond the survivors' control. The majority of survivors made it through the war through a combination of mental fortitude, health and strength, or luck and happenstance. Mostly, however, they survived because the murderers simply ran out of time when the Allies overran the extermination camps.

Less well known are the stories about Jews who were active participants in their own survival: those who escaped a ghetto or a camp and survived as fugitives on the Aryan[1] side. Yet thousands did choose the escape path. Some bought their way out of the captivity and into a hideout; others, without sufficient means, relied on their own resourcefulness and took their chances. Historian Gunnar S. Paulsson estimates that in Warsaw alone, at one time or another, there were more than 28,000 Jews, living either in hiding or in the open but under assumed names, among the Polish population.[2]

This story of escape and survival is an account of my life and experiences as a Jewish teenager in Nazi-occupied Europe during the Second World War. It is about my escape from a small forced labor camp in Tomaszow Mazowiecki, Poland, and my life under false Polish Catholic identities, first in Warsaw and later in Vienna. It is a story about betrayal by friends and rescue by strangers, about living in constant fear of being recognized as a Jew and denounced to the Nazis, about the struggle to find lodging and work and efforts to blend in with the local population, and story of a double life working for opposing resistance groups and of opportunities to help others survive. During the Warsaw Uprising of 1944 I was recaptured and deported to a camp in Vienna where, after another escape, I found a job as an electrician in a Nazi-owned firm and a room with a family where the parents were secret Communists and their young son was a member of the *Waffen* SS. Finally, on 13 April 1945 Vienna was liberated by the Soviet Army and I could reclaim my true identity. I was free.

Escape to the Aryan side in Poland was neither simple nor easy, not for me and not for the thousands of others who managed to flee. It was hampered by a multitude of factors: risks and conflicts, fears and conflicts, and many preconceptions. But perhaps the biggest obstacle to taking this step was that for a long time and for most of us, the notion, the idea, of escaping hardly ever entered our thoughts. As the Nazis herded the Jews into ghettos and, later, labor camps, we did not know nor could we even imagine what the Nazis had in store for the Jewish people. We did not know what awaited us. Most people thought that it was a matter of weathering a bad storm, a question of enduring war-dictated hardships; we thought the war would be over within months. Some entrusted their fate to God and prayed for a miracle. Others just waited. As a result, most of us were slow in recognizing the danger to our very lives and hence a need for any action, including escape. Later, when we learned about the extermination camps, most people did not believe it, and when the truth was too real to be ignored, tragically, it was too late. Escape was then possible only rarely or not at all.

In contrast to the risks that escape represented, remaining in a ghetto or labor camp seemingly had its advantages: a sense of comfort derived from being with family and friends in the same situation; the minimum necessities to live; and the illusion that the Jewish Council (*Judenrat*) in the ghetto might provide a measure of protection or the hope that Jewish labor was of such value to the Nazis that they would spare our lives. There was solace in predictability and comfort in knowing where the next meal would come from or where one would spend the next night. Also, leaving behind spouses with children, younger siblings, or elderly parents was out of the question, it was unthinkable.

Those of us who did decide to escape faced a multitude of concerns and uncertainties. We had many questions with no answers. We worried obsessively over how the local population would receive us. Would it be safe to reveal to a former neighbor or even a friend that you planned to escape and ask for his or her help? Would they agree to help? How much support would you need from others after the escape in order to survive? When my money ran out, would I be able to get work without risking exposure? We all knew that there were risks and dangers. But how real were they? How real was the danger of being blackmailed, denounced, or killed?

Like many Jews, and especially because I was young, I knew little about the non-Jewish world around me. Because of centuries of anti-Semitism in eastern Europe and the consequent isolation of Jews from the rest of the Polish population, the Aryan side became unfamiliar and unknown, mostly perceived as an alien or outright hostile world. And as always, we fear the unknown, and we fear most what we know least.

Although the two communities had lived and worked together on the same land for centuries, they were often separate and distinct from each other in language, custom, and appearance. This was now significant. It led to a situation where many Jews lacked what were considered main prerequisites for blending with the Polish population: Aryan looks and demeanor, the ability to speak fluent and unaccented Polish, and contacts with friendly Poles. However, while these differences were valid and important, they were not absolute. I certainly did not meet all of the above requirements and I do not know of any other Jew on the Aryan side who did.

As I found out later, after my escape to Warsaw, German-occupied Poland was particularly fraught with dangers, even if one was Aryan-looking or spoke proper Polish. Strict laws and drastic punishments for disobedience ruled the country.

Escaping, residing outside the ghetto and possessing false identity papers were all crimes punishable by death. The same punishment applied to any Pole who hid, fed, sold food to, or assisted a Jew, and proclamations were plastered on the walls of Warsaw and in all other cities and towns to remind the population of the price they would pay for violating these laws. Thus, finding safe lodgings, establishing a support network, and just everyday living among the local population were daily, perilous challenges. There was a constant fear of being either caught by the Germans, or denounced to the authorities by the subservient Polish 'blue police', Polish fascists, collaborators of various nationalities, or just plain criminals. One particular group posed the most insidious and constant threat: gangs of blackmailers. Daily, they were on the lookout for Jews in hiding or those who lived submerged within the local population. Some were common criminals, others opportunists, corrupted by the war. They roamed the entire Polish countryside, big and small towns even villages, but were especially prevalent in Warsaw where most of the escapees chose to hide. They were our worst scourge.

Also, in Warsaw, besides being caught, betrayed or murdered as a Jew, one could easily be caught or killed as a Pole. Here, the Germans carried out frequent round-ups on the streets and searched homes for young Polish men to be used as hostages, and who were then often shot as retaliation for any and all acts of resistance against the occupation.

While the vast majority of Poles seemed indifferent to the plight of the Jews, and many were outright hostile toward them, there was also a measure of goodwill and compassion among many. There were thousands of individual Poles, including some who had been vocally anti-Semitic before the war, who, at great personal risk, helped thousands of Jews survive. Some help was also provided by organizations. There were several underground Jewish organizations in Poland that provided financial and other support to escapees, and there were even some Polish organizations, such as *Zegota* (the code name for RPZ, *Rada Pomocy Zydom*, Council to Aid Jews), dedicated to helping Jews in hiding.

My own experience with Christians on the Aryan side who knew or may have suspected that I was a Jew was, on the whole, more positive than negative. I found that despite the laws that prohibited their actions and despite the risks, there were people who were willing to help. I also found that life on the Aryan side, in general, including living conditions, work opportunities, and the blending with the population, was easier, and the chances for survival better, than my friends and I had anticipated when we were still in the ghetto. As I reflect now, with the benefit of hindsight, and as I recall believing then, many more people – including my parents, my relatives and my friends – could have been saved themselves had they taken the path of escape to the Aryan side. Not everyone would have survived, far from it, but at least their chances for survival would have been greater. Escape from ghettos and camps in Nazi-occupied Poland was a hard and dangerous choice and, at best, it was a choice for the few not for the masses. Yet the alternatives proved to be incomparably worse. We now know, from Paulsson's and Leo Cooper's estimates, that of the 28,000 Jews who hid in Warsaw, 41 percent survived the war, compared to approximately 3 percent, or less, of those who remained in the camps.[3]

In retrospect, I attribute my survival to a multitude of factors and situations. Fortuitous circumstances, planning combined with lucky choices, a youthful tendency to be daring, some recklessness, and some ingenuity – all contributed to my being saved. Above all, though, I ascribe my survival to incredible good luck and to meeting several compassionate and courageous people who were willing to help me.

I am writing this story primarily for my family and friends, and I am doing it now before the characters and emotions of those days fade from my memory and before the remaining yellowing pages of my wartime diary become totally illegible. I am also telling my story in the belief that each witness's testimony may shed a different light, add a new aspect, or offer a new perspective on events and people of this period, and that the cumulative total of these testimonies may contribute to a better understanding of the tragedy that befell the world during the Second World War.

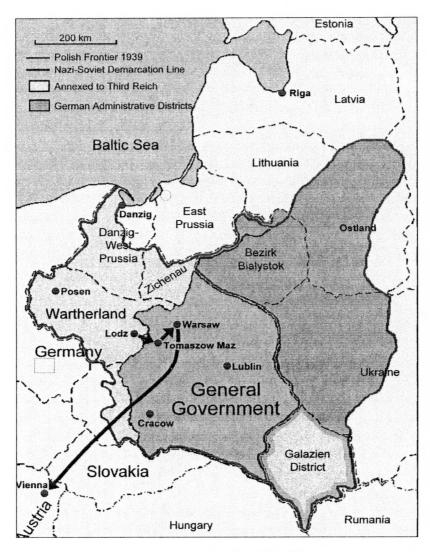

Poland under German Rule (1939–1944)

1 Leaving Home

The war broke out on 1 September 1939, and a few days later, the German Army occupied my hometown of Lódz (pronounced wooj), the second largest city in Poland, about 70 miles southwest of Warsaw. Before the war, Lódz was a major industrial city, about 750,000 in population, manufacturing primarily high-quality textiles; a thriving, vibrant city sometimes called the Manchester of Poland, after England's textile center. About half of the city's residents were Polish, one-third were Jewish, 10 percent were ethnic Germans, and the remainder were Ukrainians and other minorities.

Lódz, as I remember it, was never beautiful. It was gray and drab, with only a few large, ornate buildings, few historical monuments, and only three or four large parks. The most distinctive structures in its skyline were very tall, blackened brick chimneys spewing dark gray smoke. While the city had an extensive tramway system as well as buses, cars, and taxis, I remember more vividly horse-drawn wagons for transporting various goods, and dorozki, old-fashioned horse-drawn carriages. The wagons and carriages competed with the motorized vehicles for the limited space on the narrow city streets, while building concierges, as part of their job and much to their chagrin, constantly collected the horses' droppings.

My memories of living as a youth in Lódz are happy ones. I was surrounded by a warm and loving family: my mother, Bronia my father, Feliks and my sister Rena, who was two years older than I, plus some aunts, uncles, and cousins. I also had many friends, mostly schoolmates. My life centered on my education, a prime concern of my parents, and was complemented by a few outside activities: occasional sports, such as ice skating in the winter and swimming in nearby lakes in the summer, and several hobbies, such as collecting stamps and butterflies or building model airplanes, model steamboats, and crystal radios. Like most boys my age, I was fascinated by fire trucks, especially by the fireman in the passenger seat who would announce the emergency by playing a trumpet with one hand and ringing a bell with the other. I would often run after the trucks until I was completely out of breath.

Our middle-class milieu was typical of the time and place: our living conditions were modest and lacked many conveniences such as a refrigerator, a telephone, central heating, or elevators, but my sister and I attended private high schools, our family spent our holidays in the countryside every summer, and we always had a maid. Our last holiday before the war started was spent in Sokolniki, a small but beautiful and serene resort some ten miles north of Lódz, in a rented two-story villa, surrounded by beds of colorful flowers in the midst of several acres of birch forest. The owner of the villa, a police captain, rented it out for the summer while he and his family stayed in a small guesthouse.

Culturally, we were both Polish and Jewish. My parents felt a strong bond to our Jewish identity, traditions and heritage, but my sister and I spoke only Polish and studied almost exclusively Polish history and literature. Nonetheless, I would sometimes accompany my parents to a theater: the last show I saw was a Jewish musical comedy titled *Yidl mitn Fidl*, featuring two noted comics, Dzigan and Schumacher; it was performed in the city's largest theater, the Philharmonic Hall on Narutowicza Street. As for religious activities, my parents had rather tenuous ties to Judaism; my father and I attended the city's main synagogue only once a year, for the Jewish High Holidays. Politically, my father was a democrat and a Zionist. In terms of nationality, my family felt Polish with Jewish ethnicity and believed themselves to be as loyal and patriotic citizens of Poland as any non-Jewish Pole. Although my parents knew Yiddish, they used it only when speaking with my grandparents or when they did not want my sister and I to understand. At home we spoke only Polish.

Even as a child, I was aware that there was anti-Semitism in Poland, either by hearing it discussed at home or, when I got older, by reading about it in the newspapers. In 1936 and 1937, I read about pogroms in the small town of Przytyk and a couple of other towns; I was also well aware of the Numerus Clausus at all Polish universities, a limit in the admittance of Jews to these universities, with consequent boycotts of classes by Jewish students and frequent fights with the Polish students. I was also aware that only a token number of Jewish students were admitted to state gymnasiums, which had very high standards and were free. Finally, I was aware of the '*Bojkot, owszem*', the officially sanctioned economic boycott of Jewish businesses, proclaimed in the Polish Parliament by the last prewar prime minister of Poland, Slawoj-Skladkowski, in 1938.

However, my direct exposure to these various forms of discrimination was limited and inconsequential, as the environment in which I lived was predominantly Jewish. In my high school, Szwajcera Gymnasium, only a few employees and two teachers (one an ethnic Ukrainian) were Gentiles, and all the students were Jewish. At home, the few neighborhood friends I had were Jewish. My parents had some non-Jewish acquaintances and my father had Gentile business associates, but my direct contacts with ethnic Poles were limited to our maids, who were mostly country women, and people I met outside my home in city-wide school events, on summer holidays, or during frequent visits to my grandparents in the town of Tomaszow Mazowiecki.

I remember one instance of personal anti-Jewish discrimination, when a friend of mine and I wanted to learn how to swim better and decided to join the local YMCA, the only youth club in town with a covered swimming pool. They signed us up, but on our second visit, we were told that the directorate had not approved us. No explanations were

3

offered, but the reason was clear: we were Jewish. (They deduced it, most likely, from the combination of our school affiliation and our names.) There were also many shops in town with big signs on the doors proclaiming them 'Christian Stores', implying that Jews were not welcome, and there were graffiti on walls and buildings with the recommendation 'Do Not Buy From Jews'. There were other derogatory slogans, some with political content but many anti-Semitic, scrawled at tram stops, on benches in parks, or in public toilets.

From the very beginning of German occupation, the walls of the city were plastered with official proclamations in German and Polish announcing a variety of restrictions and the particular punishments for noncompliance with the new laws. The penalty for many violations was death. New restrictions were added regularly, and each affected our daily life a little more: each added a little more pain and each was more severe than the preceding one. It was a tactic we called 'slicing the salami': each day another slice of our freedom was taken away.

Some orders applied to the population at large, but most were intended only for Jews: all Jews had to wear armbands with the Star of David; Jewish secondary schools were closed (later, in most ghettos, that was also true of the elementary schools); businesses were either shut down or forcibly transferred to Aryan ownership; bank accounts were frozen and assets confiscated. I still vividly remember helping my father carry a large Philips radio console to a collection center when the possession of radios became illegal. I also remember standing in line at a bank to exchange 2,000 Bank Polski zlotys, the maximum allowed per person, for new, Bank Emisyjny zlotys. When my sister Rena took 2,000 zlotys to another bank, she came home crying. As she stood in line, a young German soldier had approached, flirted with her for a few minutes and then offered to carry out the exchange for her, bypassing the line. After taking her money, he disappeared, and she never saw him or the money again.

At home, we built special storage shelves and hiding places

and started to gather food. One day, my father arranged to have an enormous barrel of salted herring delivered to our home; he remembered that during the First World War, salt became a scarce commodity. Another day, several cases of Wedel chocolate bars were delivered; I guess there was then also a shortage of sugar and sweets. Both supplies came in handy but did not last long.

Within a month or two of the occupation of Lódz, random beatings in the streets, nightly arrests, and sudden disappearances, especially of prominent community leaders, became commonplace. Punishments ranged from fines to torture and execution. To show they were serious about the new edicts, the Nazis picked up three Jewish men at random and hanged them from specially erected gallows at the Baluty Market, one of the city's public squares. As part of the escalating campaign of terror and as a warning, their bodies were left hanging for several days. I visited the macabre scene, and as I gazed, revolted, at the lifeless bodies of these innocent men, I felt, for the first but not the last time, an ice-cold fear in the pit of my stomach.

In late September 1939, my school opened its doors for only one day to announce its 'temporary' closure in accordance with the new German edict that all secondary schools must be closed immediately. The school director gave a speech to the assembled students, encouraging us to pursue our education elsewhere, wherever and whenever possible. 'Till we see each other again,' he concluded, his voice trembling with emotion. Neither he nor any of us imagined that this would be the last time we would ever see each other. Distraught, I returned home in tears.

Expecting that worse was still to come, my parents decided it would be wise for the family to move to Tomaszow, my mother's hometown, located in a semirural area about 40 miles from Lódz. In a large two-story house surrounded by a front yard, a vegetable garden on the side, and a fairly large field of arable land at the back, lived my 92-year-old maternal grandfather, three aunts, Rena, Rachela, and Celina, and a 10-year-old cousin named Olek. Their house, situated at the edge of the town, allowed easy contact with the nearby farms and small villages where food could be purchased outside the ration card system. I had visited my grandfather in the past, usually with my sister during the summer holidays or for family gatherings, and enjoyed the fresh air and the beautiful fields and forests that surrounded his property.

In November 1939, two months after the war began and three months after my fifteenth birthday, I boarded a rented truck that was to take me to my grandfather in Tomaszow. I took all my possessions with me, along with as many house-hold goods as the hired truck could carry. My parents and my sister, together with the rest of the household, were to follow shortly. But they kept postponing their departure. It must have been very painful and difficult for my parents to abandon what they had built over two decades: a home and business, a circle of relatives, friends, and neighbors. But there were other reasons for the delay. My father, a wise man with extensive war experiences in Russia and Germany during the First World War – he was a veteran who spent four years fight-ing with the Russian Army and then an additional three years in a German prisoner-of-war camp – had predicted that the war would last much longer than people expected and hence thought that there was little need to hurry with the planned move. While his prediction on the length of the conflict had been correct, he had grossly misjudged the attitudes and the plans of Nazi Germany. He did not anticipate either the oppressive rule that the Nazis would impose on Poland with special persecution of the Jews, or the terrifying nightmare that this war would turn into.

That November I said goodbye to my parents and my sister and left my hometown. At my grandfather's house in Tomaszow, I began a long wait for them to join me.

2 Tomaszow

In Tomaszow, I quickly realized that I was the de facto head of the household, with more duties and responsibilities than I had ever thought possible. Almost without noticing, I had moved from boyhood to adulthood. It was not an easy task for a 15-year-old 'big city' boy who, up to now, had led a sheltered, carefree life and whose only responsibility had been to be a good student in school and to keep good company outside of it.

Tomaszow was a quaint, small textile town on the Pilica River, with a population of about 60,000, where the Polish Catholic majority and the Jewish and *Volksdeutsche*⁴ minorities had lived and worked harmoniously for decades. Although most of the people I came in contact with were Jewish, my best friend during the early months of the war was Mirek Stec, the son of a Polish father and a *Volksdeutsche* mother. We were next-door neighbors and spent entire days together, either in his large backyard competing in various sports – we improvised all of the track and field events of the Olympic Games – or in each other's houses, playing games and discussing books we had read. We also lamented the Nazi occupation of our homeland and wondered how we could fight the oppressor. (During the second year of the war, in mid-1941, life changed for all of us: my family and I moved into the ghetto; Josef Stec, the father, was sent to a concentration camp; the mother signed the *Volksdeutsche* list; and Mirek joined the *Hitlerjugend*.) We were brought together by the fact that his father was the principal of Elementary School No. 6, where my Aunt Rena was a teacher. The Stec family resided on the school premises.

The winter of 1939–40 was bitterly cold. The temperature dropped as low as –15°F, causing our water pipes to freeze. Two or three times a day, I had to carry buckets of water from an artesian well half a block away, and by the time I got home the upper layer of the water's surface had frozen solid. Another of my daily tasks was to chop wood each morning for our wood-burning stove. I was also the one who stood in line for bread, margarine, or soap. There was a lot of pushing and shoving in these lines, because even though we all had ration cards, there was never enough to go around.

During the first months, though life was difficult and challenging, it was bearable. We had enough food for regular meals, most utility services were available, and there were no major physical restrictions on our daily movements. The only notable changes to our lives were a general curfew and the requirement that in public Jews wear a white armband with a Star of David. Otherwise, during the day people would meet with relatives and friends, read books, or engage in endless discussions of current events. Sometimes we traveled to nearby villages or towns to supplement whatever food or other products were not obtainable on ration cards. I felt completely unprepared for my new role but generally content, expecting my parents and sister to join me shortly. In the meantime, my family and I corresponded at least twice a week, exchanging greetings and keeping each other informed about the deteriorating situation in both towns.

But within weeks after my departure, major changes occurred in Lódz: the city was renamed Litzmannstadt and was incorporated, with its surrounding area, into the Third Reich. Most importantly, there were new German restrictions for the Jews, including among them that all travel out of the city was prohibited. Gradually, I lost communication with my parents. At first, the frequent correspondence dwindled to an occasional, pre-printed, signed postcard reporting, 'All is well here, wish the same for you.' Then, the transfers of money, which I was getting once a month, became erratic and finally stopped. It became increasingly apparent that, at least for the time being, I would have to take charge of my future and start making my own decisions much sooner than I had planned.

The first decision I made under these new circumstances regarded the continuation of my education. In Tomaszow, as elsewhere, clandestine classes were being held for about eight to ten students per class at private homes in the evenings. We had lectures and homework, and we studied using old textbooks, but of course there were no school facilities. In addition, since curfew was at 9 p.m., the study sessions were short.

The school lasted only a few weeks, however. One night, our group was leaving one of the homes when it was met by a bunch of uniformed *Hitlerjugend*, thugs from the local German youth organization, armed with pipes, chains and sticks. A fight ensued and, I'm sorry to say, we lost. Bloodied, with our books and notebooks stuffed under our coats, we eventually managed to escape into the night. But this incident marked the end of the clandestine schooling, as no parent was willing to host such classes. It also marked the end of my secondary education. My only alternative was to enter the work force.

Ten months after moving to Tomaszow, at the age of sixteen, I went to work for a local construction company, whose super-intendent was a friend of my Aunt Rena, a man named Mr Sowinski. He was a tall, broad-shouldered man who projected physical strength and authority. Aryan firms were prohibited from employing Jews except under special circumstances, when particular qualifications were indispensable, which, of course, was not my case. But Mr Sowinski accepted the risk and hired me out of friendship for my aunt. As it was illegal for me, as a Jew, to be employed there, each day when I left for work, I took off my armband and took on the identity of a Catholic Pole. I had to be careful not to be recognized by anyone who knew me as a Jew, as they might give me away. It helped that I was a newcomer to the town, so not many people knew me; besides, conscious of who I was, I worked hard at being inconspicuous, staying on the sidelines and avoiding idle conversation with my co-workers, who only knew me by my first name, Zenon, a Polish name.

The construction company employed me for more than a year. Working for this Aryan firm, located close to the edge of town, had advantages beyond its wages. Because of its location, I was able to barter directly with peasants from the nearby villages, buying food or trading household items in exchange for food.

I performed a variety of jobs, from digging ditches and laying foundations to painting and roofing the finished structure. One of my first jobs was assisting bricklayers by carrying mortar and bricks up the scaffold and loading and unloading 100lb cement sacks. The work was demanding and hard, but I was young, healthy, and eager to learn new trades.

After a few months, during the winter of 1940–41, the firm assigned me to its ice retrieval and storage project. Because home refrigeration in Tomaszow consisted of iceboxes, it was necessary to store pieces of ice during the winter for distribution in the summer. The ice was retrieved from nearby frozen lakes and transported to a storage facility, a specially built pit. The storage site was located in the backyard of a large apartment building on Krzyzowa Street, close to the center of town. The pit was a 40×40-foot hole in the ground, four stories deep, with a low, inclined roof about three feet above ground at the edges. There were three or four small openings between the roof and the ground through which the ice pieces were tossed into the pit. The stairway to get inside the pit was a rickety, wooden scaffold that looked like a zigzagging ladder in a chicken coop.

For the first part of the job, we stood in the middle of the frozen lake and broke the layer of ice into pieces; we then carried the pieces to the waiting trucks. At first, the ice we stood on was dry, but as the hole in the ice grew bigger the water from underneath rose up and spread over the surface, so that, after a few hours, we were walking in up to two inches of ice-cold water. This task was followed by a half-hour ride to the Krzyzowa facility, sitting on the ice pieces. That, plus the low winter temperatures and the windchill, turned us into human icicles by the time we arrived. The job was tough and could also be dangerous. One afternoon, one of our co-workers slipped and quickly slid into the ice-cold lake. Frantically, he shouted for us to help him, but despite our efforts we were unable to save him. We watched helplessly as he disappeared under the freezing water. The company notified his family, but that was all. The next day a new employee took his place.

The second part of my job was to stand at the bottom of the pit and break the incoming blocks of ice into smaller pieces; then, using a heavy mallet (a large tree trunk with a handle-bar attached to it), pound layer upon layer of ice into the rising floor. Sawdust was spread between the layers of ice to prevent the pieces from adhering to each other. The pit was almost completely dark, lit only by one small electric light bulb, and the temperature was always below freezing and the humidity constantly high.

This work was hard and monotonous. I worked 10 to 12 hours a day, usually with one other person. My shoes and feet were always cold and wet, and chills penetrated my body to the bone. I went home so cold and tired that I would lie down just for a short rest, without taking off my clothes, too exhausted even to eat dinner, only to wake up the next morning in time for a new day's work. Needless to say, only the very strong and very healthy survived these conditions for more than a month or two. Although I was young, strong, and healthy, I still had to ask for a reassignment.

My new assignment was another construction job that took me to Ujazd, a little town about ten miles from Tomaszow. I was brought there by truck each morning and returned home to Tomaszow in the evening. The construction site, an area about a mile square, was located in the midst of a densely wooded forest next to a railroad siding. There were all kinds of buildings being erected, barracks and permanent brick structures. I was back working as a bricklayer's helper, once again carrying bricks and mortar up the ladder. Polish workers under German supervision did most of the work, although some work was also done by German paramilitary personnel from the Org. Todt.[5]

11

I was still working there in the summer of 1941, when, after the start of the conflict between Germany and Russia, the construction site became a transit camp for Russian prisoners of war. The prisoners arrived in cattle cars in ever-greater numbers, thousands upon thousands. Some of the prisoners were assigned to work with us, and, with this daily contact, I began to pick up some Russian vocabulary. The big problem, however, was that this site was in no way prepared to house and feed such a large number of prisoners: there was little food available; the water, obtained from a few hand-operated pumps on top of the wells, was insufficient; there were hardly any barracks or tents for the prisoners to sleep in; and, finally, the prisoners had no hygienic facilities.

The captured soldiers were imprisoned here in the middle of nowhere and left to fend for themselves. Within weeks, even days, we encountered sick, starving, and dead prisoners when we arrived for work in the morning. The bodies were scattered everywhere and the stench was unbearable. This was my first personal experience of Nazi Germany's inhumanity to man on a large scale. In Ujazd, thousands, if not tens of thousands, of Russian prisoners starved to death and were then buried in mass graves.

Yet as brutal as the Germans were everywhere, including Ujazd, I experienced, quite by accident, a dose of human kindness from one of these Germans that made an indelible mark on my thinking and even on my character. Paul Biebow, a middle-aged paramilitary man who was my supervisor, liked to engage me in short conversations. We spoke in German, as I had studied it in school and had heard my father, who was fluent in the language, speak it often at home with a couple of his friends. At first, Mr Biebow would start the conversation with a question about my family or me, or on a more general subject, such as our accommodation in Tomaszow. When he found out that my parents were in Lódz, he wanted to know about them and why we were separated. 'When was the last time you saw your parents?' he would ask, or 'Have you heard from them?' I answered in my broken German, wondering why someone was taking such a personal interest in me.

Soon this developed into something of a father–son relationship. Every day, as I arrived at the compound with a group of other workers, he stood in the doorway of his office building and called out for me to join him. Once there, he would take me to a dark corner of the hallway, out of sight of the others, and fill my pockets with a variety of items: a can of food, a chocolate bar, or cigarettes. One day, I mentioned casually that I had a toothache. The next morning he had money ready for me with 'instructions' to see a dentist immediately. Initially, I was wary of associating with a German, but, eventually, I looked forward to both our conversations and the gifts.

After a time, his kindness prompted me to reveal my true identity and my illegal status in Ujazd to him. Unaware of the risks of doing so, I assumed that he was a friend and, therefore, could be trusted. My instinct, fortunately, turned out to be correct, and our relationship continued as before. Although I was too shy to ask him directly, I often wondered why he was being so kind to me. The only clue he ever gave me was when he mentioned that one of his sons, a boy approximately my age, was fighting on the Russian front. Perhaps by his kindness to me, he was hoping that someone in Russia would be as compassionate to his son. Perhaps he was just a good man.

By the end of August 1941, after having worked illegally for more than a year, going to work for the construction company and pretending to be a Pole became too dangerous. The Jewish quarter, which had been a largely ill-defined ghetto, was becoming more and more closely guarded. The Jewish Order Police and German police with dogs were posted at strategic points; leaving the area without the armband or without authorization could mean death. I now had no other option but to quit my job.

Within four months, the Jewish quarter of Tomaszow was transformed into a closed, walled ghetto. Shortly thereafter, the entire Jewish population of Tomaszow, about 13,000 in total, was forced to find accommodation within this quarter, a small and impoverished area, already overcrowded, with many wooden houses and no running water. A few houses and apartments were vacant because the Polish inhabitants had been forced to move out of the area. In many cases, people were assigned to move in with relatives and friends or to sublet.

The allocation process was harrowing. Everyone wanted larger and better quarters, and everybody felt more deserving than the next person. People quarreled with the members of the Jewish Council, with the Jewish Order Police, and, most of all, with each other. Sometimes there were physical fights to prevent allocations from being carried out. The best accommodation went to relatives and friends of the council members, to other people with influence, and to those who knew how and whom to bribe. I did not count much at all because I was an outsider. In the end, my grandfather, aunts, cousin and I had to move from our big, comfortable two-story house to two small one-bedroom apartments. I stayed in one of them with my Aunt Rena and cousin Olek.

When I could no longer sneak out or be seen outside the ghetto without the required armband, I looked for and soon found work inside it as a carpenter. I hardly knew what carpentry was all about, but luckily the requirements to prove one's qualifications were very lax. My new job with the Org. Todt, near Polna Street, paid me a small salary and, even more importantly, provided a measure of safety. When requested, the Germans of the Org. Todt issued an employment certificate that protected the bearer from being assigned to a forced labor battalion.

Life in the ghetto grew increasingly worse. Food supplies were meager. People lived from hand to mouth, never knowing where their next meal was coming from, and many began to die from malnutrition. To supplement the food obtained on ration cards, people, including my family, sold personal and household possessions and made purchases on the flourishing black market. I did not know the financial state of my relatives, but apparently we could afford the supplements. I have no idea how the black market managed it, but almost anything was available, and some very rare items, like coffee beans or tobacco, were found more easily inside the ghetto than outside. There were a few instances when German supervisors at work, through a Jewish intermediary (and on occasion I was that intermediary), purchased coffee beans or tobacco for shipment to their families in Germany.

Another source of supplemental food was the packages from relatives abroad that we were allowed to receive in the early months of the war. Wonderfully nutritious and scrumptious packages came to us from Vilno, Lithuania (annexed then by Russia), from my Aunt Rena's husband, Julian. Three of my uncles, Julian, Henryk (my aunt Marysia's husband), and their brother-in-law Max, had fled to Russia when the war broke out.[6] They were among the tens of thousands of other Jewish men, mostly young or middle-aged, who had crossed over to Russia to avoid becoming forced laborers for the Nazis. Packages weighed up to ten kilos and contained a myriad of food items, such as smoked meats and bacon, canned foods, bars of chocolate, and biscuits. Sometimes there were even lemons and oranges, items unavailable in the ghetto. Similar packages, but fewer, arrived from our Uncle Enrico in Italy. Enrico, my mother's brother, emigrated to Italy after the First World War where he became a successful businessman in the film industry. At the start of this war and because he was still a Polish citizen he was interned in a camp for enemy nationals. But what a different camp it must have been, for him to be able to send packages full of delicacies to us!

A few days before Christmas 1941, the German who had befriended me at the labor camp, Mr Biebow, unexpectedly came to the ghetto gate, requested that a Jewish policeman on guard find me, and then delivered an enormous Christmas package that had been prepared by his wife, back in Germany. It was brimming with canned food, homemade cookies, and even winter clothing. I was completely overwhelmed by this kind gesture and extremely grateful for the contents. For a uniformed German to bring to the gates of a ghetto a package with food provisions was an extraordinarily courageous act,

15

an act that restored in me some measure of faith in humanity.

As conditions deteriorated, it was not long before a typhus epidemic swept through the ghetto, felling dozens of people daily, including my grandfather. He was admitted to the hospital, but we were not allowed to visit him, as the hospital was quarantined. His daughters bribed the nurses to deliver to him some of his favorite dishes in the hope that the home cooking would help him recover his health. Invariably, the nurses came back telling us how much he enjoyed the food and that he had asked for more. And so we sent more. In spite of his advanced age, my grandfather got better and was released. It was only then that we learned that he had never tasted, or even seen, any of his favorite dishes; the nurses, not expecting him to live and tell, had consumed every meal that we had sent to the hospital. A few days after his release my grandfather died, at the age of 94. Out of 30 family members who died during the war, he was the only one who died of natural causes.

It was not only drastic food shortages and disease that made life in the ghetto so chaotic and perilous. My memory of the men rounded up in Lódz and hanged on the gallows was revived as random executions started to occur, mostly targeting the so-called intelligentsia: teachers, doctors, lawyers, and engineers, i.e. those perceived by the Germans as potential organizers and leaders of a resistance. Once, in the middle of the night, I was awakened by gunshots. In the morning, on my way to work, I saw the results: several bodies lying motionless on the pavement near my house, in pools of blood. My heart seemed to stop beating for a second as I realized that I recognized three of the victims. Two of them were brothers, both lawyers, by the name of Hirschbrung. The third was the son of one of the lawyers. I later learned from witnesses that when the Gestapo agent had come to take the men away, the son ran after him, begging him not to kill his father. That is when the son, too, died.

But regardless of my sorrow, it was too dangerous to show any sympathy for the victims. My stomach churning, I, like the few other passersby, simply crossed the street and continued to my workplace as if the bodies did not exist; I was numbed by helplessness.

In spite of the ever-increasing restrictions, constant abuses, deprivation, and suffering, most of the inhabitants in the ghetto attempted to make the best of a bad situation. Unable physically to resist, people showed a remarkable moral defiance through their composure and resilience. Life moved on. In the first and second year after the ghetto was formed, we all tried hard to maintain some semblance of normalcy.

To alleviate some of the gloominess in our lives, we sought refuge in self-organized entertainment and cultural activities. Discussion and reading groups were formed, lectures were given, and budding intellectuals organized an amateur theater. This latter group performed their own satirical sketches, poking fun at themselves and those around them, at our own ghetto leaders and sometimes, in a subtle way, ridiculing our oppressors. A young man with straight blond hair and deep greenish eyes, Adas Lichtenstein, was a major contributor to the literary and theatrical evenings. Highly intelligent and talented, he wrote satirical sketches, poems, and song parodies.

People wrote poems and songs, exhibited their paintings, and engaged in political debates. We had political groups covering the entire gamut of opinions, from left to right. More often, for entertainment, the younger people gathered in the evening in someone's home and, accompanied by an instrument such as a guitar, sang Yiddish or Polish songs, both old and new. Sometimes, if enough people knew the words, we sang Russian songs or, sometimes, even German, such as 'Unter die Laterne' ('Lili Marlene'), popularized by Marlene Dietrich and heard on a clandestine radio.

Participation in these illegal activities made us feel that even if we were physically oppressed, in spirit we had been neither subjugated nor defeated. With time, all these activities ceased, as did the receiving of food packages. Like Pavlov's gradual conditioning of animals, each day brought a new restriction, a diminishing supply, one more turn on the tightening screw. In every way, we had too much to starve, but not enough to live.

17

3 Akiba Cell

One spring evening in 1941, before the Jewish quarter in Tomaszow had been turned into a closed ghetto, Tusia Fuchs came to visit me. It was her first such visit and an unexpected one.

A classmate in the clandestine school I had attended, Tusia was a plain, intelligent, vivacious, and an unusually well-read girl, and she quickly explained the purpose of her visit: an invitation to a secret meeting of young people to be held the following Sunday in an abandoned garden shack on Krzyzowa Street. She didn't tell me the purpose of the meeting, who the other participants were, or what to expect. But, intrigued by the mystery and secrecy surrounding the invitation, I agreed to go.

Twelve of us attended: six boys and six girls, all between the ages of 15 and 18. I soon learned that the common characteristics of the participants were that we were all young and healthy, spoke unaccented Polish, and had no discernible Semitic features; we also were all known to be trustworthy and eager to take some action against our situation. The importance of language and physical appearance soon became clear: one of the main goals of the group was to escape from the ghetto and blend in with the Polish population at large. We planned either to join the underground resistance movements that were forming in the cities and forests of Poland or to try to survive under assumed identities. In either case, escape was possible only for those who could pass as Gentiles. I was invited to join the group primarily because I met these requirements; as I was new in town, most of the others did not know much else about me.

The group called itself Akiba,[7] and its main objectives were resistance, defiance, and survival through active effort and self-reliance – anything but passive submission and compliance. Our leader and organizer was Yitzhak Rosenblat, a likeable 18-year-old redhead, slightly built, with a light complexion and freckles. He limped as a result of childhood polio, but despite his physical limitations he had all the makings of a born leader. He was mild-mannered, but intelligent and articulate, clearly possessed of a strong character. Yitzhak inspired in us trust and confidence. Most importantly, he inspired us to action.

The members of the group ranged across the political spectrum in their views and so did the discussion topics. During our weekly meetings, we discussed the progress of the war and the latest German victories. We talked about the increasingly oppressive measures across occupied Poland and the particularly bad situation in the ghetto. We tried to extrapolate from the current state of affairs what might happen next and what should be done to prevent it. Some of us doubted that anything could be done. One girl wondered how God could have allowed this terrible situation to happen. Another boy philosophized that Jews had always been persecuted, that they had survived many misfortunes before, and they would survive this adversity too. Others reaffirmed their dream to go to Palestine. 'War or no war,' one young boy told the group, 'we must work towards building a Jewish state.' An ardent Zionist, he held up this goal like a beacon to be followed at every meeting.

Still others discussed how, after we made our escape, we could join the partisans in the woods or cross the border into Russia, where presumably we would be safe. Though Russia was allied with Germany at that time and was considered an enemy of Poland, the Russians were known not to single out Jews for discrimination. During the early months of the war, the Russians allowed tens of thousands of Jews to cross from German-occupied Polish territory to that occupied by the Soviets, as my uncles had done. Despite the fact that we had nothing solid to support such plans, we thought that these were real options. We were young and inexperienced and determined not to sit back – we were determined to take action.

The discussions became most animated when we dwelled on the lack of leadership by the community elders. Many of us voiced disappointment, even anger, that the members of the Jewish Council (*Judenrat*) did not have the necessary qualities to deal with the situation. They were mostly middle-aged or older and had been selected because they were well known in the community; some were even drawn from the religious leadership. While a few were opportunists, most of them were honest, intelligent, and well meaning, but to us they were hopelessly unequal to the task. We complained that they were either weak and subservient or corrupt and self-serving, that often they appeared to collaborate with the Germans in our mistreatment. The Council seemed unable or unwilling to attend to our current needs and did not impart any confidence that it could be entrusted with our future. We thought that even under occupation our human rights should be respected, and we expected the local Jewish leadership to show some contrariness, some semblance of resistance. But it never took any action to oppose the rulers. It remained, to the last, accommodating and passive, leaving the population hopeless and helpless.

We also lamented our own inactivity. Yitzhak in particular commanded us to take the initiative, to take our fate into our own hands, and, focused on this idea, he single-handedly brought us back to it whenever someone would stray onto another subject. Having never been politically active, I tended to sit on the sidelines and listen rather than talk. I was also intimidated because I was from out of town and had known the members of the group for only a short time; the others knew each other well from before the war, and many had gone to the same school. However, I was sure of one thing: I was decidedly in Yitzhak's camp. I too was ready to act.

Many ideas were tossed around, but few were practical.

We thought that we should engage in some form of sabotage. I proposed cutting the telephone wires that the German military had strung on trees along a nearby highway from Tomaszow to Piotrkow. The idea was received enthusiastically at first. Then we all realized that we could do it only after dark, but since it was summer, darkness fell after the 9 p.m. curfew. Passive resistance – slow or shoddy performance in the workplace – was an option but was already commonly practiced. As for other actions that were suggested, including acts of armed resistance, they were more an expression of our youthful exuberance than practical and real possibilities. As willing as we were to take chances, the risks were too great and we were too inexperienced. We had no weapons and there was no way for us to obtain any. Our only strength was our will to act.

Our many discussions led to one conclusion: we must leave the ghetto. Since staying on was unacceptable and any resistance impossible, escape was our only option. On this we all agreed. The next key question was, what concrete steps could we take? We had ambitious goals, but we were at a loss as to how to attain them.

Yitzhak provided most, although far from all, of the answers. In a lengthy but clear speech during our last meeting, he summarized our feelings and our conclusions. He defined the immediate goals and spelled out the practical steps that we must take:

'We must free ourselves from this nightmare. We are helpless here, lacking numbers, lacking means, lacking adult leadership. Physical resistance is out of the question. Our group has no military experience and lacks all the prerequisites for any effective action. We cannot expect help to come. But we cannot also sit idly by. We must prepare for our escape by relying primarily on our own resources. Once we are outside the ghetto, outside the city of Tomaszow, we can join other movements, an underground that is already in existence. But we must escape first. There is no other way. It won't be easy to abandon the security of our homes in exchange for the uncertainty of the unknown. It will take all our strength and all the courage we can muster, but this is our only chance. To remain here is worse. If only a fraction of the rumors we hear proves true, we are all doomed.'

Yitzhak seemed to have had a sixth sense about our agenda and our ultimate objectives, and he expressed himself with great clarity. He inspired all of us to individual action with his words. 'Rely on yourself. Take the reins of your survival into your own hands. Escape is the only path to survival,' he said.

To test conditions on the Polish side and determine general opportunities for escape, as well as to get a sense of the difficulties that awaited us, the group decided to send out a couple of scouts. Tusia was the first volunteer to be sent out into the Aryan side, picked for her resourcefulness and courage. She had prewar contacts in the city of Kraków, as she had belonged to a national youth organization there before the war. And she was a girl; if caught, a boy could easily be proven Jewish by his circumcision.

Tusia's mission was to find and establish contacts with other underground organizations, to set up a communication channel with them, and to obtain Polish ID cards for the rest of us. We all contributed funds for the trip, supplied her with our pictures and personal data, and, tearfully, bid her farewell. Deep down, every one of us envied her.

Twice she returned to Tomaszow to inform the group about the underground contacts she had made and to collect additional personal data for the Polish documents. Everything seemed to be going well. Our spirits were rising, as we felt that we were making progress. But when Tusia returned to the ghetto for a third time, she brought bad news.

'The Nazis are destroying the small ghettos and herding Jews into ghettos in larger cities. Some people have disappeared without a trace. There are rumors that there have been mass executions: that they are forcing people into the woods and killing them, burying them in mass graves,' she said and then continued. 'What they call "resettlement camps" are nothing more than extermination camps. You must tell the others what is happening to our people.' Her warning, disturbing if not totally surprising, reinforced our group's determination to proceed with our plans to escape.

Yitzhak and other members approached the elders of the Jewish Council to pass on the information we had received. We tried to warn them, but we were rebuffed and branded as 'panic mongers'. We were advised not to spread such bad, unsubstantiated news.

'It is unthinkable!' they scolded us. 'No one will believe such rumors.' We remained silent.

After her last trip, we lost track of Tusia. Some time later, Halinka Rubinek, a tall, Aryan-looking girl, with dark hair and blue eyes, followed in her footsteps. She found out that Tusia had lived for a while in Kraków, working diligently on our behalf until, one day, she was caught by the Germans, shot and killed. After her first trip back to report about Tusia, Halinka also disappeared; no one knows what happened to her. Afterwards, a boy from our group, Marek, left the ghetto in search of contacts; his destination was Warsaw. He, too, disappeared without a trace.

4 Tomaszow Labor Camp

By mid-1942, I had been transferred from the Polna Street workshop to a furniture factory (*Tischlerei*) managed and operated by Org. Todt – a large firm, located within the ghetto, that produced cabinets and other furniture for the German war machine. Mr Kramer, a short, heavy-set man with a jovial and kind face, was head of the plant. His rank, I was told, was equivalent to that of a general in the regular army. He, like all other Org. Todt members, wore a green uniform with the Nazi swastika on its arm. About four hundred people were employed at the factory: some Germans, some Poles, but mostly Jews.

At first, I was a laborer on the floor, carrying heavy wooden boards from the lumberyard to the machinery. It was a hard and tedious job. But soon I was promoted, landing a job as an assistant to the factory's chief electrician. He was a local Pole, tall and slender, taciturn but fair-minded. The new job was anything but boring: each day I learned new concepts in the magic field of electricity and became familiar with new machinery and new tools. I was learning a trade.

About the same time as I started my new job, rumors spread throughout the ghetto that the entire Jewish population of Tomaszow would be deported, or 'resettled', as the Germans referred to it. With time, these rumors became more frequent and more credible. Many such 'resettlements' had already taken place in other cities, small and large.

The official line from the Nazis was that the Jews were being sent to the newly occupied Russian territories, where they would be housed and gainfully employed. It was easy to believe it. The campaign in Russia left vast areas devastated and in need of reconstruction. It was also a fact that thousands inside the ghettos were highly skilled artisans who were now idle and could satisfy that need. Thus, the German plans appeared to have elements of rationality. To make it even more believable, the Germans encouraged people scheduled for resettlement to take with them household items, such as linen, towels, and pots and pans, and for skilled workers, their tools. They assured everyone that all these items would be needed.

The grapevine, however, told a very different story: the 'resettlers' were sent to concentration camps or, worse, to extermination camps. But the fact was that nobody knew for sure. Even when faced with eyewitness accounts from returning train operators and a few who had managed to escape, people did not believe them. It was difficult to think the unthinkable.

One day, I believe it was the last day of October 1942, the rumors of worse to come became a reality for the Jews of Tomaszow. It was a typical October day, a little chilly and gray. That morning, starting at about ten o'clock, about half the residents of the ghetto, some 6,000 to 7,000 men, women, and children, were herded into a large assembly area adjacent to the furniture factory. Slowly and in silence the assembly area filled up. As if in a daze, the Jews sat on the ground, each family surrounded by a mound of suitcases, boxes, or duffel bags. Helplessly, from the upper windows of the factory, we observed the steadily increasing mass of people. The early arrivals had been there for several hours. Without food or water, except for what they had brought with them, in fear and uncertainty as to their fate, they waited, motionless and silent. Among them were my three aunts, Rena, Rachela, and Celina, and my now 11-year-old cousin, Olek, along with a few more distant relatives and many friends and neighbors.

I did not even have a chance to say good-bye to my relatives, because the previous day, unexpectedly and without explanation, the managers at the *Tischlerei* had told us to remain on the grounds for the night. We and all the other workers from the ghetto working for German firms – a total of about 800 mostly young men and women – were exempt from the deportation.

In the middle of the afternoon, those assembled were marched to the railroad station, about two miles away, and loaded into cattle cars, where they stood, crammed together like sardines, without food, unable to relieve themselves, until sunset. At the end of the day the trains left for an unknown destination. The deportation of the second half of the ghetto population followed a couple of days later, at the beginning of November.

Weeks later the news filtered in that the destination for the 'resettled' had been Treblinka, a place of which I, as well as most others, had never heard.

The rest of us, a few hundred workers of the *Tischlerei*, camped on the grounds of our workplace for two or three days. Then, early one morning, accompanied by German gendarmes and Jewish police, we were herded into the shabbiest part of the ghetto, where the poorest of the poor had once lived. The houses were small and dilapidated, with no running water and a minimum of furniture and bedding. Chaos prevailed. Since we were left with nothing but what we had on our backs, people fought bitterly for every spoon, every dish, and every scrap of clothing.

There were similar fights for accommodation. We were left to ourselves to select a room or a tiny apartment from a cluster of shacks, usually with two or more other people. A few structures that appeared to be of slightly higher quality were already occupied. One housed a now-reduced Jewish Council; another, the Jewish Order Police and the communal kitchen. Most apartments were in disarray, with the front doors flung open; others were tidier and had padlocks on the doors: the owners expected to return. The Jewish police were supposed to keep order, but they were nowhere to be seen. They were busy requisitioning places for their relatives or friends. I ended up in a complex at 6 Piekarska Street and landed an apartment with two other men, both casual acquaintances: one was a boy even younger than myself, and the other was a man of about 40. The latter, Mr Czernow, was sadness personified. He had just lost his wife and three children in the deportation and was in an inconsolable daze.

In this new, smaller version of misery, we had electricity, but water had to be brought in buckets from hand-pumped artesian wells. Once a day, after work, a community kitchen provided food. Occasionally we would cook some soup, real soup, with potatoes bought on the black market, rather than the potato peels we received at the factory or from the communal kitchen. For cooking we used wooden stoves, rather primitive contraptions with pipes that vented the smoke to the outside. For sanitary facilities we had outhouses.

This new area became the Tomaszow Labor Camp. It was surrounded by barbed wire and guarded 24 hours a day by armed Ukrainian soldiers belonging to the Auxiliary Ukrainian Army. Although Yitzhak and the few remaining members of Akiba, including myself, remained in this camp, our Akiba activities ceased. We had lost contact with the outside and with each other. Although the labor camp was not very big, just a few city blocks, hard labor and long working hours combined with difficult living conditions were not conducive to social contact and much less to organized political activity. My time after work was spent first collecting a bowl of soup with some bread at the communal kitchen, then getting rested for the next day.

A couple of my relatives, Rysia and Felek, were among those exempted from the Treblinka transport and were now in the camp. But although they were cousins of mine, we were not close. Each had a spouse still in the camp and worked in a different place – Felek was a policeman – and I rarely saw them. Without my aunts and Olek, I felt very alone.

At the factory I met a boy about my age by the name of Ignac who was as strong as a horse and as stubborn as a mule. He was rather ugly, but quiet, thoughtful, and, as I soon found

27

out, frugal, intelligent, dependable, and diligent. I often gave him half my soup; I was glad to give it away, as I found it tasteless and Ignac was always hungry. Ignac had a contagious smile and a dry sense of humor. Fortunately, he was always willing to do more than his share, carry the heaviest box, take on the heaviest workload, and do whatever was needed. In spite of some differences, Ignac and I became close friends, almost soul mates. We complemented and needed each other.

One day, during our lunch break, I confided in him my desire to flee from this miserable and hopeless existence despite the fact that there did not appear to be any immediate danger to our lives. People really did not know where their families had been deported to or what had happened to them, so running away was not on everyone's mind. But for me, ever since my Akiba experience, there was no other option but escape. The only questions were how and how soon?

I proceeded to tell Ignac what it would take to put an escape plan into action, imparting to him what I had learned at the Akiba meetings. He must have already had similar thoughts, because it did not take much for us to agree about this. Almost instantaneously he became my co-planner and co-conspirator, and a couple of weeks later he also became a second assistant to the chief electrician of the factory.

Neither one of us knew anything about being an electrician. We bumbled through the first few weeks, not knowing a voltmeter from a circuit breaker. But we worked and learned well together, complemented each other's talents or lack thereof, and, most importantly, were completely in concert regarding the need to escape. Our utmost priority, I told him, was to obtain important Polish documents: we needed a *Kennkarte*, which was numbered and fingerprinted and included a photo; we needed a labor card showing employment, and we needed a certificate stating that we were on holiday or traveling for our company. The labor card was critical to show that we were gainfully employed; it was needed to obtain ration cards, travel permits, and other assistance.

The certificate was necessary since we expected to be away from the place of employment indicated on the labor card.

Since we already worked for a German company, we started with the labor card. Our first approach was simple: steal it. We thought it would be so easy that we didn't even consider other alternatives. We knew that every Polish worker in the factory had to have a labor card and that once a week, late on Friday, these cards were collected and registered by a supervisor and then returned to their owners. Our simple plan consisted of stealing a couple of these cards when they were on the supervisor's desk during the registration process. Our challenge was to stage some kind of an emergency in order to get him out of his office, rush in while he was gone, locate the documents, and pocket them. Afterwards, we would resume our duties as though nothing had happened.

Two locations were involved: the supervisor's office, a wooden barrack that was located in the courtyard close to the plant; and a utility room 100 yards away that contained maintenance and control equipment for the plant's electrical power. The main circuit breaker, controlling all lighting and all electrical machinery in the plant, was located in the utility room.

One Friday evening after dark, Ignac loitered in the vicinity of the supervisor's office; I was in the utility room. At a prearranged time, I pulled down the main electrical switch. Throughout the plant all the lights went out, and all of the machines came to a sudden halt. As the supervisor ran out to look for the electricians (Ignac and me), Ignac entered his office and randomly took two labor cards from a pile on his desk. When the supervisor reached the utility room, he found me already there. I was at the main switch, frantically trying to locate the problem, which I 'found' within minutes. The electricity to the factory was restored, and the supervisor complimented me on my prompt and efficient response.

Afterwards, Ignac and I congratulated each other on our accomplishment. 'Success!' we declared. The plan had come off without a hitch – or so it seemed, for we soon discovered that we had seriously miscalculated. Both cards belonged to people who were at least 15 years older than we were, and their birth dates were on the cards. At 18, even with the best of disguises, we could not pass for middle-aged men.

We thus decided to change our modus operandi: first we would find someone in our own age bracket, and only then would we attempt to steal his labor card. I soon found a young man named Alfons Machowiak who worked in the company's boiler room. One day, during the lunch hour, while Ignac engaged Alfons in a conversation in the courtyard, I entered the boiler room, found Alfons's jacket, and simply pulled the labor card out of his breast pocket. This new approach worked well. Alfons would have to report a lost document, which, without much difficulty, would be replaced, while I had been rewarded with my first Polish document. Soon after my success, Ignac obtained his labor card in a similar fashion.

But although possession of a labor card was necessary, it was not sufficient. To be completely safe on the outside, one also needed the all-important *Kennkarte*, the one with a photo and fingerprints. It bore the Nazi stamp showing an eagle and swastika and required a certificate of baptism. As this Polish ID card was the most difficult to obtain, we had to put it off until a later date.

Nevertheless, we had to be ready if the opportunity arose to obtain a card, so in the meantime I endeavored to try to get a picture taken for it. It was not a simple task. To begin with, our Polish boss, the chief electrician, had to agree to smuggle a camera into the plant. Next, I had to find a linen cloth to provide the white background mandatory for all document pictures. Finally, I had to smuggle into the factory a nice jacket, a dress shirt and a tie, obviously not standard work attire. I managed to sneak in this clothing by carrying it inside baggy pants that were tied with a shoelace at the bottom of each leg; in the meantime, the linen cloth was temporarily 'relocated' from the factory's supply room to the electricians' room. My boss also had to develop the photo. The riskiest part of this task was involving the Polish supervisor; his discretion was of paramount importance, because he knew quite well why I wanted the photo. It is understandable that I was taking a chance in asking him for help with the photo; my entire undertaking was risky. But why was he willing to take chances? I cannot answer that with any certainty, but I do believe that deep down people had compassion, and when they were confronted with an opportunity to help, more often than not they did.

Then there was the special certificate specifying permission to travel. Each of us needed one when we escaped; however, we also needed blank certificates for future use, should we find it necessary to alter our names or change travel dates. The solution to this problem lay in producing many copies. We even thought that if we could produce enough such blank forms, we might be able to find buyers for them. Thus our great printing plan was born.

Ignac and I prepared a long and ambitious list of what we needed: a *Tischlerei* stamp with a swastika and, standing upon it, an eagle with widely spread wings; a sample format of a *Tischlerei* certificate; a typewriter and the right kind of typing paper; and, last but not least, someone who knew how to type. Above all, we needed ingenuity and luck. Obtaining these items was considerably harder than we had imagined. But our mindset, our determination, and our youthful naiveté prevented us from realizing the difficulties ahead and kept us going.

Our resources were exceptionally limited. Some were practically nonexistent, considering our circumstances. The stamp had to come from the office of the general manager of the factory, Mr Kramer. The typewriter had to come from the headquarters of the Jewish Order Police, as theirs was the only typewriter in the camp. Finding a typist was less of a problem, except that it meant involving other people, which was risky. Any activity designed to promote an escape from the camp, or aiding and abetting such activity, was punishable by death. But at that time we did not even consider the possibility of being caught or how severe the consequences might be, and the question of risk came up only when we tried to solicit help from others. Friends and even relatives were often reluctant to participate in what appeared to be – and was – a dangerous conspiracy.

We started with the stamp. As electricians, we could roam the plant and gain access to any office on the pretext that we had to repair or check an electrical problem. The cleaning women, who had master keys, knew us well and were routinely ready to open any doors for us. We took advantage of that fact and, over the period of a few days, we were in and out of Mr Kramer's office several times, in order to ascertain the time of minimal activity in and around the office, as well as to determine the place where Mr Kramer kept his stamps. One afternoon, with Ignac on the lookout, I entered the office, checked the electrical outlets, tested the light bulbs, examined the switches, and then quietly proceeded to examine the desk drawers. Within minutes, I found the right drawer and there, the coveted *Tischlerei* stamp. A moment later the stamp was in my possession and I was out of the office. From that moment, the stamp became our most precious asset.

Obtaining the typewriter presented a different challenge. The Jewish Order Police performed many functions but were not in the typewriter rental business. We had to find a credible excuse to get it out of their hands and into ours. We had learned, in a roundabout way, that the typewriter at their headquarters did not work very well, so one day, we found my cousin, Felek Neumark, who I remembered was one of the policemen there, and informed him that we knew how to fix typewriters and offered to repair theirs for free. The other policemen present were suspicious of our offer, but the machine was indeed not working well and our price was right, so they agreed. In no time, the typewriter was in our hands.

Ignac's roommate Rys agreed to do the typing. The paper, the format, and the text were also ready by now. While Rys typed, Ignac and a couple of other friends and I sang loudly to drown out the clatter of the typewriter's keys. We produced over a dozen blank certificates, stamped them, and, after some practice, placed the forged signature on them: Mr J. Kramer.

At the end of the typing session, a small problem arose. We tried to mend the typewriter, as we had promised, but instead, the typewriter's state of disrepair worsened. We could not even properly reassemble it, much less repair it. When we finally brought it back to the station, the policemen on duty examined the machine, told us that we were incompetent, that we had lied to them, that we were impostors, and kicked us out.

Of course they were right on all three counts. But our task to produce a forged *Tischlerei* certificate was accomplished.

5 Plotting Escape

The most critical problem for an escapee from any camp or ghetto was finding lodging on the Polish side: a place to spend the first one or two nights after the escape, then more permanent accommodation. Some individuals and even families did survive the war in hideouts without ever acquiring false papers, but chances for survival for those with papers but no lodging were extremely low. The police curfew covered all of occupied Poland and was strictly enforced; wandering at night or hiding in public places like parks or railroad stations was extremely dangerous, even punishable by death. Poles who knowingly provided lodging to an escapee were similarly punished. This particularly applied to newly arrived escapees who were unaware of possible help available from some underground organizations. Thus, finding a contact with a safe haven outside the ghetto became our first priority and most important challenge.

Since Ignac's situation and mine were different and because it was safer to move as individuals, we had agreed to plan parallel but separate flight arrangements. For the first few days I tried to find a hiding place somewhere in Tomaszow, while Ignac, since he was native to Tomaszow, planned to leave his hometown immediately and go into the nearby forest, to join the partisans.

For my final destination I chose Warsaw. As the capital of Poland, with a population of approximately one million, Warsaw was by far the most suitable city for living incognito. It was cosmopolitan and the center for various underground organizations. It was also a major railroad junction, so there were always many travelers, including foreigners, smugglers, and transients. Many newcomers arrived daily in the city unnoticed. I hoped to be one of them.

But I had another reason for choosing Warsaw: my Aunt Marysia was living there. She had sent me a short message a few weeks earlier with the name and address of a friend of hers in Tomaszow, who, in turn, had contact names for me in Warsaw. She had not written her own address on the note, in case the communication fell into the hands of the Germans. How her message got to me, I do not know; I found it on my bed one evening when I got home from work. Most likely it was delivered by one of the Jewish policemen who periodically ventured outside the ghetto on official business.

In Tomaszow I was hoping to hide, after my escape, with the Szokalski family. Since my Aunt Rena had entrusted Mrs Szokalska with some personal items before her deportation, I was hopeful that I could confide in her and seek her help. Besides, I did not have many other choices.

The Szokalski family belonged to the *Volksdeutsche* community, whose members enjoyed many privileges and material advantages under the Germans, including the takeover of Jewish businesses. However, as the war progressed, this community was made to pay its dues, and its members were forced to send their husbands and sons off to the front, where many of them died fighting for a 'Fatherland' that was not theirs. They were also shunned and often hated by their former Polish friends and neighbors. After the war, many were branded as traitors to their native land and punished.

I sent Mrs Szokalska a note introducing myself and asking her if she would help me in my escape plan. More specifically, I wanted to know if she would allow me to hide on her premises, at least for a few days. To deliver the note I used another *Volksdeutscher*, Slazak,[8] who also worked in the *Tischlerei* factory. He was a short, wiry man in his late fifties who spoke both German and Polish; he wore the green uniform of the Org. Todt. He did favors for me in return for a few zlotys, but I always had the feeling that he was also doing it out of sympathy for our plight, for I believed no one would take the risk of being sent to the front, if caught, for a miserly few zlotys.

35

I waited anxiously for Mrs Szokalska's answer, fearful of the danger of revealing my plans for escape to a stranger, and my anxiety increased when after a few days I had still not heard from her. I sent Slazak to Mrs Szokalska with another note and, to my relief, this time he returned with a positive response.

Words cannot express how significant and crucial this affirmative response was, and in different ways it was significant to both of us. Having a place to stay for the first few nights had become the major factor in my decision to escape. As for Mrs Szokalska, she had courageously put herself and her family at risk by offering to help me. Polish (and other Christian) individuals, even entire families, were known to have paid with their lives for hiding Jews. One had to have lived during those years of German occupation, with its strict, barbaric laws and draconian reprisals, to fully appreciate the bravery and kindness that her decision represented. I have long since wondered what motivated her to take such dangerous action, particularly in view of the fact that I was a stranger, someone she had never seen or heard of, the nephew of an acquaintance.

In the meantime, Ignac was making plans with his older brother, Heniek, who was also in the labor camp. As they were native to Tomaszow and their wealthy parents had been well known before the war, they had Polish friends in town who were willing to help them and who, presumably, had already procured Polish ID cards for them.

Shortly before my final move, another fellow inmate, Ludwik, who was also toying with the idea of escape, asked me, 'How do you overcome the fear of being caught and killed? How does one find the courage to escape?'

Remembering Yitzhak's words at our Akiba meetings, and following a simplistic logic, I replied, 'The danger of dying inside the camp is far greater than being killed on the outside. It takes greater courage to stay than to leave.' I believe that this perception of what the future held for us was the motivating factor that drove me so hard and so uncompromisingly toward action, toward escape.

The only question that still remained open was when.

6 Tomorrow will be too late

I now had several elements of my escape plan in place: the promise of a hiding place from Mrs Szokalska, a labor card in the name of Alfons Machowiak, and the forged *Tischlerei* certificate stating that I was on vacation. But I had one additional trump card: an address in Warsaw where I could safely stay the first few nights, the critical pied-à-terre. This address was held for me by a Polish friend of my Aunt Marysia who lived on the outskirts of Tomaszow.

I also decided that I would make my escape from the premises of the factory rather than from the camp, which was surrounded by barbed wire and heavily guarded by Ukrainian SS. The factory, on the other hand, had a six-foot wooden fence and was guarded by only a couple of *Wehrmacht* soldiers, each on the opposite side of the complex. I still had to choose the exact location for the jump and the optimum time, i.e. when the guards would be furthest away and most distracted.

Just as my plans were almost complete, my partner Ignac began to hesitate, and his plans began to crumble. He now had a girlfriend, Tetka, a pretty 16-year-old. He was worried about leaving her behind, yet also concerned about taking on the responsibility for another person when his own fate was so uncertain. I wondered, too, if Ignac might have worried about what would be regarded as his noticeable Jewish features: short, curly hair, and dark complexion. He spoke excellent Polish, but, unfortunately, it was first impressions that counted and in our situation there was rarely a chance for a second impression. On the positive side, both he and Tetka had the all-important Polish ID cards. But, a promise from a Polish friend, Mr Zasepa, that when the need arose, he would come and take both of them to a partisan group in the forest, became unreliable. Ignac lost contact with Mr Zasepa.

Until now Ignac had been my co-conspirator and co-collaborator, but while we had worked closely together on our general plans, we had prepared our actual escapes separately. Now, in view of these new circumstances, we considered whether both of us or even all three of us should run away together. But how could all of us show up at Mrs Szokalska's doorstep when she had promised to help only me? Each additional person made discovery more likely. Just moving around as a twosome or as a group of three would make us more conspicuous and put everybody in danger. Any wrong step or action by any one of us would immediately cast a shadow of suspicion on the others. And where would we go if Mrs Szokalska refused to take in all three of us? This concern weighed heavily on all of us. Despite my misgivings, I agreed to the new plan, but Ignac and Tetka hesitated.

As determined and prepared as I was, I kept postponing the final decision, the exact day and hour of the escape. Like Ignac, deep down I was afraid of the unknown, the world on the other side of the wall. Just like many others who thought about escaping and could have escaped but never took that final step, I was afraid of the outside world and of an uncertain future. After all, I was depending on crucial help from people who were strangers. The money I had would last me a few days, maybe a few weeks, and then what?

It was because of these fears that I kept delaying the time when I would trade a life that was miserable but familiar for one that might be better, but right now, uncertain and unknown. It was a hard decision. In the camp I had a bed; I was fed poorly but regularly and had the comfort of being among other Jews, people I knew and trusted. I had never met Mrs Szokalska or the lady in Tomaszow with the addresses or any of the other people in Warsaw with whom I was to lodge, depend on for support and contacts, or work with. My Aunt Marysia was the only familiar name in Warsaw, but I did not even have an address for her.

Life in the camp was rapidly deteriorating, and conditions were becoming harsher. We existed on a little black bread, artificial coffee, and a watery soup filled with potato peels handed out twice a day. We had barely enough calories to survive, yet the work was getting harder and the work hours longer.

Acts of terror occurred more often. One of the tactics used by the Germans and designed to instill fear and despair into the psyches of both the community leaders and the population at large was to suddenly change the Judenrat leadership. One day, a Red Cross ambulance arrived at the camp and took away the head of the Judenrat, Mr Bernstein, along with his wife and their small son. Bernstein and his family had been our neighbors when we first moved into the ghetto. He was a lawyer from Lódz and had given me my first English lessons in his home, where I came to know his wife and son as well. They were told that they were being allowed passage abroad in an exchange for German prisoners. Instead, they were taken to the cemetery and shot. We realized their tragic fate only after the ambulance that had taken them away returned empty half an hour later, exactly the time needed for the 15-minute trip from the camp to the Jewish cemetery and back again.

There were other forms of terror, including what came to be known as 'actions'. During one such action, called the 'Purim Action' because it occurred close to the Purim holiday, 21 inmates were taken to the Jewish cemetery and killed. Another time, a young mother was discovered hiding her 3-year-old daughter. As children were not allowed in the camp, both she and the little girl were taken away, never to be heard from again. Another woman who was found to be romantically involved with a German supervisor, was given 30 lashes on her bare buttocks, in public, at the camp's roll call in the square.

One day, early in the spring of 1943, there was a roll call for the purpose of collecting whatever assets remained in our possession. The SS placed large baskets on several tables, then, parading up and down with a retinue of vicious-looking

39

dogs, ordered us under threat of death to place any pieces of gold, silver, or anything else of value still in our hands, inside the baskets. The SS men were shouting orders in a loud, staccato German and the dogs were barking and straining at their leashes. A shudder passed through my body as I waited, standing next to a tall, red-haired boy, no more than 18 years old. Suddenly, with a simple '*Du!*' (You!), a member of the SS pointed in our direction. My mind panicked as I tried to comprehend if he was directing his command at me but he roughly grabbed the boy next to me and pushed him to the front of the group. Four others were randomly chosen in the same way and lined up. Without any further delay, one after the other, the SS man shot all five of them in the back of the head with a revolver. The redheaded boy fell right at his feet. There was tense silence, and I noticed my hands were shaking like leaves; all I could think was how easily that could have been me. It was the first time in my life that I had witnessed killing at such close range.

We immediately deposited everything we had inside the baskets, including money, watches, and other valuables. Even fountain pens had to be deposited if they had gold nibs.

In the afternoon there was a second round of confiscation. This time the SS ordered us to deposit all valuables hidden at home. Motivated by an indescribable, uncontrollable fear, I went to my room and dug out from beneath the floorboards a pair of silver candlesticks I had found in one of the abandoned houses and hidden so that no one would find them. Now, with the terrible images of the morning's executions and the redheaded boy in my mind, I duly delivered them to the SS. I kept only my father's gold watch.

In the third week of April 1943, we were kept away from work for three full days. Soon we found out why. The Warsaw Ghetto Uprising had started, and the Germans worried that the rebellion might spread to other ghettos and camps. The Ukrainian guard contingent was increased and put on high alert.

While rumors accompanied our lives throughout the war,

they intensified in May. Each day there was a new one, each worse than the one before. It was unclear where or with whom they originated, but they kept us in a state of constant fear. The latest and worst rumor was that now, we in the labor camp would be 'resettled' – a word that sent shivers down our spines.

On the morning of 28 May I ran into Mr Kramer, the head of the Org. Todt *Tischlerei*, near his office. We engaged in conversation as we had many times before. Usually our chats were short and superficial, but now I noticed a worried look on his face and seriousness in his voice; he appeared to be in a state of discomfort. After a few pleasantries, I asked him point blank what was going to happen to us. He was evasive at first, but then, after a brief pause, he lowered his voice and said, 'My son, flee if you can. Tomorrow will be too late.' The Tomaszow labor camp was about to be liquidated and the inmates deported.

The gnawing question of when to escape was answered in that moment, the moment when my life took a crucial and unpredictable turn.

I immediately shared this news with Ignac, who in turn passed it on to his brother, Heniek, girlfriend, Tetka, and a few relatives and friends. That evening our final preparations started. We selected clothing and figured out how to carry money and a few valuables. By now my own valuables were reduced to two items: my father's gold watch with three gold covers and several blank certificate forms, complete with a swastika stamp and signed by 'Mr J. Kramer'. They had to be hidden in a secure place somewhere on my person. Ignac and I received 300 hundred zlotys each for two of our forged factory certificates, which we had sold to two fellow inmates, Felek Mak[9] and Natan Neuman. I decided to entrust the stamp, some additional items of clothing, and a few photographs that I did not intend to take with me to Mrs Szewczykowa, a Polish woman I had known for the last couple of years. We had worked together at the Org. Todt on Polna Street and then at the factory, and on a number of occasions she had told me, 'If ever I can be of help ...'

Meanwhile, there were goodbyes to say to people close to me. I pretended to be casual, but I knew that these most likely were final goodbyes. I kept my plans a secret from everyone except my cousin, Rysia, with whom I had supper that night.

The next morning, while marching to the factory, Jerzyk, a casual friend who was usually cheerful and easygoing, turned to me and said, 'Zenek, we have not even begun to live, and we are already facing the end of our lives.' In his eyes was a terrible sadness as he sensed what was about to happen to most of us. I cast down my eyes, fully understanding his fears yet anxious not to reveal my plans, as I knew doing so would be of no use to him and risky for me. I never heard from or about him again.

When we arrived at the factory, Ignac informed me that he would not escape without Tetka. But Tetka worked in another plant, and if we were to escape together, somehow she had to be brought to our factory. We approached Slazak, the *Volksdeutscher* employee who had previously carried notes between Mrs Szokalska and me. We offered him a 100-zloty banknote (about $5) to bring Tetka from her plant to ours. He agreed and, with Ignac, marched back to Tetka's camp.

An hour later Tetka was with us but she and Ignac still could not decide to make their move. The burden of the unknown was too much to face for both of them, two young people who, before all this, had never known anything but the most sheltered, comfortable, and secure lives. Determined to get started on my plan, I told Ignac, 'We must decide. We cannot wait much longer. I'm ready to go.'

At three o'clock, Ignac and I shook hands. I gave Tetka a kiss on her cheek, wished both of them good luck, and then, with my false papers in the inside pocket of my jacket, my father's gold watch safely secured to my thigh with a bandage, and a change of clothes and some toiletry items in a small leather briefcase, I headed toward the fence alone. I was about to face the defining moment of my life.

On the inside of the six-foot-high wooden fence that

surrounded the factory were several stacks of lumber and the factory's main complex, representing a wretched life and a doomed future. On the other side there was Wiecznosc Street, part of the residential portion of Tomaszow and the street where Mrs Szokalska lived. Beyond that fence was a dream world, a haven of freedom, and a chance at survival. But possibly, too, it could be my graveyard.

Separating these two worlds was an elderly, lone German soldier in a gray uniform full of Nazi insignia, trudging slowly, his rifle slung over his shoulder. The spring air was warm, the sky overcast. I waited, hidden between the stacks of lumber. Two hours passed as I observed and calculated the soldier's every move, working out the perfect time to jump over the fence. I wanted to time it just right: when he was far enough away not to hear my jump, but at the same time not yet ready to make the turn that would allow him to see me. I felt no hesitancy, even though my heart was pounding so hard that I was afraid someone might hear it, and my stomach was knotted in fear. I knew very well that a miscalculation on my part or the sheer bad luck of a sudden and unexpected turn by the guard meant disaster. Freedom and a chance for life, on one hand, a single bullet and death, on the other.

Finally, I sensed the time had come. Using the stack of lumber as a platform I scrambled up the fence and jumped, landing with my two feet firmly on the ground. I was now on the Polish side.

In my hand I carried the leather briefcase, and in my pocket I had about 800 zlotys. I walked a few steps in the direction opposite that of the marching soldier, then quickly crossed Wiecznosc Street. The side of the street closest to the fence was empty of pedestrians; on the other side, there were a few people, but they paid no attention to me. Within minutes, my rapid pace never slackening, I reached the Szokalski house two blocks away.

I stood and looked at the number 37 on the house for a few seconds, just to be sure I was at the right place. In front there was a large yard full of trees and bushes; I hid behind one of the bushes closest to the house, closed my eyes, and waited. As I sat motionless on the ground, mentally and emotionally drained, problems kept crossing my mind: What if nobody is home? What if Mrs Szokalska has changed her mind? But there was no way to turn back the clock.

When darkness fell I approached the door quietly and knocked. My heart was racing as I heard footsteps approaching. Mrs Szokalska, a pretty, middle-aged woman, opened the door, with her daughter, Lucja, standing right behind her. I introduced myself in as calm a voice as possible.

'Good evening, Mrs Szokalska. I am Zenon, Mrs Rubinek's nephew.'

Mrs Szokalska showed no surprise at my appearance. She greeted me politely but did not say much more. Matter-of-factly, she directed me to the back of the house, to a garden shack where I was to stay, only commenting that food would be brought to me the next morning. Then, as she was about to leave, she moved closer, leaned toward me, and whispered, 'Don't let my husband see you. He doesn't know that you will be staying here.' I thanked her and turned to go towards the garden shack. Inside, I rolled up my winter parka for a pillow, lay down, and soon fell into an exhausted sleep. When I woke up the next morning, rather late, there was bread with marmalade and a glass of milk waiting for me. Some soup and vegetables were brought later in the day.

At about five o'clock the next morning, I was awakened by the sound of heavy footsteps getting closer and closer to my temporary abode. I peered through a crack in the wooden shack and saw a man approaching. I could feel the sweat on my brow and the palms of my hands as I watched him come nearer. I remembered that Mrs Szokalska had warned me about her husband; now I prepared for the worst. As he reached the entrance of the shack, Mr Szokalski opened the door slightly and, with an index finger touching his lips, whispered, 'Shh, shh. My wife and my daughter think that I am deaf and can't hear anything, that I don't know about you. But I can hear enough. I know that you are here, and I am

44

glad. Here is some bread with butter for you.'

Relief flooded my body.

Later, Mrs Szokalska brought me news of what had happened to the camp and its inmates during the 'resettlement' action and what was presently happening in the town.

'The camp has been liquidated,' she told me. 'The population was taken to the railroad station by foot only yesterday afternoon, loaded into freight cars and taken to an undisclosed destination. The town is swarming with SS men and the police. The liquidation of the camp lasted three days, and then the Germans left. No one knows where the camp inmates were taken. There are rumors that two or three inmates tried to escape but that they were caught and shot.'

At the factory my escape created a logistics problem that I hadn't considered and that could have had dire consequences for me. As usual, before the workers were marched off back to the camp, there was a roll call, and that day the count would have been short by one. Luckily, Tetka was still at our factory. With her long dark blond hair stuffed into a man's hat, she took my place in the column, next to Ignac. Thus the count for the return was the same as that on arrival in the morning.

In the days following my escape I spent most of the time in a daze, completely empty of thoughts and emotions. The picture that I had formed of the camp and what had happened there during its last days, how the inmates were treated by the Nazis and their reaction to the deportation, was anything but clear – it was incomplete and incomprehensible, like images behind a cloud. Their fear, agony, and total defenselessness were beyond what I could imagine. As for me, the reality of my successful escape did not sink in, not then, and not for some time to come. In the meantime, I spent a lot of time either reading some old newspapers or just dozing.

There was no discussion with Mrs Szokalska about my plans or how long I expected to stay with them. Remarkably, considering how unsafe this was for her and her family, she imposed no limits on my stay. My plan was to stay for only a few days, but she didn't know that. How could she? It was not completely clear in my own mind when I should move on. Besides, I thought that the less the Szokalskis knew about my plans, the safer it would be for all of us. Also, at no time was there any mention of compensation for their aid, in any form, now or in the future. Although I never knew their exact motivation in helping me, one thing was certain: they were not helping me for material gain.

On the morning of the fifth day following my escape, I collected my belongings and started the next phase of my odyssey, the journey to Warsaw. I did not notify my benefactors about my departure. I like to think that it was for safety's sake, theirs and mine. It certainly was not out of lack of gratitude for what they had done for me, which was more than any payment or even thanks I could have given them.

My first stop was the house of my aunt's friend, a local Polish lady whose name I don't recall; she held the all-important contact names in Warsaw. I arrived there at about 5.30 in the morning. Even though I roused her out of bed, she received me warmly and gave me two addresses. One was for Janina, another friend of my Aunt Marysia, at whose apartment I could stay when needed; in addition, Janina knew where and how to contact my aunt. The other address was the workplace of Kuba Rajzman, a fellow Tomaszovian and a casual acquaintance who had escaped early on. When I was ready to leave, my aunt's friend, her pale blue eyes watering, wished me good luck with a traditional Polish saying: '*Idz z Bogiem*' (God be with you). She was visibly moved, but I could not tell whether it was because my visit reminded her of the dramatic events happening in town over the past four days or whether she feared for my fate. Perhaps it was because she had been awakened at such an ungodly hour.

With a flat peasant hat lowered over my face, I proceeded toward the railroad tracks, about two miles away. I made a sharp turn to the right and followed the tracks for another 11 miles, to the railroad station in Jelen. I wanted to avoid the Tomaszow railroad station, fearing an encounter with the SS or Gestapo.

The Jelen station was smaller than Mrs Szokalska's garden shack; it comprised one employee behind a cashier's window, two wooden benches, and a wastebasket. There was only one other traveler waiting, a middle-aged woman with a babushka on her head. We did not say much during our five-hour wait, but from time to time we exchanged stares: she, probably out of boredom and I, fearing that somehow she would realize that I was a Jew and an escapee. The probability of her recognizing me as a Jew, especially with the hat covering half my face, was negligible, but my terror of being recognized was real and oppressive. It was an omnipresent fear that remained with me for the remaining years of the war. There is a proverb in Polish that best describes my self-consciousness: '*Na zlodzieju czapka gore*'. It translates roughly as 'a guilty person looks guilty'; literally, it means, 'a thief's hat glows'. During the months and years ahead, I had to worry about the truth of this proverb many, many times.

The two-hour trip to Warsaw was uneventful; hardly a word was exchanged among the passengers. Some of the people in the compartment read, some looked at the scenery, but most just sat there, staring blankly into space. The people around me looked unusually strange to me, appearing to have come from a different world, a world where people were well fed, reasonably well dressed, and carefree. They had an air of contentment and a sense of security that I lacked. Their faces expressed an inner calm; their stares were clear and relaxed, quite in contrast to what I was accustomed to seeing on people's faces in the camp. They were men and women, some young, some old. Very likely many of them were smugglers, for in occupied Poland smuggling was a way of life, a means of survival. I thought to myself that I too was smuggling; I was smuggling myself. But what a world of difference divided us. If they were caught, these people would lose their merchandise; if I were caught, I would lose my life.

47

My mind was a jumble. I thought about my parents and my sister in the Lódz Ghetto. I wondered what had happened to Ignac and the others I had left behind and whether I would ever see any of them again. I wondered what the future might hold for me and how I would manage on my own. I thought about how I had felt alone in the ghetto when my aunts and cousin were deported; but now, outside the camp, I was more alone than ever before and very insecure. Never in my life had I been left totally to my own devices. I was homesick, longing for a home that did not exist; more than anything I wanted to see my parents and my sister, wanted to be with my friends. These were the only thoughts I remember. All my other senses were numb, so numb that even though I had had nothing to eat or drink all day long, I didn't feel hungry or thirsty. However, there was one exception, a part of me felt a deep satisfaction; I had a sense of having succeeded. I felt there was a chance that I might survive. I also felt free. Maybe for a short time only, but free nonetheless.

7 Betrayal

The train slowed and rolled into the main station amidst an ever-increasing number of tracks. It was about seven o'clock in the evening, and the air was still warm. I stepped down onto the platform and joined the huge number of people moving silently but rapidly toward the exit. Outside the station, masses of people, many carrying heavy suitcases, scattered hurriedly in all directions. I glanced around me, concerned that I was being watched, worried that I might look conspicuous carrying only a briefcase and wearing a heavy winter jacket in June.

A passerby gave me directions to my destination: 37 Pius IX Street. About 20 minutes later I reached the address: a tall, gray, drab apartment building in a long row of similar buildings. The concierge looked at me with suspicion. Then he directed me to the seventh floor: 'Take the elevator. When inside, close the door and push the button with the number seven.' I later learned that in Warsaw all concierges were suspicious and that they all assumed, incorrectly in my case, that first-time visitors had never used an elevator. Minutes later, with a mixture of hope and trepidation, I knocked lightly on the door. Even though I knew that my aunt and Janina were friends, and that Janina's brother had once been an employee of a hotel that belonged to my relatives, I was apprehensive. The same questions that had plagued me outside the Szokalskis' house returned to torment me again. What if Janina wasn't home? What if she refused to take me in? Where would I go with the police curfew starting at nine o'clock, less than an hour from now?

My thoughts were interrupted when the door opened and an attractive woman, about 35 years old, stood before me.

Hearing that I was Marysia's nephew, Janina called out my name, opened the door wide and warmly welcomed me in. Immediately, she prepared hot soup, with bread and butter. Suddenly aware of how long it had been since my last meal, I gulped it down in no time and then had a second helping and a third. When I finished, Janina wanted to know all about my escape from the Tomaszow Labor Camp and about my trip to Warsaw. She was pleasant, kind, and hospitable and showed a genuine interest in my stories, asking for more and more details.

Janina's apartment was modest: a small bedroom, a kitchen that also served as a livingroom, den, and dining room, and a nook with a sloping ceiling above a narrow bed. There was also a washroom consisting of a toilet and a sink with cold running water. She invited me to stay in the apartment, indicating that I could sleep in the nook. As with the Szokalski family, there was no mention of any compensation or time limit for my stay. 'In a few days I will arrange for a meeting with your Aunt Marysia; she will be happy to see you,' she added.

Later that night, as I lay on the bed in the nook, gazing up at the sloping ceiling, I felt happy, relaxed, and very much at home. Any misgivings I may have had only hours earlier had disappeared. Now I felt completely safe and was overwhelmed by the friendliness of my hostess and the comforts of my new lodging: a clean bed with a pillow and a comforter; warm meals served on a table with a tablecloth; and a washroom with privacy. What a contrast to what I had had just a few days earlier, and how lucky I considered myself now to be!

We ate three times a day. The food was nothing special: mostly soups, fried potatoes, and occasionally a piece of Polish sausage. The bread was dark and tasteless, but fresh, and the coffee was a liquid that was coffee-colored only, leaving the aroma and taste to one's imagination. Nevertheless, to me, after the paltry rations in the camp, all this food tasted wonderful, and I could not get enough of it.

For the next two days, I slept a lot, read the daily Polish newspaper, *Nowy Kurier Warszawski* – a mouthpiece of the Nazis – and chatted idly with Janina. I didn't talk about my future plans, because I had none; I didn't talk about the past because I did not want to be reminded. But neither did Janina talk about her past, or future. Our conversations were mostly about nonevents and nontopics. She did not seem to have either a job or friends; even the neighbors did not visit. From my perspective this was for the better, as she did not need to explain my being there. From time to time she left me alone to go shopping and run errands, but she always returned after a short while.

At the end of the second day, Janina notified me that the next morning she would have to leave very early but would be back around 9 a.m. 'Please, just sleep in,' she told me. I did not think much about it that evening or the next morning when I got up, washed, dressed, had some breakfast, and buried myself in the newspaper. Around nine o'clock, Janina returned as she had promised.

A few minutes later there was a sharp knock on the door. In quick succession, there was another, louder one, then still another, followed by a harsh order, in German: 'Open up! Police! Open up!'

Janina and I both froze. We looked at each other but could not utter a word. I felt the blood drain from my face as Janina opened the door and two men stormed in. Both were tall; one was a civilian who spoke German and Polish, the other a German gendarme from the *Schutzpolizei* (security police) who spoke only German. The Nazi insignia on his uniform stood out menacingly; he looked particularly ferocious with his helmet, a metal tag with a police logo hanging on a chain from his neck, and a large holstered revolver hanging on his belt. They made straight for me. 'Documents! Who are you? What are you doing here? You are a Jew!' the civilian shouted in Polish.

Trying to keep my voice steady, I told him my name and said that I was visiting a friend. I denied being a Jew, but he hit me across the face and for a moment I lost my balance. After I had pulled myself together, he hit me again and shouted, 'You *are* a Jew!' This time I tasted blood in my mouth.

The civilian told me to take my clothes off, but when I got down to my shorts he suddenly motioned to me not to undress further. He had noticed the bandage on my left thigh.

51

Immediately, he ordered me to undo it, revealing my father's gold watch. The gendarme grabbed it, admired the carved design on its cover for a moment, and then put it into his pocket. He then indicated the little bag on my back, hanging on a string around my neck. The gendarme pulled it off by breaking the thin string. Inside they found the blank certificate forms from the factory in Tomaszow, stamped with the swastika and carrying the signature of 'Mr J. Kramer, manager of *Tischlerei*, Org. Todt'. It was obvious that the blanks were forgeries and that I was a fugitive. The gendarme put this bag into his pocket, too.

They slapped my face a few times more, until I was bleeding from both my nose and my lips. From this point on I did not bother to make any more denials. After they exchanged a few sentences in German, the happiness that I had felt over the past few days was crushed as they informed me that I was to be taken to Gestapo headquarters in Aleje Szucha, a place notorious for its torture chambers and for the fact that many who were taken there never came out alive. 'We have to get our car first,' they added. 'Do not move. Wait here,' they ordered. 'We will be back in an hour to collect you.' They took the keys to the apartment and my winter jacket and left, locking the door from the outside.

During this entire ordeal I did not see or hear from Janina, but now I saw her sitting at the kitchen table, crying and lamenting my fate, her hands covering her face.

'How could this have happened? Who were they? How did they find out about you?' she asked, her voice frightened and upset, tears running down her face.

Once she had calmed down, Janina helped me clean the blood from my face and the floor; I then dressed quickly. My thoughts were racing and it took me no more than a few minutes to reach a decision: I would commit suicide by jumping from the window. Since we were on the seventh floor this would not be difficult, if only I could summon up the courage. An image of a crumpled body lying in a pool of blood splattered across the courtyard pavement flashed before my eyes. But then I thought of the torture chambers of Aleje Szucha. Why be tortured and then die? I preferred to jump.

I pushed a chair towards the window and climbed onto it and then onto the windowsill. Janina, realizing what I planned to do, ran to me, grabbed me with both hands, and shrieked at the top of her lungs, '*No, no, no!* Don't do it, please don't do it.' She was hysterical again, shouting and crying in turn. If she was saying anything else, I could not make out what it was. I felt her hands grab my pant legs, holding on with strength surprising for such a small, slim woman, and she pulled me to the floor. Gradually she calmed herself, breaking my dazed silence with an occasional 'Oh, my God. Oh, my God.'

Janina said she had a plan for me; she knew how to open the locked door and was urging me to escape. She said that I could stay with her brother Zygmunt, the one who worked in my relatives' hotel before the war. She hastily scribbled his address and directions on a piece of paper and pushed it into my hand. I didn't say anything. I was stunned and confused. I had known that my escape and life on the run were risky and that the end could come at any time. But I didn't expect it so soon.

Meanwhile, Janina had opened the door and was rushing me to get going.

'They may arrive in less than an hour. You must hurry!' she warned me.

My mind was blank. I could think of nothing else I could do, so I followed her plan. I put my regular jacket on, stuffed my few possessions into the briefcase, and with a short 'thank you' and 'good-bye' I left. Luckily, the two Germans had not noticed that hanging in the other room was my regular jacket, where I kept the labor card in the name of Machowiak and my money, a few hundred zlotys.

As I passed the concierge's window on the way out, he looked at me with even greater suspicion than he had when I had first come in. Once on the street, I merged into the crowd moving toward the nearest tram stop. There, still in a daze, I climbed into the first tram that arrived, not even knowing if it was the right one. The experience had shattered my barely acquired sense of freedom and hope. Briefly, I thought of what might happen to Janina when the Germans returned to find me gone; everyone knew that Poles who helped Jews escape or hid them in their homes were severely punished. But I was too distraught to think rationally. All I could do was wonder if I would find a safe hideout at Zygmunt's. Only after I had arrived at the address did I realize how lucky I was to be alive. I had won, at least for the moment, a new lease on life.

Zygmunt, his wife, and a young niece who was staying with them received me just as warmly as Janina had three days earlier. I had met Zygmunt a couple of times at the beginning of the war, when he would carry packages or letters between family members in Tomaszow and Warsaw. He was tall and thickset, his wife petite and pretty. Both were about 40 years old.

Within minutes, Zygmunt sent his niece to the store to buy a bottle of vodka so we could properly celebrate my success in escaping from the camp and my presence now in Warsaw, among friends.

'What a great escape story! Congratulations!' Zygmunt said, toasting me with a glass of vodka. 'One more drink for good luck in the future!'

We had some more drinks. They could not have been happier for me, and, as with Janina, I felt at home. Gulping down one glass of vodka after another – always complementing each gulp with a snack in the Polish tradition – I told of my escape from the Gestapo at Janina's apartment. Zygmunt and his wife were completely surprised.

'How could this have happened?' he asked. 'Was it the concierge who denounced you? Did someone follow you from the railroad station?'

Both were inquisitive about what had happened, but they did not seem to be at all concerned about Janina's fate, even though she could have been in serious trouble as a consequence of helping me. And since they did not worry about Janina, neither did I.

'Let's be positive!' Zygmunt said, toasting me with another drink. 'You are here and you are well. You can stay here until you find better accommodations, and on Sunday you'll meet with your Aunt Marysia. We know how to contact her.'

For the next two days our topics of conversation centered on Aunt Marysia, my good fortune at being alive, and news reports of German defeats in Russia. Conspicuously absent from our conversations was any mention of Janina.

I spent two nights with Zygmunt and his family. The place was extremely uncomfortable; it was even smaller than Janina's place, and there were four of us. There was only one bed, so the niece and I slept on mats on the floor. In order to do that, the dining table had to be moved into a corner.

Early in the afternoon of the second day I went out, telling my hosts that I wanted to look for a job. Instead, I went to look up Kuba Rajzman, the man whose address I had received from the lady in Tomaszow. I found Kuba without any difficulty; he was working in a dry-cleaning store not far from Zygmunt's apartment. We went for a walk, and I told him about my narrow escape from the Gestapo. But unlike Zygmunt and his wife, Kuba was not surprised. 'It's the first, but not the last one. We all have experienced similar situations,' he said. Right away, he suspected that the men who had informed on me were not Germans but Polish blackmailers working in cahoots with uniformed German policemen on the take.

As a precautionary measure, Kuba urged me, to leave Zygmunt's home as soon as possible; however, I had already decided not to return. He promised to help me find a new lodging, and told me to visit him the next day. In the meanwhile, I was to find some temporary accommodation to cover the situation. Even though in Tomaszow we were only acquaintances – he was a few years older than I and had his own circle of friends – Kuba was extremely supportive and helpful, and I was grateful for his friendly support, especially as I had no one else to turn to.

Finding a place to stay in wartime Warsaw was difficult for all newcomers; it was more so for fugitives like me. Nonetheless, I decided to leave Zygmunt's at the earliest opportunity, even before I found a new lodging. Somehow, after my talk with Kuba, it did not feel right or even safe to stay there. So that same afternoon, while still leaving my briefcase with my belongings there, I told them that I would not be coming back for the night.

After leaving Zygmunt's, I was homeless. With no place to sleep, wash, or relieve myself, each day and night presented challenges for which I was totally unprepared. Luckily, I was also unaware of how dangerous it was to wander around the city all day, with no home address, or proper documentation. It was especially dangerous to be without a labor card or an ID card.

The first evening I found myself in the center of the Old Town looking for any accommodation available, but I soon found out that there were no rooms for rent or, if there were, I could not afford them. I asked passersby, but they ignored me or shrugged their shoulders and told me they did not know of any. The evening got darker and darker, the curfew hour was rapidly approaching, and I still had no place for the night. I began to panic as the streets emptied.

I had reached an area close to the Vistula River, a rather seedy district, when someone directed me to a small, shabby house. Since we were minutes away from the start of the curfew, I had no choice but to go in. The entrance to the house opened directly from the alley. The facility consisted of one very big room, half in darkness, with six or seven beds equipped with straw mattresses. People already occupied most of the beds, but one was still empty.

As I entered, a short fat woman took my 40-zloty note (less than $2) and showed me to my bed. 'Are you alone?' she asked in surprise, but then just waved her hand and walked away. In the morning, in the cold light of day, I realized that I had spent the night in a bordello. During the day the beds were rented for much less money, but only by the hour.

That morning, with nothing to do until my meeting with Kuba, I decided to while away some time in Saski Park. As I sat on a park bench reading a newspaper, two German gendarmes walked by. I continued reading as they passed me. Then, after a minute, I raised my head to make sure that they had gone. They had not. They were standing some 50 yards away, watching me. When they saw me raise my head, they immediately started moving in my direction.

'Documents,' the gendarmes ordered, in stern voices, as they approached. Calmly I pulled out my labor card. They studied it carefully.

'What are you doing in Warsaw if you work in Tomaszow?' one asked.

Keeping my composure, I pulled the certificate, duly stamped with a swastika, from my wallet. It stated clearly that I was on holiday and it was signed by the head of the *Tischlerei*, Mr J. Kramer. They gave me back my documents and left. This time I did not check to see if or where they went, nor did I raise my head again. Furtively looking back or glancing quickly to the sides was a sure giveaway; that was how the hunted and the fearful acted, those who had something to hide. Such movements were well known to the German police and the Polish blackmailers, which is why the gendarmes came back to check my papers. Without question, the documents that Ignac and I had created so painstakingly in the camp were, literally, my lifesavers.

The next day, about noon, I left the same park to make my daily visit to Kuba. As I waited at the station for my tram, a young man in the uniform of a Polish railroad worker stepped down from another tram. I recognized him at once; he was Friedel Goldberg, now Fryderyk Gorniak, another Tomaszovian who had escaped early on.

I let him distance himself a bit and then caught up to him. Fryderyk also recognized me. At first he was friendly, but when I told him that I desperately needed help – a place to sleep, a job – his expression, his whole demeanor changed.

'You must leave me alone,' he declared, waving me away. 'I cannot help you, and besides, it is not safe to be seen together. Do not follow me,' he added almost threateningly. I was bitterly disappointed. For hours his words of rejection reverberated in my ears as I agonized over how a fellow escapee could be unwilling to help.

A few weeks later an obituary note in the daily newspaper, the *Kurier* announced that a certain Fryderyk Gorniak had died while jumping off a diving board in a swimming pool. The accident had occurred at a popular sports club near the

Vistula River. The next time I saw Kuba he confirmed that it was indeed 'our' Fryderyk who had died.

On my fourth day of being homeless, Kuba gave me an address: Powisle, 46 Solec Street, apartment 49. This was also in a quarter near the Vistula River, not far from the bordello where I had stayed, but in a slightly – only slightly – better neighborhood. What was available for rent was not a room, but a corner of a room. The room, though, was relatively spacious and offered a nice bed with a quilt, white linen, and a colorful bed cover. I took it without hesitation, delighted by the thought of my own bed with two soft pillows, a quilt, and a mattress.

That evening, Mr and Mrs Spoczynski, the couple renting out the corner, offered me hot soup with bread for dinner and 'tea', made of dry apple peels, with cookies for dessert. After dinner, Mr Spoczynski showed me a watch that he had received several years before the war, for 50 years of service to his company. He and his wife must have been well over 80, both of them kind and charming. Neither one could hear or see very well, but that did not bother me; in fact, as it turned out, it had its positive aspects. How could they recognize that some of my visitors, or I, were Jewish if they could not see or hear well?

The next morning, Saturday, I notified Kuba that with his help I had succeeded in finding a place to stay. I then went to retrieve my briefcase from Zygmunt. I thanked him and his wife for their hospitality and told them that I would keep in touch and after wishing them both a fond farewell and, confirming the place and time for meeting my Aunt Marysia, off I went to Saski Park. It was a sunny day and, as on every Saturday, the park was full of people of all ages and from all walks of life. I waited in anticipation for the following day, when I would finally be reunited with my Aunt Marysia, whom I had not seen for almost four years.

8 Aunt Marysia

For the whole of that Saturday, I was filled with great eagerness and anxiety. I knew very little about my aunt's life. I was not even sure if she was in hiding or living in the open under an assumed name. I also didn't know whether she was with her children, my cousins Hania and Irka. I wanted to hear what had happened to her, but I was also impatient to tell her my story about what had happened at her friend's apartment two days after my arrival.

The next day I got up early, washed, smoothed out my rumpled clothing the best I could, and set off for Krasinski Park, where we were to meet at 11 o'clock next to the fountain. The day was bright and sunny, with a light wind rustling the leaves on the trees. The sight of so many people, all in their Sunday best, cheerful and animated, was extraordinary to me. Some had just come from morning Mass, others were on a Sunday stroll. Most people were paired, man with woman, but also man with man and woman with woman, holding each other by the arm. Some were laughing, some looked more sober, but none showed an iota of worry. Children were running, playing, giggling, and pulling on their mothers' skirts. It was a bittersweet sight for someone who, not too long ago, had many little cousins and neighbors but who had not seen any children for a year and a half. As I waited for my aunt, I was absorbed in watching the children play, looking at the birds dipping their beaks into the fountain, and watching leaves drift off the trees. The half-hour flew by quickly.

At exactly 11 o'clock, from the corner of my eye I spotted a well-dressed middle-aged woman approaching the fountain.

I wouldn't have recognized her, except that she was alone and looking left and right. We saw each other. I felt goose pimples all over my body. What a thrill it was to see her, to meet a flesh-and-blood close relative after months of being alone. At last I would be with a member of my family.

We made an effort to make the meeting appear casual so as not to attract attention: a simple handshake and a triple kiss on the cheeks, the Polish way. We blended into the moving crowd. People were walking slowly, keeping sufficient distance between them to ensure their conversations remained private.

Our problem was where to start, then how to maintain an outward calm and joviality while burning inside with impatience and anxiety. I had, by now, learned little tricks of pretense that I never would have considered using before the occupation, such as keeping a light smile on my face. They had quickly become instinctive and natural.

After an initial exchange of small talk, I realized that the smile on Marysia's face hid a terrible tragedy: her two little girls, 11-year-old Hania and 9-year-old Irka, were gone. Not much was said about it in Krasinski Park or during the months and years that followed. With time, however, and indirectly from friends, I learned of the horror of her loss. Henryk, Marysia's husband, was one of my uncles who had escaped into Russia, along with Julian and Max. Marysia remained in Warsaw, ending up in the Warsaw Ghetto with her two little daughters and her sister-in-law Mania, Max's wife. While in the Warsaw Ghetto, Marysia had learned on the grapevine that only the families of those whose head of household was employed by a German company would be exempt from deportation. With the greatest difficulty and a substantial payoff, she secured such a job. But one day, when she returned home, the girls were gone. Desperate, she ran first to the police station, then to the *Judenrat*, and finally to the Umschlagsplatz, the infamous point of departure for deportations, but to no avail. Despite all her efforts she was unable to bring them back. After the loss of the girls, both Marysia and

Mania escaped to the Aryan side in Warsaw, hiding among the Polish population. A few weeks later, however, after she had been robbed several times by blackmailers and forced to search repeatedly for a new safe lodging, Mania returned to the ghetto, unable to take the stress of being a hunted person, of hiding, of being someone else. She was never heard from again.

It will remain an eternal mystery how much misfortune a human being can suffer. We had a common prayer in those days: 'Oh, Lord, please do not afflict us with as much pain and sorrow as we are able to endure.'

Marysia and I walked in rhythm with the other Sunday strollers. We touched briefly on many subjects: life in Warsaw, relatives, the general rules that governed the peculiar life on the Aryan side. Marysia's own situation as a 'Gentile' with false identity papers, working in a bed-and-breakfast inn for relatives of German officers stationed in Warsaw, appeared to be relatively safe and satisfactory.

Eagerly I told her about my experiences of the past few days that almost ended my life. She was not surprised, as she knew already what had happened to me at Janina's place. Zygmunt had told her about it when arranging our meeting. But then came my big surprise: Marysia told me that the two Germans were imposters, that they were part of a gang of blackmailers and that the true instigators and perpetrators of my mishap were none other than Janina and Zygmunt!

I was shocked, unable to comprehend fully what I had just heard. I could not understand how my aunt's friends, former employees, recipients of many favors, could carry out such a heinous and treacherous act. Unfortunately, as I learned later, such happenings were typical and occurred often. A gang would consist of one or two front people who pretended to be friendly and helpful, and then two others, usually Germans in uniform, would attack and extort money or valuables from the scared-to-death and bewildered victim.

When I escaped from the camp I knew it was possible, even probable, that I might be caught and killed by the

Germans, or that Polish Nazi collaborators might denounce me, or that common thieves might rob me. What I was not prepared for was betrayal by old and trusted friends.

Next, we addressed a pressing and important matter: obtaining an ID card for me. Aunt Marysia knew of a man who worked in the Registrar's office where birth certificates were issued. All I needed was to submit my full name, my parents' full names, a date and place of birth, and a 50-zloty bribe. A true certificate probably did not cost more than a few zloty, but that required a baptismal certificate from the priest.

I was in the Registrar's office early the next morning and within half an hour had the birth certificate in my pocket. The next steps were routine: with a passport-type picture and another 10 zloty I applied for an ID card under my newly chosen name of Zenon Matysiak. It took two to three weeks to get the card, so until then I remained Alfons Machowiak.

Marysia and I set up times and locations for regular meetings in addition to plans for contingencies, should unexpected problems arise. We described the approximate home location, without giving the exact address, and exchanged third-party telephone numbers for emergencies. I gave Marysia Kuba's work number; she gave me that of a friend's office. We said goodbye until the next Sunday and parted.

My next challenge was finding a job. I had very little money left and I had to buy food and pay my rent. Besides, a young man of 18 hanging out on the streets of Warsaw was certain to attract attention. There were almost daily roundups during which the Germans would cordon off a three-to four-block area and arrest all young and some not-so-young men. They would all be taken to the Pawiak, a large and notorious Warsaw prison known for its torture and killings. These men became hostages for future German reprisals against acts of resistance committed by the Polish Underground.

Typically, for each act in which a German national died, at least 100 blindfolded and handcuffed hostages would be taken out of the Pawiak prison, brought to the site of the skirmish, put against the wall and shot. The next morning the Nazis would plaster the walls of the city with proclamations announcing the names of those killed and warning others of similar punishment in the future. Within hours after the executions, the relatives of the Polish victims made the killing site a martyrs' shrine overflowing with pictures of the victims, crosses, candles, and flowers.

While I waited for my ID card, I returned to Tomaszow as Alfons Machowiak. I needed to retrieve some clothing I'd left with Mrs Szewczykowa and hoped she might know something about what had happened to Ignac and the other inmates after the camp was liquidated. She was the only person in Tomaszow Ignac and I knew and trusted, and she would have been the one to hear from him.

My visit was short and very emotional. I was glad to see an old and dependable friend, and she was happy to learn that my escape had been successful and that I was alive and safe. But she had no information about Ignac. Under the circumstances, all I could do was to leave my new name and address with her and hope that Ignac, if he was still alive, might somehow get in touch. I never gave anyone else who knew my true identity any information concerning my assumed name or my address. That just was not done, for the safety of either party.

When Mrs Szewczykowa and I said good-bye, I was very touched. This woman had worried about me as if I were her own child. She was concerned about my uncertain future in the big city, about whether or not I could survive living with false papers, and about whether I would encounter good people to help and protect me. A deeply religious woman, she wept for me as she placed her hands on my head in a gesture of blessing.

On that trip from Warsaw to Tomaszow, I also experienced a one-in-a-million coincidence. At the junction station of Koluszki, where I was to transfer to another train, I ran into the real Alfons Machowiak, my fellow worker from the *Tischlerei* in Tomaszow and the true owner of the stolen labor card I was carrying.

'Zenek, what are you doing here?' he exclaimed loudly from a distance as soon as he saw me. 'Didn't you go together with –' and he stopped himself in mid-sentence as he approached me and we shook hands. I greeted him cordially but answered his few questions with a long string of my own: 'Where are you going? Are you traveling alone? How are things in the *Tischlerei*?' He looked baffled, as if he was not sure he was really seeing and hearing me. But I didn't give him a chance to lessen his befuddlement or to ask me more questions. I excused myself with the explanation that nature was calling and ran to the public toilet nearby. I did not come out for a long time. By that time, his train had left, and I never saw Alfons again.

This meeting was an unusual coincidence and could have had terrible consequences. On the Aryan side one was always worried about running into someone who knew you as a Jew; such an encounter could end up giving you away, intentionally or unintentionally. But I can hardly imagine a worse situation than running not only into someone who knew you as a Jew but into someone whose identity and documents you were carrying.

9 Working at WIFO

Finding employment on the Aryan side was more than just an economic necessity; it was also a safety precaution. To spend the days at home could make the landlord or the neighbors suspicious; wandering the streets or spending a lot of time in public parks one risked being caught by blackmailers, or German police looking for young men for forced labor camps in Germany.

One morning, after reading in the *Nowy Kurier Warszawski* that a German *Baustelle* (construction company) was looking for electricians, I went to Antoninow, just outside the Warsaw suburb of Grochow. The *Baustelle* was about two miles from Grochow's tram stop, an easy walk for an 18-year-old and well worth it as I had a 20-minute interview and was instantly hired.

What attracted me most about this job was that besides paying its workers weekly, the company also gave them breakfast and lunch daily. I also liked the fact that I wasn't asked to prove my skills as an electrician; asked for my training papers, tested; or asked for references. I would have failed on all counts. What made them want me was that I knew some German.

There was an immediate problem, however: my documentation. They required an ID card, and mine was still not ready, nor the completion date known. We agreed that I was to report to work as soon as I obtained my new card. In the interim, at my request, I was given a short note stating that I was being considered for a position with their firm and sent away. This was my first document with my new last name, Matysiak. It was written on the firm's stationery, stamped with the swastika, and carried the Nazi greeting 'Heil Hitler'. It was also the first Aryan document I'd owned that was neither stolen nor forged. The importance of this piece of paper cannot be overstated. In wartime Warsaw, obtaining a genuine German document was like winning a lottery. Moreover, this new note, except for my last name and place of birth, had nothing phony on it.

To support my new identity I needed one more element: a new history. Where did I live before the war? Which school(s) did I attend? Was I born in Warsaw? How many siblings did I have? Where were my parents? What did they do for a living? Why did I live alone? I had to be careful with the answers to these questions; the story had to be the same every time I was queried. So I was better off claiming that although I was born in Warsaw, I really had grown up with my grandfather in a distant small town and came from a very small family.

On the day I picked up my new Polish ID card, the *Kennkarte*, I was ecstatic, beaming from ear to ear. I felt great satisfaction, a sense of major accomplishment. For years, first in the ghetto and then in the camp, my friends and I had dreamed of owning this document. People were willing to pay exorbitant prices to buy one. Akiba members risked – and lost – their lives to procure them for our group. Many did not dare to escape because they had had no opportunity to obtain a *Kennkarte*, or a promise to get the card remained unfulfilled. And now I was holding one in my hands, with my picture and fingerprints, a Warsaw address and an official stamp bearing the hated swastika; it also stated clearly on the 'religion' line that I was Roman Catholic. While not a guarantee of survival, this document was one of the most important prerequisites.

Besides being a necessity for those living on the Aryan side, the ID card was a useful document for other reasons. It legitimized one's residence, qualified the bearer for ration cards, facilitated travel, and in general, afforded greater protection from being sent to Germany as a forced laborer. To me, it also meant that I could start my new job.

66

My new company's name was WIFO (*Wirtschaftliche Forschungsgesellschaft*). Its business was to construct and maintain fuel oil storage tanks for military use. Civilian Germans supervised and managed the company, security was in the hands of the *Wehrmacht*, and the workforce consisted of Poles, Russian prisoners of war, about 200 Jews from the nearby camp of Kaweczynmen; and women who were delivered to the *Baustelle* in trucks every morning. Another company, Schmitt and Junk, occupied the same premises. That was also a construction company, with no clear distinction between its functions and responsibilities and those of WIFO. Both companies had their main offices in Germany, with branches throughout occupied Europe.

I was introduced to my two German supervisors, one civilian and one military, as well as to six fellow Polish electricians, given navy-blue overalls, and shown a four-room house on the side of the road that was the electricians' workshop. I wanted to jump for joy; everything seemed so rosy, so perfect. Then a disconcerting thought crossed my mind. Did I know enough to be an electrician? What would happen when they discovered I had no real training in the field, just six months' experience as an electrician's helper? However, luck was again with me. The German supervisor announced that I would be in charge of the battery room and the tool crib – perhaps because I was the youngest and therefore least experienced – charging batteries and allocating tools. Only occasionally was I to do repairs on simple electrical devices. My skills would not be put to any major test.

This was a perfect assignment for me, and I could not have been happier. I was paid as much as any of the other men, yet I was single and was renting only a corner bed. The other electricians had families to feed and had to pay rent for bigger and more expensive accommodation.

My gnawing problem at WIFO, as elsewhere, was that I was haunted by fear and forever insecure about being recognized and betrayed. Each day I faced a new environment, met new people, and was thrown into new situations. Each presented potential danger. The interaction with German employers as an employee (rather than a slave), the close working proximity to the electricians and other Poles, the close quarters in the cafeteria, all were a constant concern. I worried over how I would answer personal questions, how would I react to an offhand anti-Semitic remark. Did I behave and react the way a Pole would behave and react? Could they somehow discern that I was not one of them, that I was a Jew? I fretted over my demeanor, conscious of my conversations and my facial expressions. This worried me to the point that my anxious look itself probably became a source of suspicion.

Besides the electricians, I made several new acquaintances while at WIFO, some in the cafeteria at lunchtime, others while walking after work to the tram stop. One was a blond, blue-eyed boy, who was about my age, named Wladek Warzajtys; the other was called Roman, tall and slim with sandy-colored hair and freckles, a few years older than I. Roman always carried a briefcase with some papers, which may have been just to show off the fact that he was more important because he worked in the office. (See Chapters 13 and 14, where I discuss the role these two played in my wartime activities.)

The six electricians I worked with were more or less a congenial group, mostly family men, professional in their work, with a live-and-let-live attitude. During the lunch hour (which lasted only 30 to 40 minutes), the men chatted about trivialities or swapped dirty jokes. Two of them stood out from the group. One was a man named Szemanski, exceptionally affable and pleasant, who always carried a dog-eared paperback book in the side pocket of his jacket. With an almost permanent smile on his face, he read his book whenever there were a few minutes of free time. We all had the impression that he was reading a suspense novel that he could not put down. He was intelligent and obviously educated, as his command of Polish was excellent. He was also very helpful to me whenever I was stuck with a problem or did something wrong. Most of the others were also helpful, but he was more discreet than the others, whispering advice in a fatherly way.

The other notable figure was Urban. Tall and husky, he was the opposite of Szemanski, always grouchy, rude, loud and domineering, often cursing and never smiling. He was also, for me, the most dangerous of my co-workers. He was a vicious anti-Semite whose every second sentence contained some derogatory reference to the Jews, using the insulting term '*Zydki*' (Jew boys). He was particularly nasty to me. I didn't know whether he disliked me personally or if he hated me because he suspected that I was a Jew. In either case he posed a daily danger, and I tried to avoid him as much as possible. One day, not long after joining the group, after I had finished repairing an electric iron, I plugged it into the receptacle to ascertain that it now worked. To my surprise, at that moment a cloud of white smoke rose from the iron. I became concerned, of course, until I saw Urban nearby puffing cigarette smoke into a narrow rubber tube attached to the bench where the iron was sitting. Everyone thought this to be a funny practical joke – all except Szemanski and me.

On my first visit to Warsaw after the war I made a special effort to find Szemanski. I wanted to tell him that I was a Jew and to thank him for being always so friendly and sympathetic when we worked at WIFO. I found him living in a modest apartment in Praga, the sector of Warsaw on the eastern bank of the Vistula. When I entered his home, his smile was broader than ever before.

'I knew it all along,' Szemanski said when I revealed my true identity. 'Before the war I was a high-school teacher in a school with many Jewish students, and you looked like one of my students.' He then told me in how much danger I had been because of Urban. 'As nasty as he was in your presence, Urban was outright threatening behind your back. He did not want you in our group,' he told me. 'More than once I had to scold him for accusing you of being Jewish. "I taught in a Catholic school and Zenon was in that school, so I know that he is not Jewish," I told Urban and the others.' Szemanski also told me how delighted he was that I had survived the war.

10 A Life with Substance

About six weeks after my escape from the Tomaszow Labor Camp, and feeling well settled in Warsaw, I decided to try and join the Jewish Underground in hope of taking an active role in the struggle against the Nazi enemy. Yitzhak's inspiring appeal at our last Akiba meeting, his call to take a stand against passivity and quiet compliance, to act with purpose and initiative to bring about our own survival and that of others, had prepared me to take on additional risks, and to join the Jewish Underground movement seemed a logical next step.

I approached Kuba, whom I was now seeing two to three times a week. Although he did not belong to any resistance organization, he seemed to have the contacts; he always had the latest political and world news and occasionally shared with me newsletters produced by the Underground movement. When I asked him to arrange a meeting with a member of the movement, he did so promptly. Within a few days he informed me that the following Sunday I was to meet a representative of the *Zydowska Organizacja Bojowa* (ZOB) at a tram station on the corner of Aleje Jerozolimskie and Nowy Swiat. 'He will be waiting for you on the bench,' Kuba told me. 'But what does he look like? How will we recognize each other?' I asked. Unable to give me any details or any descriptive features of the man I was to meet, Kuba replied, with a slight smile, 'You will recognize each other. I don't know how, but we always do.'

I spent the next four days in restless anticipation. I wondered who the mysterious man might be. I tried to imagine the secret and daring missions on which I might be sent. In my mind, the word 'resistance' conjured up all sorts of ideas and images of fascinating intrigues and dangerous, daring situations.

Sunday finally came. As excited as I was about my new undertaking, I kept it secret. When I met Marysia that Sunday morning, as I did every Sunday, I did not say a word about my imminent meeting with the man from the ZOB. For her own safety and perhaps mine, I kept that information, as well as all other underground activities, secret from her throughout the war, though I think she guessed at much of it.

Anxious to allow myself enough time to find the location, I left Marysia a little earlier than usual and arrived for the meeting at least an hour and a half before the appointed time. I went to the meeting place and found the correct bench. As I still had plenty of time, and to distract my mind and ease the tension, I strolled around Warsaw, taking in the beauty of the city, rich in historical landmarks, palaces, and monuments, replete with verdant parks and innumerable churches – a lovely contrast to my hometown of Lódz. The serene Vistula River, without a single ripple, snaked placidly through the northeastern part of the town. On the other side of the river was the Praga district, and beyond it, the suburb of Grochow, where I worked.

At two o'clock sharp, I returned to the meeting place. Already sitting on the bench was a rather short, skinny, middle-aged man with a flat peasant hat that was lowered all the way to his eyebrows. We made contact with each other at once. The mystery man suddenly did not appear very mysterious after all. He introduced himself simply as Czeslaw, and at his suggestion we went for a walk toward the river, in a direction that had few pedestrians. I learned later that his real name was Jacob 'Celek' Celemenski; he had already been a leader in the Jewish labor movement before the war and was now a leader in the Underground. With his blondish hair, light eyes, pale complexion, high cheekbones, and small nose, he blended easily into the Polish population. What was surprising, however, was that he was able to continue his activities on the Aryan side in spite of the fact that he spoke Polish with a distinct Yiddish accent.

Czeslaw asked me the minimum number of questions about my living and job situations, my place of origin, and my family. Then he abruptly turned toward me and asked if I was prepared to carry out underground activities. With my unequivocal 'yes', Czeslaw proceeded to explain the organization's goals and two main activities: aiding the partisans in the forests and general support for the remaining Jews, both those in the few remaining ghettos and those in hiding on the Aryan side. He then suggested that given my relatively secure situation, I should remain at my workplace and lodgings in Warsaw. As my main goal was to participate in the anti-Nazi struggle in any way I could, I was agreeable to any assignment, anywhere.

Czeslaw and I agreed to meet at the same place the following Sunday, when he would introduce me to my direct superior. He shook my hand, and we parted. I was in a daze but ecstatic, remembering how in the Akiba meetings we had talked about making contact with the Underground, like a dream that we all wished but dared not hope would come true. And now, I had not only made contact with it, but was a part of it.

The next Sunday brought a delightful surprise: my direct superior turned out to be a young attractive brunette named Ala. Ala was from Warsaw and was an active member of the ZOB while still inside the ghetto. Her job now was that of courier, and I was designated to assist her. Our association, however, did not last long. Within the same week she was reassigned to another task, and at our second meeting a week later, she introduced me to my new superior, Krysia.

Krysia was another attractive young woman of about 21, blonde, with sparkling brown eyes and a perpetual Mona Lisa smile. She gave an impression of quiet intelligence; when she did speak she mostly asked questions and, as a result, she learned all about me, while I learned little about her. I knew her first name, that she was from Warsaw, and that she lived with her ailing mother. What I did not know at the time was that hiding in her home was her fiancé, Henryk, whom she later married, or that she also had a brother living in hiding at a different address and for whom she also was responsible.

Over the many months that followed, I learned that Krysia was a true Jewish heroine. A full-time courier for the ZOB, she was courageous, selfless, and totally devoted to the cause of resisting the Nazis and helping Jews survive.

Here is how one of Krysia's superiors, Vladka Meed, a known ZOB activist and a heroine in her own right, described her after the war:

> Krysia Mucznik of Warsaw was the most active and diligent of these aides. Beautiful, slender, blond, about twenty-two years old, she shared her living quarters with her ailing mother, whom she often had to lock in, to hurry off on some errand with which she has been entrusted.[10]

Krysia and I lived about two miles from each other, on the eastern side of the Vistula, and we took the same number 27 tram home. When we got off at the Washington Square station, we briefly chatted, agreed on our next meeting's time and place, and said goodbye. Krysia waited until I disappeared completely before starting home. This was not an uncommon precaution in those days, especially if you had others to protect, but it was also typical of Krysia, who was always responsible, always careful. During more than a year of working together, work that almost always entailed the danger of being unmasked and taken away, I became a great admirer of hers, awed by her courage and dedication.

Although I did not know it then, the ZOB was an umbrella organization for various political parties, and Czeslaw represented only one of them, the Bund, a socialist, non-Zionist, Yiddish-promoting group, also known as the Jewish Labor Party. Neither did I know that there were considerable inter-party rivalries within the ZOB or that one major Jewish organization was not even part of the ZOB. That organization,

73

the *Zydowski Zwiazek Wojskowy* (ZZW), which was on the right
of the Jewish political spectrum, was a separate fighting force
in the Warsaw Ghetto uprising and remained separate on the
Aryan side. The ZZW partisans and the Bundists were bitter
ideological enemies. At the time, however, the political
distinctions between the parties, their often opposing
agendas, and their infighting were of little concern to young
people like Krysia and me.

My assignments as Krysia's assistant consisted mostly of
delivering packages, small suitcases, and occasionally
envelopes containing monthly subsistence money to various
destinations for people in hiding. These individuals, or at
times small groups, maybe two or three members of the same
family, could not provide for themselves because their
appearance or accent made it too risky for them to leave their
hideouts. The deliveries, even if routine and less glamorous
than the assignments I had dreamed of before I had joined the
Underground, were crucial tasks. Although I was not privy to
the content of the packages, typically they contained food and
medical supplies, sometimes documents or other necessities
critical to their survival.

The more difficult and considerably more risky work was
making deliveries to safe houses on the outskirts of town. For
these deliveries, the suitcases were considerably larger and
heavier, as they contained supplies, ammunition, and
weapons for the partisans fighting in the woods. But it was
not the weight that worried us. In wartime Warsaw, people
who carried suitcases always attracted attention, and not only
from the Germans. The Polish police were on the lookout for
smugglers, so that they could either confiscate the illegal
goods or extort a bribe for not taking them. Then there were
common thieves, always ready to snatch a valise – the heavier
and bigger the valise, the better.

Generally, it was assumed in the Underground that it was
safer to work in pairs. In cases where arrest was threatened,
one could distract the arresting party while your partner
could discreetly slip away with the contraband. Or, should

74

one get arrested, your partner could provide a report stating who did the seizure and where you had been taken. Krysia and I pretended to be a young couple, newly arrived from out of town. Arm in arm, we walked and talked, trying to look cheerful, carefree, and oblivious to our surroundings. One rule we agreed on was never to glance, never to look around, and especially never to look back. However, to my best recollection, we didn't have an escape plan, reluctant as we were to think about what might happen to us if we got caught.

Transportation was our biggest challenge. We traveled mostly by tram and after work hours, at exactly the time when Warsaw trams were particularly crowded. To make the situation worse, some trams were designated for Germans only and were off limits to us. Those passengers who got on the tram in the central parts of town often had to resort to traveling 'grape-style', i.e. hanging on the side of the car, holding onto a window or anything else protruding, with one foot on a step or a wheel axle. A variation of this arrangement was to stand on the junction equipment that connected two trolley cars. For Krysia and me, because we always carried a suitcase or other loads, to stand on the junction equipment was the only option. While we worried about losing our balance or slipping 'on the grape', at least we did not have to worry about being caught as smugglers or, worse, being recognized as Jews. Typically, policemen, blackmailers, and thieves thought this way of travelling too risky and left those who did it alone.

Financial assistance to those in hiding came from two sources. A small amount of funding came from the Polish government-in-exile in London and was channeled through the Warsaw Delegatura (its representative in the underground) and from a newly established organization called *Zegota*, a Polish committee to help Jews. The largest donations, however, came from Jewish organizations abroad: the American Joint Distribution Committee, the Jewish Labor Committee, and others. The money was provided to the government-in-exile in London, transferred to the Delegatura in Warsaw, then distributed by the Jewish National Committee. As the war progressed, increasingly larger amounts were made available to the Jewish Underground. Unfortunately for many Jews on the Aryan side, however, the Underground's distribution process had serious problems and a significant number never received any financial help. Many were unaware of the existence of the Jewish organizations and their funds; even fewer knew of the existence of *Zegota*. Typically, an escapee arriving in Warsaw knew only a few Jews or Poles and sometimes knew no one; for example, when I got to Warsaw I had only two contacts, an address for Janina and a telephone number for Kuba.

The organizations, on the other hand, while aware that there were many needy people in hiding, did not know how to reach them. Naturally, they couldn't publicize their funds except by word of mouth, and they always had to be extremely careful not to risk exposure. For a long time I did not know about assistance funds, and neither did the Jews closest to me. Yet, according to Celemenski and Paulsson between 8,000 and 9,000 Jews in Warsaw were receiving monthly subsidies.[11] How did this happen? Based on what I learned after the war from other Aryan-side survivors and from other sources, the recipients of regular subsidies were either party activists like Krysia, party members who were unable to earn a living in the open and therefore were confined to hiding, and people who happened to have learned about the money from those who were receiving it. Each political party within the ZOB received subsidies and each strongly favored in many ways its own members.

Distributing financial aid to the ghettos and camps had its own problems. By the end of 1943, almost all of the ghettos and small labor camps in Poland had been liquidated. Their populations had either been sent to the few remaining larger ghettos, such as Lódz or Częstochowa, or been killed in extermination camps such as Treblinka, Auschwitz, or Belzec. The few remaining camps and ghettos were rigidly guarded and hermetically sealed, with Jewish, Polish, or regular German police guards replaced by SS and Gestapo troops. The result was that all reliable contacts within the ghettos and camps were lost, and the establishment of new channels was almost impossible. Although money was available, providing financial help to the ghettos and camps was extremely difficult, as the surviving inmates were constantly being moved within the camp and out to other camps. In the end, the only channels available to maintain contacts were couriers sent by the Underground.

Distributing aid to those on the Aryan side also had its problems. Some, like those in complete hiding, never ventured outside and never saw anyone except one or two protectors who were providing their basic necessities. And even if they heard about aid, they did not know how to obtain it. Because of the essential secrecy, the contacts were made by word of mouth, and only a few knew the right names and places. Conversely, the ZOB did not know who was in need and where to find them. There were others, like me, who lived in the open and neither sought help nor needed it. People in this category either worked and earned money or had sufficient means of their own. During the time Krysia and I carried envelopes or packages and suitcases to and fro, I never even knew what was inside them. Only after the war did Krysia reveal their contents to me.

The financial help from abroad or from local sources ameliorated some situations and saved some lives. But more often it was too little, too late. Too little, because the early limited amounts were insufficient either to buy off the Nazis or to prevent starvation in the ghettos. Too late, because by the time the amounts became substantial, in the millions of dollars, the great mass of European Jewry had already been murdered.

In the spring of 1944, Krysia told me that the ZOB had more money than it knew what to do with. Yitzhak Zuckerman, one of the few surviving leaders of the Warsaw Ghetto uprising, reports that during the Polish uprising in August and September of 1944, when a ZOB safe house at 18 Leszno Street burned to the ground, more than a million dollars went up in flames.[12] How many more millions in other safe houses were lost, how much money remained at the war's end, and what happened to it, we may never know.

One of the Jewish workers from the Kaweczyn camp brought to WIFO in trucks every morning was a sweet 16-year-old girl from Berlin named Eva Schuster. She worked in a building right across the street from mine. Eva was pretty, bright-eyed, vivacious, and full of life. It was hard not to feel sorry for her. On some mornings, I would bring her an apple or a chocolate bar and exchange a few friendly words. I tried to show her a little compassion, cheer her up, and encourage her. But what I really wanted to do was to rescue her. I enlisted the help of Kuba and Krysia, and together we devised a plan. We saw no major problems: we knew by now how to obtain forged Polish documents, especially the *Kennkarte*, and we had some ideas for a hiding place, at least on a temporary basis. Eva's fair complexion meant that she could easily pass for a Pole, and even her Polish was adequate. Escaping itself was quite easy. The *Baustelle* was a vast area with hundreds of workers, and the building she was working in was unguarded. It was a promising situation.

Toward the end of July we heard rumors that the Kaweczyn camp was to be liquidated. Our plan was ready, and we made arrangements to carry it out in the first week of August. But we were too late. One day, at the beginning of August, neither Eva nor the other Jews returned for work at the *Baustelle*. Nobody knew what had happened. The general response was one of silence and indifference. Outwardly my reaction did not differ from that of the others, but the fate of these Jews, and especially Eva's fate, greatly preoccupied me.

Three days later we learned what had happened to them, when our supervisor drove up with a truck and ordered all the electricians to take their toolboxes and accompany him. 'The Jews are gone, and we are going to dismantle all the electrical equipment in their camp,' he said.

Within minutes, we reached a cluster of barracks located a

short distance from the *Baustelle*, on the edge of a small forest. As we opened the wide double doors of the barracks, we saw a wall of small black insects slowly rising from the floor. A black tidal wave of fleas – thousands upon thousands – was moving toward us, randomly changing form within itself. As we entered, they swarmed and attacked us. At first, we tried to repel them with hand motions or tried to kill the ones that attached themselves to the exposed parts of our bodies. We waved cardboard in front of us, but to no avail. They were everywhere, crawling under our clothing, sucking our blood. They had not eaten for three full days, and now they were going after us to satisfy their hunger.

The inside of the barracks was a scene of misery and desolation. The barracks were pitifully bare. For some semblance of privacy, the inmates had crisscrossed the space with strings and attached blankets or linen to them to create rooms and cubicles. The floor was bare ground. There were cots to sleep on and boxes of various shapes and sizes serving as chairs and tables. Papers, clothing, and other items were strewn all over. It was clear that the inmates had had to get ready at short notice and, surmising their destination, had been in a panic.

In one room, on the floor, I found two pictures. One was of a shadowy figure of Eva standing in the doorway of the building where she had been working next to her German supervisor. The second picture was of an attractive dark-haired young woman, gazing intently and lovingly at a pretty girl, about 8 years old, who was staring defiantly at the camera. I turned the photograph over and found the names written neatly on the back. It was a picture of Eva with her mother. I slipped both photographs into my pocket.

Without delay, we completed dismantling the electrical equipment, loaded it up, and returned to the *Baustelle* whereupon some of us headed straight for the local lake. Except for our shoes, we jumped in fully clothed, hoping that the fleas from the camp would drown. Unfortunately, that didn't happen, and I had fleas on my skin and in my clothing for several weeks.

I was reminded of the people from the Kaweczyn camp some 40 years later in Los Angeles, when I attended a social function sponsored by a local survivor organization, 'The 1939 Club'. One of my companions at the dinner table was Fred Kort. The conversation drifted to the question 'Where were you during the war?' It turned out that Fred was one of those 200 inmates of Kaweczyn and was a 'next door neighbor' to Eva and her mother. As we had suspected then, and as Fred confirmed, all inmates of the Kaweczyn camp had been sent to Treblinka, where most of them perished. Fred was one of the very few who managed to escape and survive.

My work in the Underground lasted just over a year. It seemed routine and, on the surface, of little significance. Even the constant fear of being caught became so routine that it ceased to preoccupy my mind. Yet this period and that work were the most exciting and most meaningful of my entire life, before or since. I was filled with a passion and a sense of purpose that had no equal. Life was full of danger at every corner, with every encounter, but it was also filled with an incredible sense of accomplishment and satisfaction. I gave of myself the most one could give, and I knew that, in a small way, I was helping people survive. Although Krysia and I spent many hours discussing various topics, from ethics to the war situation and from our lost youth to future dreams and hopes, we never talked about how we felt about our work or our feelings of the present. Yet I am quite sure that her experiences evoked the same feelings of purpose and satisfaction that I felt. Many years after the war, we were sitting in a hotel coffee shop across from the main railroad station in her new hometown of Zurich, and Krysia described those times in Warsaw in her uniquely succinct way: 'It was a life with substance.'

11 The Hotel Polski Trap

On the third or fourth Sunday after my arrival in Warsaw, Aunt Marysia arrived at Krasinski Park for our regular meeting unusually happy, yet agitated.

'Zenek!' she exclaimed. 'Our worrisome days are over. We're going to be exchanged for Germans held in Allied countries.'

'What are you talking about?' I asked, dumbfounded.

She proceeded to tell me about the Hotel Polski, where organizers had set up their headquarters, and where each candidate for exchange was to register. She had already started arrangements for herself and she wanted and expected me to do the same.

'We will be getting real visas,' she told me, 'Even new foreign passports. We will have the status of aliens.'

She explained that the documents were genuine, from South American countries and Palestine, and had been issued to Jews who were no longer alive. The Gestapo, who took possession of these visas after killing the rightful owners, was now ready to sell them to Jews hiding on the Aryan side in Warsaw. To give credibility to the scheme, Marysia pointed out that some prominent Jews were involved. One of them was a certain Mr David Guzik, the head of the American Joint Distribution Committee in prewar Poland; others were from the Jewish Underground. Another reassuring fact, she explained, was that people could enter and exit the hotel freely. Finally, those who had gone on such an exchange earlier had confirmed, by letters, their arrival at a transit camp in Vittel, a city in France, where they claimed the conditions were quite acceptable. 'The Germans are treating prospective

Jewish emigrés with the same courtesy they normally accorded foreign citizens,' they wrote to their friends who remained in Warsaw.

'This is a unique opportunity to reach the outside world, to reach real freedom, to survive,' Marysia said, trying to persuade me. 'Yes, one has to "buy" a place on the list, but don't worry. We'll find the funds. Such funds are available from the various underground organizations, Jewish and Polish.'

For Marysia, it was not a question of if I would sign up, but when.

She asked me to accompany her to the hotel, as she had agreed to meet some people there. Reluctantly, I consented, even though I was not convinced that what I had just heard was for real. I could not fathom the notion that all of a sudden the Germans should be trusted again. As we walked in the direction of Dluga Street, where the Hotel Polski was located, I suddenly had a change of heart. 'I'll wait for you here, Marysia,' I said, when we were not far short of the hotel. 'I'll just walk around the block. Spend as much time there as you need; I'll be here, waiting.'

She agreed and walked on.

While I waited, I got curious. I walked closer to the hotel and began observing the people at the revolving doors. Indeed, there were no Germans in sight. Men and women, presumably all Jewish, walked in and out of the lobby completely unhindered. Some of these people clearly did not have to take this chance; they were well dressed and appeared to blend well with the Polish population. And images of past experiences were spinning in my head, such as the fate of the Bernsteins in Tomaszow, the family who had been promised exchange with German nationals from Switzerland but instead had been taken to the Jewish cemetery and killed.

My understanding of this Gestapo 'emigration' plan was not very clear, nor did I know many facts or details about it. But my conclusion about what to do was clear and firm: I would throw in my lot with the Poles of Warsaw rather than reveal my identity to those whom I hated the most and trusted the least.

The whole exchange scheme did not make one iota of sense to me, and when Marysia returned I told her that I would not be signing up for it. She was visibly unhappy, as she did not want to go alone, but I stood firm. Another week or two passed and Marysia, too, reconsidered her plans and decided not to go.

The Gestapo, which organized the whole affair, went to incredible lengths to give the 'exchange' an authentic appearance, as was illustrated by the following incident. A week before his departure, one of the Jewish registrants went to the home of a Polish acquaintance to retrieve his belongings, which he had left there for safekeeping, but the acquaintance, knowing that the man was about to leave the country, refused to return them. This was not an uncommon occurrence on the Aryan side. What was uncommon in this case was that when the registrant complained to the Hotel Polski organizers about the dishonest Pole, they sent two uniformed Germans to the cheat's home to help the Jew, apparently now a respected and protected foreigner, reclaim his property.

With their foreign visas in hand, those who signed up for the 'exchange' were led to their deaths, in various camps or in the courtyard of Pawiak prison. Among those who perished was my friend Adas Lichtenstein, from Akiba, the only member of our group whom I encountered in Warsaw. A week before departure, I met Adas in Warsaw on the Aryan side, shortly after my arrival there. He said he was tired of pretending to be a Pole, tired of being on the run, tired of hiding, tired of being in constant fear of discovery. He was tired of living, he told me. My fresh zest and enthusiasm did not raise his sinking spirits. On the day the Gestapo offered Jews in hiding the chance to be exchanged for German prisoners in Allied hands, he accepted the offer and joined others at the Hotel Polski. He tried to persuade me to come with him. But I had arrived in Warsaw only a few weeks before and was neither tired nor dispirited. I stood by my decision not to go and tried to convince him to do the same.

Of more than 3,500 Jews who assembled at the Hotel Polski, only about 40 survived.

12 Friends Helping Friends

In the Tomaszow Ghetto, I had known Ludwik only casually. I knew that he was at least seven or eight years older than I was, that his name was originally Fredek Lenga, and that he came from a prominent and well-to-do family. I also knew that he had graduated from law school at an unusually young age because of his exceptional intelligence. However, as I later discovered, his intelligence did not extend to practical matters that were essential to surviving on the Aryan side. Although Ludwik had escaped from the Tomaszow Labour Camp a few weeks before I did, his situation was one of continual minor and not-so-minor problems.

One day in the late summer of 1943, during one of my periodic visits with Kuba, he informed me that Ludwik was in a terrible situation and urgently needed help.

'What kind of help?' I asked. 'Lodging? Money? Job?'

'Everything; all of the above,' Kuba answered. I promised to do what I could.

When I saw Ludwik the next day, he was glassy-eyed and on the verge of a mental breakdown. I brought him to the Spoczynskis', where he slept on a cot that we borrowed from a neighbor: exhausted, he slept for two nights and two days. My own accommodation on Solec Street was not for two people and, at best, only temporary, so I went in search of new lodgings. Finding a home in wartime Warsaw was a major problem, especially for fugitives. There was a scarcity of places, the city was overcrowded, but, most importantly, apartment owners were afraid to rent to strangers for fear that they were Jews. Since personal recommendations and references were also hard to get, I resorted to a second best source:

the local church. Since moving into the room on Solec Street, I had attended church to establish my new Catholic identity. Attendance at church, particularly for Sunday Mass, was part of my cover. From day one I wore a cross around my neck, and at home, above my bed, there hung a crucifix. Every evening, before going to bed, I knelt and said the *pacierz* (evening prayer). My problem was that I did not know the words to the various prayers, especially the prayers in church. In such cases I would just move my lips. In time, I learned the number count that was equivalent to the length of a given prayer; the *pacierz*, for example, required me to count to 52.

It was at the church that I noticed a bulletin board with all kinds of advertisements, including rooms for rent, one of which was in the Grochow area on Osowska Street, close to my place of work. I managed to rent this room even though my landlord knew nothing about me; he assumed that I attended the church where he placed the advertisement. It was a reference of sort.

I quickly moved into my new home, which meant that Ludwik was able to take over my corner at the Spoczynskis'. I continued to sleep there on occasion, when my busy schedule did not leave me enough time to get to Grochow before curfew. I also used it as my mailing address. My rule at this time was to split my life into more than one compartment and to keep each compartment as separate as possible from the others. Marysia did not know where I lived or worked, although she had a telephone number where she could leave messages for me. The Spoczynskis would not know where to find me if their life depended on it, and some of my friends only knew where to find me on specific days and at specific times. These safety precautions were sometimes difficult to keep track of, but somehow they all worked. It is amazing how complex problems find easy solutions when one's life depends on it.

Ludwik was still in a state of semi-shock, but he was slowly recovering. He had no problem passing for a Pole; his features, his Polish pronunciation, and his demeanor aroused no suspicion. He easily won over the Spoczynskis' hearts, judging by the many complimentary remarks they made about him. Providing food for him was also no problem, as staple items were relatively available and affordable.

Little by little, Ludwik told me his story. While still in the Tomaszow camp, he signed a promissory note to sell one of his family's houses to a Polish friend after the war. In return, he received a substantial sum of money. Being financially secure, he and his young wife, who also had Aryan features and spoke flawless Polish, managed to escape to the Polish side of Warsaw. Shortly thereafter, they moved to a nearby resort town, Otwock, settling in one of the many boarding houses used by holiday-makers before the war. They led a normal and comfortable life, regularly taking long walks through the picturesque countryside. Life was pleasant and carefree and, to all appearances, secure.

One day, when they returned from their afternoon walk, their landlords, anxiously awaiting their return, informed them that the Gestapo was looking for them. Further, the landlady told them that she could not let them in because it would endanger them, the landlords, and their family. They were told that they must leave town immediately and never return. She closed the door in their faces, not even allowing them to retrieve their belongings.

With only pocket money and the clothes on their backs, they left. For three days they hid in the surrounding fields. Then, dirty, hungry, and exhausted, his wife could not bear it anymore. Despondent, she took her own life with a cyanide pill.[13] In despair and confusion, Ludwik left her body in the potato fields. Somehow he managed to get to Warsaw to contact some friends, among them Kuba.

Slowly, at the Spoczynskis', things began to improve for Ludwik, and he regained a measure of self-confidence. At the first opportunity, he returned to Otwock to search for his wife's body. He looked everywhere, but there were many potato fields and they all looked the same. He even made some discreet inquiries, but without success. He learned, however, that the Gestapo had not been looking for him. The landlords had turned to blackmail, and had invented the Gestapo story to rob Ludwik and his wife of their possessions.

After a few weeks of physical and mental rest, Ludwik applied for and got a job as a clerk at the *Baustelle* where I worked. He was assigned a room in the company's barracks, got a certificate stating that he was employed in a war-important enterprise, and was fed breakfast and lunch each day. In time, he regained some sense of safety and self-worth, a measure of hope and faith. But not completely. The memory of the tragic loss of his young wife – and a fear of blackmailers – lingered.

When Ignac and I said good-bye to each other at the Tomaszow factory on 28 May 1943, our paths diverged into the unknown. We did not know if either path would lead to a chance at life or to a certain death, and we wondered if we would ever see each other again. The prospect seemed remote.

Although the question of what had happened to Ignac and other friends from Tomaszow was often in my thoughts, I didn't know how to find out where they had been taken, if they were safe or even alive, and to some extent I was afraid to find out. So many before had been taken away and never heard from again.

But one day in December the gnawing question of my friend's fate was answered. That evening after work I stopped at the Spoczynski residence to pick up my mail and found a letter from Ignac. I couldn't believe it. He had found a way to communicate with the outside world from inside the Blizyn Labor Camp and had located Mrs Szewczykowa, our co-worker in the *Tischlerei* in Tomaszow and the only person to whom I had given my address.

In his letter, he inquired about my health and well-being, about Warsaw, about work opportunities, about living conditions, and about many other topics. His numerous questions were in code but very clear to me: he was now ready to join me and wanted to know what prospects for survival one could expect in Warsaw. I responded without hesitation or delay that I was doing well, that he and Tetka should 'come IMMEDIATELY' and that 'in Warsaw one CAN survive!'

I received one more letter from Ignac. But to my astonishment, before I managed to mail my response, Ignac arrived in Warsaw, on 16 December 1943.

Ignac turned up at 49 Solec Street, the address that I had left with Mrs Szewczykowa, but by that time I was living in Grochow. I didn't visit my old lodging very often, but on that day I stopped by to pick up my mail. As I entered, I greeted the elderly Mrs Spoczynski. Then I saw Ignac. He was sitting with his back to the entrance door, but I recognized him instantly. I couldn't believe how quickly he had managed to get there.

Though I greeted him casually, as if I had expected him, we were at a loss for words. Ignac appeared to be in a daze and at the point of exhaustion. He looked like someone who had had no food or sleep for days. His eyes expressed uncertainty, apprehension, and confusion; his clothing was in tatters. I repeatedly patted him on the back and whispered, 'It's good you are here, it's good you are here.' I was overcome with happiness that he had taken this critical step toward survival.

The Spoczynski apartment had a large room, a corridor, and a kitchen. It did not provide much privacy for a conversation, but Ignac managed to whisper something about the critical situation 'they' were in. When he used the plural, I thought that he was referring to Tetka and wondered where she might be hiding. Then Ignac said something about escaping from the camp with another man, a friend named Stasiek.

In the two letters I had received from Ignac, Stasiek's name was never mentioned. I asked Ignac where Stasiek was, but he was fearful of saying it in my landlord's presence, blurting out something about 'downstairs' and 'public toilets'. At first I did not fully grasp what he was trying to tell me, but then I realized that Stasiek was hiding around the communal toilets. I was incredulous. What could be more suspicious than a stranger hanging around all night in such an unsavory place? I couldn't begin to explain to Ignac how dangerous it was.

Indeed, Stasiek was at that moment curled up in a wall recess, close to communal toilets and above a large trash bin, both on the ground floor of our building. Ignac and Stasiek had spent most of the day there, hungry and cold, waiting for me. After their escape from the camp, they had walked for miles from one village to another, sometimes on and sometimes off the road, through fields and forests. In the dark, local blackmailers, thieves, and other criminals had robbed them of their few possessions. Even their meager winter clothing had been taken from them. Penniless and with no place to spend the first few nights, their future looked hopeless.

As the day was rapidly coming to an end, many problems had to be resolved. The main dilemma was lodging, but they also needed food, clothing, documents, and a place to spend their time during the day. They had to be educated about the dos and don'ts of life in hiding and how to keep themselves and others safe. The problem in Aryan Warsaw was that the sum of one plus one was greater than two. There was a saying at the time: 'One Jew looks like one Jew, but two Jews look like three.'

Quickly, we had to dispense with niceties and determine what to do. I turned to Mrs Spoczynska and asked, 'Is my bed still available?' 'Yes, of course,' she answered. 'We would like to take it for Ignac; I'll pay the rent for now. Later we'll find him a job, and there will be no problem paying the rent.' She immediately agreed. I had always gotten along well with her and her husband, and they happily tolerated my frequent switching of tenants for their rental bed; Ignac was neither the first 'sub-boarder' nor the last. At different times, over the year or so of my stay in Warsaw, the Solec Street lodging had had a total of six Jews: four friends, one relative, and myself. This modest corner was their safe haven in time of dire need.

But what about Stasiek? Putting him and Ignac in one bed would have been not only awkward but suspicious, especially since his name was never mentioned before. Taking him to my place was too risky for both of us. Stasiek would have to remain in his current accommodation for at least that night. The curfew hour was soon approaching, and I had to get home to Grochow. 'I will be back tomorrow, early; I'll see what I can bring,' I told them.

The next morning, I collected food and some pieces of clothing – some of which I'd bought just days before – packed it all into a small suitcase, and headed for Solec Street. I could not stay long, as I had to rush back to work.

We had to get Stasiek out of the restroom area. It was not only unsavory but also outright dangerous. On the second or third morning, at about 6 a.m., while Stasiek was sound asleep in the recess above the rubbish bin, a tenant in the apartment building had entered and noticed the stranger. He woke him up and asked what he was doing there. Stasiek mumbled something and then began repeating: 'I am a Pole, I am a Pole.' Luckily, this man was the only other Jewish tenant in the building, the one who told Kuba Rajzman about the bed at the Spoczynski apartment when I was first looking for lodging. (He and I never met, but he often complained to Kuba that with all the strangers I was bringing home, I was endangering the entire neighborhood.) The man told Stasiek sternly to move out from there, to move on, but also wished him good luck. Then he added, 'I am from the same parish' (*Jestem z tej samej Parafji*), the equivalent of saying 'I am a member of the same tribe.' Had anyone else discovered Stasiek, we all might have been in much worse trouble.

I needed to enlist help. At the top of the list of those to contact were my Aunt Marysia and Maciej Monszajn, a family friend who was always helpful. He was blond and blue-eyed, with a pug nose and a light complexion, and exceptionally enterprising. For most of us it was difficult enough just to survive on Aryan papers, but during the war Maciej managed to start several successful businesses. Because of his perfect Aryan features, I 'adopted' Maciej as my uncle and enlisted him as an occasional visitor, making sure to introduce him to my landlord and neighbors, in order to dispel any suspicions they may have had about me. I always made it clear that he was from my mother's side, in order to explain his different surname.

The next evening, Stasiek, Ignac, and I met at Maciej's latest place of business, a vinegar distributors on Chlodna Street, to see if he could help with the newcomers' needs for lodging, documents, employment, more clothing, and cash. Luckily, Ignac had a diamond that his mother had sewn into his long johns, which he now vowed to sell. In the meantime, Maciej not only allowed Stasiek to stay overnight, but also offered both of them temporary jobs. 'You boys are too young to die,' he told them.

Slowly, and with the help of many people, Ignac and Stasiek's problems found resolutions. They were fed and received warm winter clothing, and the process of obtaining Polish ID cards was set in motion. Fortunately, the Underground organizations had become very skilled in producing authentic-looking cards without the major involvement of the applicant. In many cases all that was needed was a proper photo. Ignac sold his diamond through Maciej for about 20,000 zloty, so even money problems were resolved.

Yet, while Ignac had a place at the Spoczynskis', Stasiek's accommodation remained a problem. Finding him a place of his own was extremely difficult, and besides, he had no money. Any temporary or shared lodging was likely to arouse suspicion. Because he spoke Polish with a Yiddish accent, he needed a hideout where his landlord or host would be aware of his identity. We tried hard and did what we could. Stasiek stayed a few nights with Ludwik, who now had a room at my *Baustelle*. In the evening, Stasiek entered the room through a back window and went out the same way in the morning. Then I found him a place for a few days with a distant relative of mine, Helenka Flattow, who lived in Mala Wies, near Warsaw. Helenka was my cousin Marta's aunt who, with her little son Stan, also lived on Aryan papers. Her husband, an officer in the Polish Army, had been taken prisoner by the Russians in the 1939 campaign and killed, along with 15,000 other Polish officers, in the Katyn Forest. (Stasiek found and visited Helenka in a nursing home in Israel some 50 years later. He wanted to thank her for her wartime hospitality.)

The long-term problem was how to settle these two men without exposing them – and all of us – to the danger of being recognized as Jews. Both Ignac and Stasiek had problems blending in with the Polish population. Ignac's Polish was unaccented, but he had stereotypical Jewish looks. Stasiek's problem was just the opposite: he looked very much like a Pole, with blue eyes, straight blond hair and sharp facial features, but his Polish was faulty. There were only a few words that he pronounced differently from ethnic Poles, but those few words were enough to reveal that his mother tongue was Yiddish, not Polish. The Germans would not have recognized the accent, but blackmailers listened for it and became extremely skilled at detecting Jews from their speech.

One idea we had but never put into effect was to have Ignac and Stasiek always walk together, with Ignac pretending to be blind and Stasiek acting as if he were deaf and mute. In accordance with local custom, Ignac would carry a white cane and wear large dark glasses (in addition to an oversized peasant hat that would cover half his face), while Stasiek would wear a yellow armband with three black dots. If the need arose, Ignac would be the only one to talk.

Before we could implement this rather bizarre plan, a better solution appeared. The *Baustelle*, for which I was working, was in the process of establishing a new branch in Riga, Latvia. The company needed workers in various categories and for this purpose they had opened a special recruitment office at Wiejska Street in Warsaw. We jumped at the opportunity, especially since I knew one of the clerks in the new office: Roman, my friend who used to work at the *Baustelle* in Grochow. Still, this was also a risky undertaking; each prospective worker would have to go through a registration process and a possible medical examination. Also, there could be a police investigation upon crossing the border into the vast territories of the Soviet Union. But Ignac and especially Stasiek didn't have many alternatives. Stasiek became our guinea pig.

We were hopeful that a workplace outside occupied Polish territory would provide a safer refuge for hunted escapees and others who had difficulty finding a haven in Warsaw. As we correctly assumed, the people who ended up working in Riga were of many nationalities and ethnic backgrounds and spoke a variety of languages. Blending in there was considerably easier than in homogenous Warsaw, where most, if not all, workers were Poles. In Riga, everybody had an accent.

Three and a half weeks after his arrival in Warsaw, Stasiek was on his way to Riga, and Ignac and I anxiously awaited his first letter. We were sure of one thing: at least Stasiek would no longer have to sleep in a public toilet or above the communal rubbish bin. Soon letters from Stasiek began to arrive and we were relieved to discover that the messages were consistently positive.

Ignac decided to join Stasiek in Riga, but before leaving Warsaw he decided to make an attempt to rescue his girlfriend Tetka and his brother Heniek and Heniek's wife, Halinka, from the Blizyn camp. Barely three weeks after his own escape, and with barely enough time to obtain the three false ID cards, Ignac embarked on a trip back to Blizyn. Given the risks and dangers involved in such an undertaking, and Ignac's Semitic features, this venture was so daring and courageous that it bordered on madness. But he went. In Blizyn, with the help of a local Polish peasant, Mr Wrona, the same man who had helped him carry on our correspondence, he delivered the three sets of false documents to Heniek.

But something went terribly wrong. Heniek may have been denounced, because the SS caught him with the false ID and threw him into the camp's jail, a bunker. Tetka and Halinka avoided a similar fate by sheer luck: Heniek managed to deliver their ID cards to their barracks before his arrest. In the bunker for two or three weeks, Heniek was beaten and interrogated daily by the Gestapo – they were trying to find out who delivered the false ID card, what was his contact's address in Warsaw where the ID card was issued, and how had he communicated with that contact person. But they failed to find out any information. Heniek remained silent as to the identity of the mysterious bearer of the document; and as for the address in Warsaw – Solec 46, apartment 49 – he swallowed the piece of paper with the address on it. To put additional pressure on him to talk, the Gestapo also arrested and jailed Halinka.

Knowing their ultimate fate and not wanting to go through torture, both Heniek and Halinka attempted suicide by cutting their veins at the elbows. As their blood slowly seeped away, they lost consciousness. The Germans discovered their almost lifeless bodies when they came to interrogate them. They were sent to a hospital, and the personnel were ordered to resuscitate them, as the SS desperately wanted to trace the documents to their source before putting them to death. They knew full well that false documents had been produced by the Underground. What they wanted to know is by whom and where.

A few days later, in a surprising move, the Blizyn Labor Camp was transformed into a concentration camp, and an entirely new administration, from Radom, took over. The new camp commander ordered that Heniek and Halinka be spared and after they had left the hospital, they joined the other inmates.

Ignac's attempt to rescue his loved ones, however, had failed, and he returned to Warsaw safe but heartbroken.

On 10 February 1944, Ignac departed for Riga: Schmitt and Junk employed him as an electromotive mechanic. His letters confirmed Stasiek's earlier assessments regarding not only the living and working conditions but also, more importantly, their excellent chances for survival.

Stasiek and then Ignac were the first of my friends and acquaintances with Aryan papers to go to Riga's *Baustelle*, but not the last. Next to go were Ludwik, then Janek, and then a few others whose names I don't recall. Whenever I heard that someone was in trouble, I would direct him or her to Riga. I also spread the word through Krysia, Kuba, and Maciej. One day I received a letter from Ludwik with a plea: 'Zenek, do not send any more of "ours." We are now in the majority.' He added that Jews numbered 13 out of 25 foreign workers at the company there.

Every hidden Jew who went to work for the Schmitt and Junk *Baustelle* in Riga – all 13 of them – survived the war.

13 Miecz i Plug

Although I had volunteered for the Jewish ZOB, I was drawn by circumstances into two additional organizations – both affiliated with the Polish Underground. One was *Miecz i Plug* (the Sword and Plough), the other, *Gwardia Ludowa* (the People's Guard). These two organizations were extreme enemies that fought each other almost as much as they did the Germans. Moreover, if it were known that someone belonged to both groups, he or she would be suspected of being a spy by one of them and could be killed by whichever organization discovered it first. But when I joined these groups I did not know any of this. I thought that all underground organizations were groups of Polish patriots, fighting against the same German enemy. I was 18, but, politically, my naiveté and inexperience were that of a much younger boy. Neither of the two organizations knew of my work with the ZOB.

My involvement with the *Miecz i Plug* organization happened quite by accident. I was introduced to it by Wladek Warzajtys whom I met soon after I started working for WIFO. He was rather shy, but pleasant and intelligent, was devoutly religious and interested in furthering his education, but his first and overriding interest and devotion was to fight the Nazis; he was a true Polish patriot, ready to sacrifice himself for his native land. No matter where our discussion started, it invariably ended on what we could do to sabotage and defeat our bitter enemy. In this, we were in total agreement. In the weeks that followed, Wladek provided me with leaflets produced by the Underground daily and kept me informed about world news from Allied sources.

As time went by and Wladek and I became close friends, he suggested that I join his Underground group, the *Miecz i Plug*. I had never heard of the group and assumed that this was just one of the several organizations that belonged to the main Polish Underground, *Armja Krajowa* (Home Army). Apart from joining the group for obvious, patriotic reasons, I signed on also because to refuse could have made me suspect, not only to him but also to his superiors, who knew of the invitation. I kept from him my membership in the ZOB, simply because secrecy regarding any resistance movement was paramount. I attended a couple of gatherings in a dark basement in the center of Warsaw and met a couple of his friends, but it was mostly Wladek who was my contact. There was no formal induction of any kind and, as with the ZOB, only first names were exchanged. I never saw the other members again, but I continued to see Wladek but because we both worked at WIFO.

One day, Wladek announced that the organization needed a motorcycle and that he and I had been designated to get one. The plan was that I would find a motorcycle at the *Baustelle*, somewhere within the pool of motor vehicles, and take it to the side of my work building, presumably to charge its battery. That was the easy part. For the rest, one day Wladek would remain hidden behind my building until after dark, at which time he would move the cycle quietly, without driving it, to my lodging at 37 Osowska Street. He would spend the night with me and then, after the curfew was over, would drive the motorcycle to its destination.

Contrary to reason and elementary caution, I agreed to every last detail of the plan, even though in wartime, stealing a piece of military equipment, transporting stolen military goods, or harboring those who did so was sabotage of the first order and punishable by death. I did not ask Wladek any questions and, more importantly, I did not prepare any answers in case I was caught. I had a vague notion that my inability to operate a motorcycle might somehow mitigate my culpability. Today, when I think of this venture, and a few like it, I can only conclude that I had more luck than brains. In any case, we accomplished what we had set out to do without incident, and the operation was a complete success.

Early one morning, a few days after the motorcycle affair, Wladek approached me.

'I have something for you,' he whispered. 'I'll see you after work.'

My curiosity was piqued, and I couldn't wait for the workday to end. When we arrived at my lodging on Osowska Street, Wladek handed me a Parabellum revolver, telling me that it was mine to keep for possible future actions or for self-defense. This was the last thing I had expected, and I was not sure how to react. I thanked him as if this were a predictable reward. Although I had no idea what I would do with it, I recognized its real as well as its potential future value. Krysia had told me that when the Jewish fighters in the Warsaw Ghetto were preparing to resist further German deportations, the ZOB requested from the *Armja Krajowa* a shipment of weaponry for the forthcoming uprising. After lengthy negotiations and at a substantial price, the Polish Underground agreed to provide the ZOB with a meager ten revolvers, although later there were other larger shipments. That demonstrates how valuable guns were in wartime Warsaw. And now I held a revolver, my own, in the palm of my hand.

A few weeks later, Wladek provided me with another weapon: a grenade. Then, while walking to work one day, I found a second grenade lying by the side of the road. I picked it up as casually as if it were a rock, slipped it into the pocket of my jacket, and marched on. Inexperienced as I was, it never crossed my mind that it could have exploded, killing me and others around me.

The revolver and the two grenades constituted my 'war' arsenal.

One day in the late autumn of 1943, I found out from Marysia that my cousin Marta was alive and well and that she too had been living in Warsaw, on the Aryan side. I was pleased at the news. Marta was my first cousin, she came from my hometown Łódz, and she was my age; we knew each other well. 'How did you find out about her? Where is she? Where can I meet her?' I showered Marysia with questions. She hesitated for a moment and then blurted out: 'She is in jail, imprisoned in a Polish police precinct station, in Ursus, a small town near Warsaw.' Of course, I wanted to know why she was in jail and next, how we could get her out. But Marysia had no answers. She was sad and perplexed as to what could be done about her since it was an unwritten law on the Aryan side that fugitives should stay away from police stations, German or Polish, as any involvement, typically, not only did not save the prisoner, but created new victims.

A couple of days later I mentioned to Wladek that a girl, an acquaintance of mine, was in custody at the police station in Ursus. Almost immediately, a plan was born and Wladek and I embarked on another risky and reckless adventure: Marta's rescue from the precinct jail. The following Sunday afternoon, armed only with a bag containing half a dozen apples, Wladek and I made our way to Ursus. For my part, I failed to consider the consequences for me either if Marta was in jail for being Jewish or if, somehow, she revealed that we were related. And, of course, I did not think about how Wladek would react if he knew my true identity. All these possibilities could have affected our friendship, jeopardized my membership in the Underground, and even endangered my life. But as these scenarios never occurred to me, I never sought answers to them, and we proceeded with our plan.

With Wladek acting as lookout, I went into the precinct's courtyard and faced a one-story building. At the far end of the building was the jail with three windows, each with bars except at the very top, where there was an open wooden slat. I called out 'Miss Marta? Miss Marta?' and from the second window a voice came back, 'Who is it?' I said that it was Mr Zenek, that Marysia sent me, and that I wanted to know if she needed anything. We exchanged a few words, I gave her my landlord's name and the Solec 46 address, threw the six apples into the top opening, said good-bye, and left. On the way back to Warsaw, Wladek and I considered the possibility of a rescue attempt. But we had no idea how to go about it.

A week later, without informing me of his plan, Wladek returned to Ursus with a friend of his. Late in the evening, they cautiously approached the low, gray police station and cut the telephone wires to the building. While his friend remained in the entrance hall on lookout duty, Wladek, drawing a revolver, entered the office and confronted the lone policeman.

'We want Marta. Don't ask any questions,' Wladek had demanded. Fully aware that he was dealing with the Underground, the policeman knew better than to ask questions. There was, however, a minor problem: Marta was no longer there. The German police had taken her and some others to Warsaw for interrogation. Wladek and his friend returned home empty-handed. Nonetheless, when I learned about this second escapade to Ursus, I was tremendously impressed and felt deeply indebted to Wladek. His effort was beyond anyone's obligation to a friend, and he proved to be not only a good friend but also a courageous young man who was willing to risk his own life to save another's.

Within a few days, on a moonless evening and ten minutes before the curfew, there was a knock on the door at the Spoczynski residence, where I was visiting and planning to remain for a few nights. It was Marta, and she needed a place to spend the night. I introduced her to my landlords as a family friend and asked if she could stay. 'Yes, of course, what else can she do?' Mrs Spoczynski answered. So Marta stayed in my old bed in the old corner of the room while I took up a new corner, on a small cot. We spent two or three nights like that, and then I returned to my lodging in Grochow. Marta became a new renter at the Spoczynski residence.

During those few days, Marta and I had many conversations on a variety of topics, including politics, philosophy and religion, yet never, not once, did we talked about why she was in jail in Ursus, what had happened during her interrogation by the Gestapo or other police agency, or how she managed to be released. It sounds incredible and I could not explain it if my life depended on it. But that is what had happened; some subjects were just never touched. These were strange times and we all behaved in strange, odd ways. What Marta did tell me, however, was that her mother and older sister were still in a small labor camp in Skarzysko-Kamienna and that she wanted to go there to see if she could help them. I don't remember why but I volunteered to make the trip for her, and a few days later I took a train to Skarzysko. I located the camp, a row of two-story barracks behind barbed wires in a lightly wooded area. I walked around trying to find someone to talk to but there was no one. The surrounding silence was a bad omen: indeed, the inmates were no longer there.

When I came to see Marta and pick up my mail a week or two later, she was gone. Now it is quite true that on the Aryan side, discretion and secrecy were the order of the day. But Marta brought these qualities to a new level; she disappeared just as mysteriously and unexpectedly as she had arrived.

After the war I found out that the *Miecz i Plug* organization, an offshoot of the NSZ (*Narodowe Sily Zbrojne*), was politically far to the right, was militantly anti-Semitic, and that after the war, its leadership was accused of wartime collaboration with the Germans and persecuted.

At the time, though, I knew nothing about *Miecz i Plug*'s attitude or policies toward Jews or its extreme animosity toward the Polish left. I never heard anything derogatory either about Jews or about the political left, from Wladek or anyone else. What I do remember, however, is reading in one of their newsletters an article that, in essence, said: 'Germany is enemy number two; Russia is enemy number one.' But this was late in the war and these slogans were not uncommon; I paid little attention to them. I know only that, then, I did not feel that my association with this group endangered my life. Only after the war did I realize that by joining them I exposed myself to enemies on all sides: within the group as a Jew and outside the group to their enemies on the left, all in addition to the Germans' threat to me as a Pole, as a Jew, and as a member of the Resistance.

Yet in all likelihood, even if I had known all this background, I still would have joined. First of all, I was ready to join the devil himself to work against the Nazis. Secondly, doing otherwise would have been very suspicious and thus dangerous to my own survival. It was rare in those times that a young, healthy Pole would refuse to join any Resistance when invited to do so. But, had I known, I would have probably kept my distance from the other members of the organization, even perhaps from Wladek.

I have always wondered what Wladek's reaction to me would have been if he had known that I was a Jew. I am quite confident that he would have remained a good friend and that he would have helped me if I needed help. I am equally sure that he would never have involved me in his group.

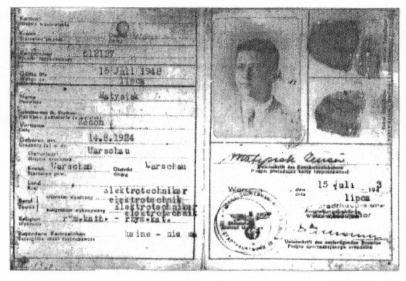

1. Polish Identity Card (*Kennkarte*)

2. Labor Card (*Arbeitskarte*)

3. Zofja Szokalska (right) with Lucja Szokalska, 1960s

4. Proclamation declaring death penalty for Jews who escaped and for non-Jews who assisted Jews with lodging or food. This proclamation best defines conditions on the Aryan side.

5. The author, posing for a photograph for a false ID, Tomaszow Labor Camp, 1942–43

6. Paul Biebow, Organization Todt, Ujazd (near Tomaszow), 1941

7. Electricians at WIFO: Szemanski, with a book; Urban, bottom right; the author on top, Warsaw 1943

8a. Aunt Marysia, Warsaw, 1942

8b. Maciej Monszajn, Warsaw, 1942

8c. Ignac Bierzynski, Tomaszow, 1942

8d. Stanley (Stasiek) Grosman,
Warsaw, 1943

9. Jacob (Czeslaw) Celemenski (ZOB), Warsaw, 1943

10. Krysia Mucznik (ZOB) and the author, Warsaw, 1944

11. Krysia Mucznik (third from right) and Jacob (Czeslaw) Celemenski (second from right), at a Catholic cemetery for the burial of a Jewish ZOB activist

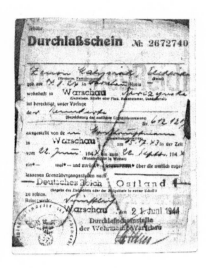

12. WIFO's certificate for a 'business' trip (*Dienstreise*) to Lódz, June–July 1944

13. Border pass for crossing between General Gouvernement and the Third Reich. Lódz, renamed Litzmannstadt, was incorporated into the Third Reich

14. The author, during the trip to Lódz, July 1944

15. Roman Malinowski (*Gwardia*), Warsaw, 1950s

16. Wladek Warzajtys (*Miecz i Plug*/AK), Warsaw, 1944; he fell in the Warsaw Uprising

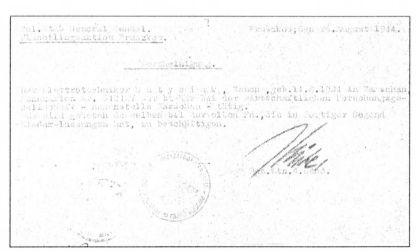

17. Certificate, obtained from the SS in Transit Camp Pruszkow; it sent the author to a labor camp near Vienna (most males of the author's age in Pruszkow were sent to concentration camps)

18. Letter to Ignac imploring him to join the author in Warsaw 'immediately'. It was instrumental in his and Stasiek's escape and survival

19. Sample pages from the author's wartime diary

14 Gwardia Ludowa

Roman was the other co-worker at WIFO whom I befriended. We mostly ran into each other walking towards Grochow after work. He was usually better dressed than most workers and, as I found out later, held a degree in civil engineering, although at WIFO he was working as a clerk. He was always aware of current events but overall was a bit of a mystery. From the time we first met, there was a strange affinity, which was soon explained: we had each figured out that the other one was Jewish.

After several weeks, Roman was transferred to our company's offices in Warsaw proper. The number of our encounters diminished but did not stop. One day, he confided in me that he was involved with yet another Underground organization, and asked if I would help. Without asking the name of his organization – it was only later that I found out it was *Gwardia Ludowa* – or its political agenda, I simply answered, 'When do I start?' As it turned out, he already had an assignment in mind for me similar to the one that he had performed when he was working at the WIFO *Baustelle*. After the war, when I questioned Roman about how he had found enough confidence in me to reveal his underground activities, he replied, 'Out of carelessness!' meaning that he had not scrutinized my background properly, particularly my work in the other two Underground organizations.

From the window of the room in which I worked, there was a clear view of the main east–west railroad track. Every hour or two, the track would carry trains heading in one direction or the other. The eastbound trains were freight trains loaded with all kinds of war equipment and weaponry, from motorcycles with side baskets to tanks and heavy artillery. The westbound trains were either freight trains full of wood cases or passenger trains with large Red Cross markings, carrying soldiers wounded on the Russian front. My job was to keep a record of the number of trains, the number of cars on each train, and the type of weapons or load it carried. Similarly, I was to record the trains with wounded soldiers. Twice a week, in the evening, I traveled to Warsaw to deliver the information to Roman. Usually we would meet in front of the polytechnic building. Waiting for my data, but standing on the opposite side of the street, was Ignacy Loga-Sowinski, Roman's superior.[14]

One day, as I was scribbling and rearranging some records for Roman at my desk in the battery room, my German military supervisor, Ernst, walked in. I quickly put the sheets of paper I was working on into a book, placed the book on a shelf, and pretended to be cleaning my desk. Ernst appeared to be suspicious and asked that I fetch something for him from a nearby storage building. When I came back, the book was back on my desk, and Ernst, pointing his finger at the sheets of paper inside, asked, 'What are these, Zenon?' I mumbled something about playing a game, a numbers game, and apologized for doing it during working hours. He did not seem convinced but could not figure out what the numbers and scribbling meant. Nervously, I continued to apologize for playing on the job, and finally, he shook his head and walked out.

A few weeks later, on my way to Warsaw carrying my reports for Roman, German gendarmes stopped the tram in the middle of the Poniatowski Bridge. 'All out,' they ordered. I swiftly folded the three pages and stuck them behind me, between the upright and the horizontal parts of the seat. I was not only scared because of the reports I carried, but also worried that I would be taken as a hostage just for being young, male, and Polish. In this case, however, the Germans were looking for someone specific, and after checking our documents they let us back on the tram. When I returned to the tram, an elderly woman sat down in my seat and no words of persuasion, no pleading, would make her change seats with me. While people did not understand why she was so stubborn, neither did they understand why I was so insistent. Uneasily, I waited until she got off the tram, then I returned to the seat to retrieve my papers. I arrived at my appointment an hour late.

One day in May 1944, when I returned home to my Osowska Street lodging, I found on my table an empty telegram envelope. It seemed a little odd to me – a telegram usually implied an emergency – but I did not think much of it. However, later that evening my landlord, Zbig Janowski, professing regret, informed me that he wanted me to move out, preferably as soon as possible but no later than a week or two. He said he had received a telegram that his father was coming to stay with him. But I suspected that this was not the reason for the eviction. In all likelihood, he or someone else in the building had figured out that I was a Jew. Usually, in such cases the eviction would be instantaneous, sometimes with the explanation that the tenant's presence endangered the landlord and his family's life; other times, it could be worse, with the landlord denouncing the tenant to the Germans in exchange for a small reward. But Janowski did not denounce me; more than likely he was a good and decent man, simply concerned with his family's safety. He might also have been worried about my activities in the Polish Underground, of which he was quite aware as I made it a practice to leave copies of Underground leaflets scattered around my room. This was useful for a number of reasons. It earned me respect from landlords who were patriotic and, at the same time, provided me a with cover for being so tight-lipped about my comings and goings. I know that such was the case at the Spoczynskis', and I had hoped it would also be true at the Janowski lodging. Another possibility was that Janowski had discovered my revolver and the two grenades hidden in the corner of my straw mattress. Or he may have been afraid to denounce me or evict me publicly, so he tried to do it quietly and amicably.

In any event, within days I moved to another house at 5 Kiprow Street, in the same general area. I found new accommodation the same way I had found the last one and how most Polish renters did: through the bulletin board at the local church. My new landlady was a young mother with a 5-year-old girl; her husband was a prisoner of war somewhere in Russia, taken in the 1939 campaign. My new lodging was a considerable improvement on Janowski's and a giant step above the Spoczynskis' corner bed. The apartment had indoor plumbing, a small refrigerator in the kitchen, and even a small balcony. In addition, my rent included a daily supper prepared by the young lady. My biggest problem was that I had to find a new hiding place for my revolver and the two grenades; the place had to be inconspicuous yet easily accessible, so that I could retrieve the weapons at a moment's notice. For this I built a false bottom in one of the corners of a large standing wardrobe.

Late in June 1944, after the Allied invasion of Europe, an unexpected caller visited me at my battery room. Mr Miertsching was the vice president of WIFO, a tall slim man, about 50 years of age, with dark hair, piercing brown eyes, sunken cheeks, and an olive complexion. According to the grapevine, where each executive had a stamp of approval or disapproval by the employees, no one seemed to know much about him or why, at his relatively young age, he was not in a uniform somewhere on the front. He might have been wounded and released from service or possibly was a specialist and, as such, exempt from service, or perhaps he knew somebody very high up. However, my immediate concern was why he was now visiting me.

Miertsching sat down, leaned close, and in a low voice whispered, 'Zenon, I need a contact with the Polish Underground. Can you help me?'

A sickening wave of fear rolled over me, and my mind

raced as I tried to think of how to react. I was frantic: did my
German employers know about my Underground activities?
And, if they did, did they know more than that? Conscious of
my demeanor, I hardly knew how to react. I prayed that my
facial expression would not reveal my utter terror. I searched
the face of the man sitting calmly in front of me, looking for
any sign that would tell me if he was sincere or whether this
was a trap. He stared back at me intently, waiting for an
answer, his hands relaxed on his crossed leg. Instinctively, as I
looked at Miertsching, I felt that he was truthful. But how
could I get involved in something so risky and complex? How
could I risk my life and the lives of others in the organization
based just on my instinct? I searched quickly for an answer.

'But Mr Miertsching,' I told him politely but firmly,
conscious of keeping my voice steady, 'I do not belong to the
Underground or know anybody who does. I work at this
German *Baustelle*, and I would never have anything to do
with an illegal resistance organization.' I threw in a few more
denials for good measure, but he was not dissuaded.

'I expected you to say that,' he said. 'But I'm determined. I
want to join the Underground and help to bring this shitty
war to an end. I was never a party to it, and I never believed
in this crazy adventure. I need your help, Zenon.'

I concentrated on remaining calm, insisting that I had no
contacts. He was equally composed, insisting that I find one.

That same evening I had arranged to meet Roman. Still
unnerved by Miertsching's visit, I eagerly told him about the
conversation. We wondered how sincere Miertsching was and
what might have motivated him to make such a risky request;
whether it was simply a case of him switching sides as the war
swung toward a victory for the Allies. Roman's first reaction,
like mine, was negative.

'What if he's a spy?' Roman questioned. 'What if the whole
thing is a setup?'

We certainly didn't want to get caught in some kind of
trap. To lose our lives, lives we had so laboriously and
carefully reclaimed, at this late stage of the war was unthink-

able. We knew that the Russian front was only 40 to 50 miles from Warsaw, that the end of the war was near. But then, we thought, could he offer something that would help our fight? Maybe he had information that might be of special value or could provide weapons, which were always critically needed. In the end, Roman left it more or less up to me to decide what to do; it was, after all, my life on the line. I went home distraught and confused: Why was this happening now? Why had he picked me?

My tendency to foolishly disregard risks and dangers prevailed. Combined with my desire to do some good for the cause, I hoped that the Underground movement might be able to benefit from his help regardless of his sincerity or motives. I decided to continue my conversation with Miertsching cautiously, assuming him to be a shrewd opportunist aware that the Germans were on the verge of defeat.

Two days later, when Miertsching showed up again, realizing that I might be signing my own death warrant, I told him that I knew somebody who knew somebody who knew somebody, adding that what they said the Underground needed most was weapons, especially automatic weapons such as machine guns. I told him that my contact knew nothing about him and that, in my opinion, this entire undertaking was much too risky. I waited for his reaction, for some indication as to my fate. To my dismay, he did not react or respond except to say that he would be back. The next day, when he did not return, I agonized over my decision to trust him, expecting any moment to be arrested by the Gestapo. To my relief he returned the following day, asking for a list of weapons the Underground needed.

In the meantime, the situation was changing rapidly. Roman was nowhere to be found. The Russian front was now so close that at night, when silence normally engulfed the city, the rattling of machine guns and periodic fire from heavy artillery could be heard. In Warsaw, there were persistent rumors that a major action by the Polish Underground was expected to take place in anticipation of the imminent entry of the Russian Army into Warsaw. The Poles had no desire for their capital to be liberated by the Russians.

The *Baustelle* was ordered to close, and Miertsching and all the other German employees were commanded to start preparing for transfer to one of WIFO's branches in Liebau, near Vienna. Hardly any of the workers were showing up. On my last day of work, I was about to leave when I noticed that leaning against a wall was the company's military bicycle that had been assigned to me for work purposes. I looked around me and, seeing the area was deserted, quickly jumped on the bike and headed away from the *Baustelle*. Satisfaction at the successful coup was heightened by my knowledge that the *Baustelle* personnel were scheduled to depart the following day, so my chances of being caught and punished for the theft of the bike, a serious offense, were slim.

I waited a day and then, expecting that the Germans had left, I decided to take a ride toward Warsaw. Several blocks later, as I turned the corner, I heard my name called and was alarmed to see Miertsching in the company of two other high officials of the WIFO. I had been caught. In time of war, and especially in the frontline zone, this was considered sabotage, and I could be shot for my action – something that I had not considered before. I sat on the roadside as the three men discussed my fate, lamenting my rash foolishness. After some time it was clear that Miertsching had persuaded the others not to make an issue about the incident. To me, this meant either that he was serious about his desire to help the Underground or that he was worried about my revealing our conversations to his associates. In any event, they merely pointed out the gravity of my misdeed and ordered me to return the bike to the *Baustelle* immediately.

I didn't follow their instructions, however. As I watched the three men disappear down the road, I hesitated; I couldn't bring myself to give back the stolen bike. Even more frightening to me than disobeying these officials was the thought of returning to the *Baustelle* to admit the theft. Doing so might mean all kinds of punishment, including being shot. Instead,

I waited impatiently at the roadside, close to the *Baustelle*, for the return of Miertsching and his companions. When they reappeared, I waved for them to stop, apologized for my conduct, and pleaded with them to let me keep the bike. In return, I offered them one kilogram of tobacco, a scarce commodity at that time, which I had in the meantime purchased on the black market. They consulted briefly and, in the end, agreed to the deal. Since they all were ready to pack up and leave Poland, it was easier to add a kilogram of tobacco to their luggage than a bicycle. I suspected, however, that Miertsching again may have had something to do with their decision.

Once more, I felt the potentially disastrous consequences of my foolish and careless actions. Once more, luck and fortuitous circumstances were with me. And once more, my life had been spared.

15 Mission to the Lódz Ghetto

My everyday underground activities were limited to Warsaw and its suburbs, although from time to time an operation took me outside the city, usually only for a day or two. But there were two trips I undertook outside Warsaw in 1944 that were longer, lasting one week each. They were more complex, more daring, and more dangerous than my assignments in and around Warsaw: these were trips to my hometown of Lódz, now inside the Third Reich. My first trip was personal; I wanted to try to contact my family. My second trip was sponsored by the ZOB.

I yearned to help my parents and my sister, who had been confined in the ghetto for the past four years. I had had no contact with them for three of those years and did not know what had happened to them. I didn't know if they were still there or even alive. The ZOB wanted to establish a channel of communication with the ghetto and possibly a conduit for delivery of money and weapons. All we knew at the time was that the ghetto still existed and that it was large, overcrowded, isolated, and sealed. Because it was now part of the Third Reich, it was particularly inaccessible; with respect to occupied Poland, it was like a foreign country.

The Lódz Ghetto was established in February 1940 and remained in existence until the late summer of 1944. It was first set up for the indigenous Jews of Lódz, approximately 250,000 in number, and later became a gathering place for those from surrounding villages and cities. Finally, Jews from Germany, Hungary, Czechoslovakia, France, and other places were included in the Lódz Ghetto. Typically, ghettos were just places of confinement. This ghetto, however, was organized to be smoothly run and productive, almost a city-state unto itself.

A powerful Jewish Council and Jewish Service Police were put in place, and a complete civic infrastructure was established. At the head of the *Judenrat*, the Germans had placed a prewar community leader, Chaim Mordechai Rumkowski. Within months, the ghetto became a huge work camp for the German war machine. Manufacturing workshops were established and new machinery was brought in; experts were sought out from among the inmates, and new ones were trained. Under Rumkowski's reign the ghetto also attained a degree of autonomy and self-rule that was unknown in any other ghetto or camp. Apart from basic facilities, such as hospitals and utility services, it also had its own courts, a prison, an orphanage, and a sanatorium. In contrast to other ghettos, Lódz offered high-school level education and a variety of cultural activities, such as concerts.

However, in addition to the useful institutions and functions, others were established that were of questionable value. For example, the ghetto authority had a post office and printed postage stamps with Rumkowski's image, although during the last two or three years the inhabitants were not able to send or receive mail. Banknotes in marks (nicknamed 'Rumkies'), bearing the Star of David and Rumkowski's signature, were also issued; they were used to barter inside the ghetto but carried no value elsewhere. There was also a department that was responsible for trams, even though there were none in the ghetto. Two tramlines from the outside did pass through the ghetto but did not stop there. The ghetto's only motor vehicle was a fire truck. I had learned about the goings-on in the Lódz Ghetto early on, from my parents' letters and, later, from people who escaped the ghetto and came to Tomaszow.

Rumkowski organized the ghetto into what appeared to be a Jewish mini-state where he was an absolute ruler. Under the motto 'Productive work in exchange for survival', he created a slave labor camp dedicated to the support of the German war machine. Rumkowski believed that under the rules imposed by the German authorities this was the only way to save the ghetto, its inmates, and himself.

The ghetto, established in the poor northern section of Lódz, soon became greatly overpopulated. Of the Poles living in Lódz, many were either deported to the occupied Polish territories or forced to relocate to the city's suburbs. Local ethnic Germans, together with newly arrived Third Reich and foreign Germans, took over the houses and apartments in the central, nicer parts of town – homes, for the most part, left by the Jews.

Soon after the Germans conquered Poland in 1939, they separated the area to the northwest including Lódz, from the rest of the country and annexed it to the Third Reich, calling it Warthegau and Danzig-West Prussia. They gave the cities German names, with Lódz becoming Litzmannstadt. The rest of occupied Poland was designated as General Gouvernement (GG). The GG–Germany border was controlled like any international border and required special documents for entry or exit.

My two trips to Lódz, a mere 70 miles from Warsaw, were now considered international trips; they required a passport (in my case the ID card) and a visa-like document for border crossings. Traveling across these new borders also presented unknown dangers because few Poles, if any, ventured to travel to Germany of their own volition. Mostly, they crossed the border under supervision as forced laborers for Germany's fields and factories, as smugglers, or on their way to Nazi concentration camps.

Despite my keen awareness that the Germans were committed to the total destruction of the Jewish people, I nurtured the hope that the Lódz Ghetto would prove an exception, that perhaps it would survive the war, my family with it. This ghetto, I thought to myself, with its own money, postage stamps, and Jewish-guarded prison was such an anomaly that maybe it would survive. I wondered often what I might do to help my parents and my sister – how I could contact them, help them to escape, or, at least, advise them how to avoid being deported. I also wanted to let them know that I was alive and safe. Although I knew it was an extremely risky undertaking and that it had a low probability of yielding results, I decided to go to Lódz.

The first thing I had to do was obtain travel documents. Because I knew some German, I had made several acquaintances among the German employees of the company, including secretaries and some officials. I had also acquired a certain status within the WIFO organization; German workers usually came to me with their electrical problems so that I could translate to the other electricians what needed to be done. Similarly, my Polish co-workers came to me to translate their problems and present them to the Germans. Some Germans used me as a translator. One used to bring me love letters he had received from his Polish girlfriend.

The Germans at the *Baustelle* were generally proper and businesslike toward the Polish workers; they needed us as much as we needed them. Some were always friendly, and others became noticeably friendlier starting in early 1944, when German forces were suffering one defeat after another and were forced to withdraw on all fronts. I often exchanged a few words with these Germans whenever our paths crossed, usually on the way to and from the cafeteria or at lunchtime.

Mrs Follman, a secretary to one of the vice presidents, was particularly nice. She always had a warm expression and greeted people with a smile. A woman in her thirties from Breslau, Mrs Follman had a 10-year-old son living with her. Although she was very Aryan-looking, her son was not. Rumor had it that Mrs Follman had been married to a Jew, that they had been forcibly separated or divorced as demanded by the Nuremberg Laws, and that her husband had been deported to the Warsaw Ghetto, where he perished. It was also rumored that, at the same time, her own father was serving in a police battalion that had fought against the Jews in the Warsaw Ghetto uprising.

I approached Mrs Follman for help, confiding in her that I had a fiancée in Lódz and wanted to visit her but that I needed the necessary travel documents. She was very sympathetic to the idea and promised to intervene on my behalf with the president of WIFO, Mr Stüpnagel. To my delight, she succeeded. In March 1944, I obtained an official WIFO document stating that I was traveling to Litzmannstadt on company business and requesting all German authorities to facilitate my travel and render assistance, if needed. Specifically, it stated that I be provided with accommodation and the Reich's ration cards. This document, in turn, allowed me to obtain the second necessary pass: the border-crossing visa. Within days of receiving the documents, and with the hope that I would soon see my family again, I made my first exploratory trip to Lódz.

The morning train I boarded was bound for Berlin and was packed with Germans: civilians and military on home leave and some women with children, most likely returning home after visiting their husbands and fathers. For all I knew, some may have been concentration camp officials or guards. Chattering and laughing, they paid little attention to a Pole in their midst. To avoid being included in their conversations and to make it clear that I was not one of them, I held my Polish newspaper in front of me. Forever conscious of who I really was and the irony of the situation, I was bitterly aware that I might be sitting next to the murderers of my own family and friends. I felt disgusted but relatively secure. Who would look for a Jew in the midst of a group of happy Nazis?

My documents were foolproof; the border controller accepted them without even looking at me, and more and more, I felt completely at ease. But as I arrived in the city itself, my mood changed. A constant, dull pain accompanied my every move. The city looked so different from the way I remembered it, sad and lifeless. The streets were half empty and the few passersby walked in grim silence. Lódz was never a pretty place, but now it was ugly and ghostly. I registered in the hotel assigned to me by the Military Travel Aid kiosk at the Lódz Kaliska railway station and immediately went for a walk in the direction of the ghetto. Ferocious-looking German police guards in full military gear prevented anyone coming too close to the barbed wire or the entrance gate, their rifles constantly at the ready.

Two tramlines ran through the ghetto, one through Nowomiejska Street to Zgierska Street and one through Franciszkanska Street and Brzezinska Street. However, while passing through the ghetto the doors of all trams were locked at all times. I traveled on both lines, up and down, up and down, for hours. It was by sheer luck that no one noticed my repeated aimless traveling through the ghetto or my intense stares at the people there.

Inside the ghetto, masses of emaciated, distraught, shabbily dressed people were everywhere. The sight made my heart ache. I searched eagerly for my family, friends, or neighbors, but I didn't see anyone I knew. I felt so close to them and yet so far away. Helplessness weighed on me like a sack of lead. My only hope for contact was to attempt to send letters to my parents with a sign that I was alive and with a warning: 'Don't let yourself be taken away!' Back in my hotel room I wrote several such letters, folded them up, and placed them sometimes inside little rolls and other times into matchboxes. Then, back on the trams speeding through the ghetto, I would bend down, pretending to tighten my shoelaces, open a cover over the tram's step, and throw out a roll or a matchbox. I made several trips but did this only once or twice during each tram ride, so as not to attract attention. With each letter there was also a cover note addressed to the finder of the roll or the matchbox, asking him or her to deliver the letter to my parent's home at 10 Brzezinska Street. Of course, I had no way of knowing whether any of my notes would be found or delivered.

My travel permits were soon to expire, and I was ready for my return trip. But I decided on one last deed before returning to Warsaw. There was an epidemic of typhus at the Blizyn camp and Tetka, Ignac's girlfriend, was already ill. Anti-typhus serums were presumed to be effective and therefore were very much in demand and almost impossible to find. I eventually found and bought them in a German pharmacy and immediately took a train to Blizyn to deliver them through Ignac's Polish contact, Mr Wrona. The Pole promised to make the delivery.[15]

After that meeting with Mr Wrona, I walked across the railroad tracks and down the narrow country road toward the Blizyn concentration camp, as if somehow drawn to it. I do not know and do not understand why I wanted to go to this horrible place where people might recognize me, a place surrounded by SS men. It was dangerous not only for me but for others, including Mr Wrona, and totally without purpose. Luckily, halfway there I ran into a column of camp inmates accompanied by a Jewish policeman whom I knew, Jurek Rosenberg. It was the Loading Commando, the one from which Ignac and Stasiek broke away when they escaped to come to Warsaw. Recognizing me, Jurek urgently signaled that I should go no further, that I must go back. Heeding his advice, I turned around and took the next train for Warsaw.

My second trip to Lódz, in July 1944, was a mission that I instigated and carried out for the ZOB. The goal was to establish a contact inside the ghetto with Jewish community activists and to set in motion the transfer of money and, perhaps, weapons for resistance. We wanted, at the very least, to find a means to provide material help to the suffering ghetto population so that the remaining Jews of Lódz could resist any deportation and take an armed stand, if at all possible. These goals were loftier and more ambitious than those set for my first trip, but with an equally low chance of success. To the best of my knowledge or Krysia's, the ZOB had no contacts or anchors there at the time, which compounded the problem, but we felt it was our duty to try.

I presented my plan to Krysia , and she passed it on to her superiors. Approval came within days in the form of two $50 banknotes, equivalent to about 4,000 zlotys. With that in hand, I endeavored to obtain the required documents and to search for contacts in the city. Getting a set of travel documents from WIFO was easier this time; after all, they already knew that I had a fiancée in Lódz. Once again Mrs Follman was helpful, and I was able to obtain an official visa for border crossing without too much difficulty.

A more difficult problem was finding a trustworthy contact in Lódz. I needed local residents who would be willing to help and, hopefully, already had an established contact inside the ghetto. I also needed a safe place to stay, a base. All these were tough orders; all the people involved would have to be prepared to take enormous risks. Here, as elsewhere, any activity related to contacting or assisting people in the ghetto was punishable by death.

I decided to use my other Underground connections to help me in my mission. Juggling my membership in the three opposing organizations was nerve-wracking and burdensome, but, luckily, I never fully understood the potentially fatal consequences of the situation I had created for myself. Only intuitively did I know that asking for help from *Miecz i Plug* was out of the question. The revelation that the purpose of my trip had anything to do with a ghetto would have betrayed my identity immediately, and any mention to *Miecz i Plug* that I was involved in the two other organizations would have been dangerous beyond description. I could have been killed as a traitor or agent provocateur or both.

I settled on the other Underground organization, *Gwardia Ludowa*, and approached Roman, who knew that I had parents in Lódz and understood my desire to help them. Regarding the other, broader objective of the trip, establishing a channel to the Lódz ghetto, I left him in the dark. I could not reveal the ZOB involvement. If Roman knew that I needed the contact for a mission sponsored by the ZOB or that I even belonged to that organization, he would provide no help. Moreover, I would be dismissed from *Gwardia Ludowa* without hesitation.

Believing that I was traveling to Lódz only to find my family, Roman readily agreed to help. As he held a high position in *Gwardia Ludowa*, and his superior, Loga Sowinski, knew who I was and was aware of my services, when Roman requested a contact in Lódz for me, Loga granted it as a personal favor. I was given a name, an address, and a password: 'Wlodek sent me.' So, equipped with documents from the Germans (WIFO), money from the ZOB, and a contact from *Gwardia Ludowa*, I took off. It was amazing how helpful each party was when they were unaware of each other.

This time, there was a huge crowd on the train, and I had to stand for the entire journey. As the Russian armies pushed ever closer to the Reich's territory, a massive stream of refugees moved westward. This time there were not only Germans on the move but Latvians, Estonians, Ukrainians, and White Russians. Some were fleeing to the West because they were German collaborators, while others were simply fearful of falling under Communist rule again. Crossing the border was no problem; because the train was so packed, there was simply no room for the border controller to pass through the car. After a two-hour journey I arrived at Lódz Kaliska station, where, as expected, I was told that there were no hotel rooms available. Once again, I asked for assistance at the Military Travel Aid kiosk, an organization that served military personnel. Shown the documents indicating I was traveling on official business, they tried to help, but all they could offer was a bed in a large room of a hostel hotel, with three others in the room. It crossed my mind that the roommates could be Gestapo agents spying on me, that perhaps I was being followed. But that was not the case. When I arrived at the hostel, I found that they were three *Hitlerjugend* boys. I was not happy. It was bad enough I had to look at swastika-marked uniforms everywhere I turned, but to have to spend several nights with them in the same room was too much.

'Lousy luck,' I thought to myself. But I had no choice. The encounter ended without incident, except that in my absence they rummaged through my suitcase.

Early the next morning, I set out to locate my contacts. I was apprehensive, acutely aware of the magnitude of my assignment. Never during my yearlong stay on the Polish side had I volunteered or admitted to anyone that I was Jewish, but this was exactly what I was about to do. I was to divulge my secret to the strangers to whom Loga and Roman had sent

119

me. I knew that they all were members of the Underground and assumed that they were patriotic and trustworthy. But it was also possible that they were patriotic and anti-Semitic, which was not at all uncommon. I was worried, but again there was no turning back.

I arrived at the address I had been given, a small apartment house in the working-class suburb of Chojny, a manufacturing sector. I was expecting to meet two brothers, but a woman answered the door, and I gave her the password. In a matter-of-fact manner, as if I were a neighbor who had come to borrow a cup of sugar, she muttered 'Come in, come in.' Inside, there were two other women in a typical workers' apartment: two rooms and a kitchen with beds everywhere. I waited about six hours for the two brothers, the key members of the cell, to come home from work. During that time we ate a modest lunch, not saying much. We did not even introduce ourselves. Did they have other visitors like me, I wondered? Were they expecting me? Or were they just sizing me up, trying to figure out what kind of dangerous adventure I was on? In the end, the women never asked why I came, and I never told them.

When the men finally arrived, I told them why I was there and what I hoped to accomplish. They listened attentively but, like the women, said little.

When I finished, one of them said curtly, 'Tomorrow, we will take time off from work to look for contacts for you.'

They asked no questions about who I was, what was so special about the people called Neumark, or why the Underground wanted to help them. The word 'Jew' was never mentioned, but it must have been obvious to them that I was one. But somehow my fears were allayed and I felt, instinctively, that I could trust them.

I spent the night there, and the next morning one of them made the rounds with me. We visited a tram conductor who occasionally had the job of operating one of the trams traveling through the ghetto and we went to a food deliveryman who had a permit to enter the ghetto; we talked to a bureaucrat with undefined connections. They were all sympathetic as to my quest and emphasized how difficult my task would be; however, they all promised to help. But they did not deliver. One of them did come back with the information that my family was fine and that my sister was working in a communal kitchen.[16] Others pleaded for more time.

When these first few contacts didn't pan out, I tried an alternative plan, which was to find my Aunt Stenia, who lived in Lódz but not in the ghetto. Stenia was the only Christian in my family, married to my mother's brother Jozef. From the beginning of the war she had helped her husband and, indirectly, my parents. The problem was that I could not remember her maiden name or her address. I knew her brother-in-law, Franek, but, again, I did not know his last name or address.

I made one last attempt in the search for a contact by visiting a well-known Italian ice cream parlor, Chlodnia Wloska, on Piotrkowska Street. An Italian family, the Serrafinis, had opened it many years before the war. Normally, I would not have exposed myself to an unknown merchant or a casual acquaintance but I was desperate. And Mr Serrafini was not a complete stranger, as my father had known him for many years and had had numerous business dealings with him. Whenever my sister and I stopped by for ice cream – our favorite was the multi-flavored cassata in a metal container shaped like a champagne glass – Mr Serrafini would never let us pay.

I walked in and asked the young, dark-haired man behind the counter if I could speak with the owner.

'I'm the owner,' he told me, and, probably seeing my confused expression, explained that he was Mr Serrafini's son and had taken over the business.

Although I did not know the son, I risked confiding in him. I asked to talk with him in private, and he led me to the back room. I told him directly that I needed help in contacting the Neumarks in the ghetto, that I needed a contact in any shape or form, at any cost, and that I needed one now, as my stay was coming to an end. He acknowledged that he knew my father and said that he would like to help, but he knew of no way. There was no discussion as to why I wanted to help them

121

now or why I felt so desperate – that was understood. Before I left, he insisted that I have a cassata ice cream. Later, when we said good-bye, I felt the same hopelessness and helplessness that I experienced in the Tomaszow Labor Camp.

Two days before my scheduled departure, I made one of my routine trips through the ghetto on a tram going down Brzezinska Street. As with my first trip to Lódz, I was dispensing the usual letters, hidden in a roll or a matchbox, calling on my parents not to let themselves be taken away, under any circumstances. During one of these trips I looked up and saw a familiar face sitting right across from me. I was sure that I knew the man but could not place him right away. As discreetly as possible, I continued to stare at him, willing myself to remember his name. He was of medium stature, slim, with a rather dark, olive complexion, and totally bald. When he got off the tram a few stops later, I decided to follow him. Then, it suddenly dawned on me who he was: a teacher of handicrafts from Szwajcera Gymnasium, my high school. Although the school was Jewish, he was an ethnic Ukrainian, one of two non-Jewish teachers in the school.

Conscious that someone was following him, he soon stopped and turned. I quickly approached him and told him that I knew of him, that he had been a teacher at Szwajcera Gymnasium. Breathlessly, I explained that I knew that from a friend of mine who had been a student in the school. I could not tell him that I myself was from there, because that would have revealed I was Jewish. To my great surprise, he vehemently denied he was that teacher and ordered me to stop following him. But I didn't. I continued to follow him and he stopped again. Angrily, he turned on me, and demanded, 'Why are you following me? What do you want from me?'

Hesitating slightly, breathless with fear at the risk I was taking, I told him, 'I need to contact the ghetto elders and one of the families in the ghetto. I was wondering if you could help.'

Without admitting who he was or agreeing to help, he thought for a minute and then said that he would meet me again. He proposed that we meet the next day at noon at the corner of Pomorska and Kilinskiego streets, close to where Szwajcera Gymnasium used to be and not far from the ghetto wall.

That night I did not sleep a wink, tormented by images of uniformed Gestapo and SS men descending from all directions as I stood alone on that corner. Images of torture, reprisal against my family, and finally death filled my thoughts. But the die was cast, and there was no going back. I was determined to stay with the plan. Now and then I forced the pictures out of my mind and asked myself: What if he can help? What if he will help? What is the downside of meeting with him? My mind would not stop swirling. I wished all night that I could turn the clock forward to noon.

I arrived early for the meeting the next day and waited, observing from a distance. He arrived on time, but I waited a few more moments to make sure he was alone. Satisfied that no one else was around, I approached him. I didn't know if by then he had recognized me as his former student, but he was friendly and agreed to help, adding that he had some leads for me. The tension from the night before dissolved into a flood of relief and elation, and I had renewed hope that I might find my family and help the ZOB.

My former teacher took me to an apartment about three blocks away, where we met two middle-aged sisters. He mumbled something about the sisters working outside the law, perhaps meaning in the Underground, and that one of them had only recently been released from jail.[17] They gave me their full names, which I no longer remember; I introduced myself only as Zenon. The women were friendly and listened attentively, even sympathetically. For my part, I spilled my entire plan: that people in Warsaw wanted to help individuals, groups, even the entire ghetto and that I had a personal interest in saving one specific family. I revealed that money was available to pay for the help and that we had repeatedly failed to find secure channels into the ghetto. Again, I was told how difficult it would be. But I also heard about possible contacts they had.

'We need time, a few days, perhaps even a few weeks,' they insisted. But for me, time was rapidly running out. It was July 1944, the front was no more than 100 miles away, and my permit was about to expire.

The next morning, the day of my departure, I visited the ladies again. Several possibilities were mentioned, but nothing specific. There was one hopeful note, though. A lady friend of theirs, whose husband was in the ghetto, was supposed to visit them the next day. But I could not wait. My permit was expiring and I had to hurry back. Tired, discouraged, and emotionally drained, I left for Warsaw in the early afternoon without leaving either my last name or my address.

At the station I went to board the train, my mind preoccupied with my visit and my return to Warsaw. Suddenly, the German railway police stopped me. Looking around, I realized that I was the only passenger whom they stopped and I had no idea why. With a feeling of dread, I did my best to appear unconcerned and casual. They took me to a small room and stripped me to my underwear, searching every piece of clothing and examining every piece of paper they found. I had no idea what they were searching for. Weapons? Smuggled diamonds? I still had the two unused banknotes, well hidden in a tube of toothpaste. My main worry was how I should answer if they asked me what kind of business trip I was on or whom I had contacted in Lódz, realizing that my answers could have been checked. But they did not ask, and after a thorough search of all my belongings, they let me go. In the meantime, the train waited for me, and we finally left the station almost an hour late.

Although traumatized, once safely settled in my seat I had a moment of satisfaction: single-handedly I had managed to wreak havoc on the railway schedule of the Third Reich!

The evening of the day I departed for Warsaw, the two sisters had a visitor. It was their lady friend, whose husband was in the ghetto; she was first on their list of people with contacts within the ghetto. The two sisters related to their guest the events of the preceding two days: they told her

124

about the visit by their friend, the Ukrainian teacher; the visit from a young man from Warsaw on an urgent mission to contact the ghetto; and the young man's desperate plea for help for one particular family. Then they described me. At that point the lady friend almost fainted.

'But that was Zenek, my nephew! Where is he? How can I contact him?' she cried. The lady friend was my Aunt Stenia.[18] If only I had found Stenia on my first visit to Lódz; or my meeting with the two sisters had happened just a couple of days earlier, who knows how my mission might have turned out.

On a trip to Poland in the summer of 1990, I spent considerable time trying to find my former teacher, but I did not succeed. I couldn't find a single old classmate or teacher from the Gymnasium; the school itself was now a Technicum, and I was told that all the records from the Gymnasium period had been shipped to the school district administrator. There, I was told that due to a shortage of space, all records had been transferred to an unknown location. More recently, I tried to find him or his family, again unsuccessfully, through a Ukrainian club and an Underground members circle. I would have liked to thank him from the bottom of my heart for trying to help me and for being a decent man.

Although I had failed in my mission to the Lódz Ghetto, I still had faith that, by some miracle, my family would survive this war. The Russians were moving closer and closer, and the fate of Germany was a foregone conclusion. Its forces were in retreat on all fronts. Maybe the few remaining ghettos would be spared, not so much by a change of heart or change in the Germans' plans or design, but by circumstance: by a breakdown of order, by the avalanche of refugees moving westward, or by the need to throw all available manpower – including the SS, police, and Gestapo who were running the ghettos and camps – into reinforcing the front lines. I hoped and prayed.

The Lódz Ghetto lasted longer than any other large ghetto in eastern Europe. However, in the end, the Lódz Ghetto, its people, and Rumkowski shared the same fate as all the other ghettos: destruction.

16 The Calm before the Storm

In July, the pace of life in Warsaw accelerated. Tensions and anxieties escalated. The number of German military personnel in the streets doubled and military equipment moved in both directions: eastward toward the front and westward toward the Reich. The Nazis constructed bunker-like entrances to major buildings that were occupied by Germans. In front, they also wore full military gear, which seemed heavier than usual; the guards looked more ferocious and there were more of them. German civilians at the *Baustelle* and elsewhere were packing to go west.

The Polish Underground was conspicuously quiet, yet one could sense in the air that something was brewing. Radio Moscow blared repeated appeals for the populations in all occupied lands to rise up and revolt against the oppressor. Radio Swit (meaning dawn in Polish), the official voice of the Delegatura in Warsaw (the representative of the Polish government-in-exile) appealed to the Polish people not to lose hope, to endure a little longer, that the hour of liberation and revenge was drawing near. In actuality, Radio Swit was located somewhere in the vicinity of London, England, and only pretended to broadcast from Warsaw to mislead and frustrate the Germans. Thus, the radio equipment in Warsaw consisted of a receiver and re-broadcast stations, not a transmitter, and was moved frequently, sometimes hourly, to avoid being captured by the Germans.

One Saturday at 10 a.m., on the corner of Grochowska Street and Szembeka Square, a few people gathered under a large speaker hanging from a lamppost to listen to a broadcast of German propaganda. This type of loudspeaker was distributed throughout Warsaw and was the main source of our daily news (other than the daily *Nowy Kurier Warszawski*), owing to the fact that private ownership of radios was prohibited. All of a sudden, the regular broadcast was interrupted, and a few seconds later a new station came on, a clandestine Polish station playing the Polish national anthem, '*Jeszcze Polska nie Zginela*' (Poland is not yet lost). The few became a crowd, all standing to attention with their hats or hands over their hearts. Tears streamed down people's faces, lips moved in unison with the words of the broadcast. I was one of the crowd, and the event moved me every bit as much as it moved the others. I, too, felt my face wet with tears and as much a proud Pole as any Catholic Pole.

The atmosphere became more anxious each day. We (the remaining Jews) felt optimistic that the end was near, but our hopes were tempered, not only by the many reversals and disappointments of the past but also by the stark, sad reality we knew, subconsciously, we would have to face in the future: the tragedy that had befallen our people. We all felt ambivalence, a fervent desire to fight and defeat our bitter enemy, yet also a fear of confronting the destroyed world of yesterday and the expected emptiness of tomorrow. Even if we did not know it, we sensed it. Our thoughts kept returning to those dear to us, far away and nearby.

In the last days of July I saw only Krysia, Marysia, and Maciej. My friends Ignac, Stasiek, and Ludwik were in Riga, and Wladek had joined the partisans in the woods; his prime task now was to bring wounded partisans to Warsaw to be treated in the Underground's makeshift hospitals. Communications with Roman, as well as with a few other friends, fell silent. Krysia, too, lost contact with her superiors and, thus, my own underground activities ceased. Even my *Baustelle* co-workers, the electricians, had dispersed. I went to work only now and then, spending more time at home socializing with my neighbors, reading books, and attending church functions regularly.

Father Sztuka, the priest from the local parish church on Szembeka Square, which I had been attending now for almost a year, was someone I knew personally. I had made his acquaintance by chance through his 17-year-old niece, Zosia, who was a friend of my landlords on Osowska Street and a frequent visitor to their home. Zosia was very pretty: medium height with light complexion, honey blonde hair and dark blue eyes. She always wore a cross around her neck but never any makeup. Her beauty was natural, characteristic of many Polish girls, especially at that age. On occasion, she would ask me to accompany her to a store or on an errand but more often than not we would veer off towards a small neighborhood park, forget whatever we set out to do, and look for a secluded bench, where we would usually end up flirting with each other.

Earlier that year, for Easter, my landlords gave a holiday party, which was mostly celebrated in my room, the biggest in the house, and which included, among other things, the Easter dinner. There were several guests at the party, including Zosia. Besides the traditional food and egg-hunt, there was plenty of vodka flowing, which was rather unusual for wartime. Soon, not many guests could stand up straight because they were drunk, too drunk to find their way home. So, as it was late, and with the police curfew hovering over us, about ten people, including Zosia, remained in my room, all sleeping with their clothes on, on the two available beds, on an armchair, or curled in a corner against the wall. I fell asleep in one of the free corners of one of the beds but when I woke up the next morning, Zosia was next to me.

That morning, I was designated to accompany Zosia to the parish house, partly for company but mostly to provide the necessary explanation about where she had spent the night. That's when I first met Father Sztuka, a round, short, stocky man, jovial and pleasant, of peasant origin. He invited me to join him (and Zosia) for breakfast – he too must have been celebrating the night before to have such a late breakfast – and I accepted. It turned out to be the most sumptuous breakfast I

128

had had in years and it was not difficult to figure out where Father Sztuka's roundness came from. After breakfast, we engaged in small talk. I don't remember the topics of our conversation, but I know that neither Jews nor religion nor the war itself were mentioned.

Towards the end of July I decided that I would have to stop my visits to the Spoczynski house. During my last visit, Mrs Spoczynski informed me of a big scare I had, unknowingly, caused them. Very early one morning, around 3.30, the Gestapo had come to arrest me. She told them that I had moved out several months ago and that no one had heard from me since. They asked several questions as to my current whereabouts, new address, place of work, relatives, and so on, but since she didn't have any answers, they left. I had no clue as to what they were after – it could have concerned my underground activities, or someone might have denounced me as a Jew in hiding – but I was not about to stay to find out. I left hurriedly, never to return. From then on, 46 Solec Street, which had provided an anchor of safety for me and quite a few others, and which had always filled me with deep affection for the Spoczynskis, became off limits.

During the last days of July, the traffic in and around Warsaw became unusually heavy. It contained not only German military and civilians, but also the Polish population at large. Some Poles wanted to avoid the front and the expected battle for Warsaw. Some, afraid that the food supply to the city would be cut off, headed for the countryside. Some sought safety by joining relatives in other towns. Still others crowded into the city because they could not return to homes that were now on the other side of the front lines, in the area already liberated – or occupied, depending on one's point of view – by the Russians.

As August approached, fresh news swamped the city: the German armies were suffering defeat after defeat on all fronts. The Russian army east of Warsaw was poised for further advances. Everyone expected them to march into

Warsaw any day. German tanks, armored vehicles, heavy artillery, and grim German troops headed westward. In Grochow, the front was no more than seven to ten miles away. During the night, only the crackling of machine-gun fire interrupted the thunderous sound of artillery.

Attacks by the Polish Underground against the Germans increased in frequency and boldness. There were daily assaults on German officers and Nazi agents. Railroad tracks were blown up, sabotage was rampant, and retaliation by the Nazis was not long in coming. In this chaos, the Germans executed Polish hostages for the smallest acts of sabotage or resistance. But we all knew that the hour of vindication was near. The Polish Underground, especially the largest of the various groups, the *Armja Krajowa*, was mobilizing fighting units for a general uprising against the despised German occupiers.

We were awaiting the coming storm. The only question was when.

17 Warsaw Ablaze

Finally, at 5 p.m. on 1 August 1944, the storm broke.

I was in Warsaw, visiting with Marysia and running some errands, when I heard the distant wail of sirens, followed by gunfire coming from all directions. A crackle of anxiety went through the crowds of people on the street as they hurried to reach their homes. I was trying to get back to my home in Grochow on the eastern side of the Vistula River, but it was impossible to find a tram; some of the streetcars had been requisitioned for use as barricades and others were so overcrowded that no one could get on, so I started on foot. I had crossed the Poniatowski Bridge and reached the end of the Paderewski Park when I saw a group of 15 to 20 young underground fighters moving in my direction, single file, from a building across the street. They wore light Polish military hats and civilian clothing with white and red armbands, and they carried rifles. Within minutes they had crossed the street and taken up positions behind the park's wall, pointing their guns at German cars moving eastward. The cars accelerated, not stopping to engage in a fight. I rushed over to the group's leader, a lieutenant, and said, 'I want to join you. I am a member of the Underground, the *Miecz i Plug*. Please, I want to join the fight against the Nazis.'

I was unceremoniously turned away with the explanation that they had no arms for me and no permission to accept volunteers; I should go home and wait till I was called. But I was never called, for two reasons: I had never been formally inducted into a combat unit of any of the three organizations with which I was working; and, except for a few skirmishes like the one behind the Paderewski Park, no significant battles were fought in Grochow or in any area east of the Vistula. At least not while I was still there.

The Warsaw uprising was ordered by the *Armja Krajowa*, the umbrella organization for the main underground groups. Smaller underground organizations, such as the *Gwardia Ludowa* and the *Miecz i Plug*, immediately joined the insurrection. The start of the uprising was carefully timed: ahead of, but close to, the anticipated entry into Warsaw by the Red Army, which was now close to the city's outskirts and was expected to reach Warsaw in a few days. The *Armja Krajowa* Command, although it did expect the Soviets to help, wanted the Polish people themselves to liberate their capital.

Sadly, this strategy turned out to be a major miscalculation. The Soviets refused to assist the uprising. Instead, they made a strategic decision not to intervene in the battle for Warsaw and halted their offensive, even retreating a few miles to enable part of the German forces facing them to turn around and fight the Polish insurgents. They also forbade Allied planes to land and refuel on their territories after dropping ammunition and other supplies to the *Armja Krajowa*. Finally, in spite of pleas by the Polish government-in-exile and its prime minister, Mr Mikolajczyk, who flew to Moscow to make a personal appeal to Stalin, they declined to provide their own supplies to the Poles. Stalin had his own agenda: to prepare the ground for a takeover of Poland by a pro-Communist, pro-Soviet government that was being established in the territories already occupied by the Red Army. We heard about this complex and tragic situation, in part, on clandestine radios; the rest we learned only after the war.

At the time, we were shocked and dismayed that the Russians didn't help. After all, Poland was allied with Russia against Germany. People struggled to explain the failure. Some thought that the uprising was not properly coordinated, that the Red Army, with its troops exhausted from the previous offensive and its supplies low, had not planned to advance into Warsaw at that time. Others insisted the reason was political, a result of the stark, centuries-long antagonism between Russia and Poland.

Still another explanation was offered to me many years later by a former Russian officer who was with the Red Army at the very gates of Warsaw exactly at the time of the uprising.[19] He had been there when the Poles gained control of almost the entire city. He was also there when the insurgents became low on food, water, and ammunition and – under constant, relentless bombardment – had to surrender. 'Why in God's name didn't you come to our rescue?' I asked in a pained voice. 'Didn't you see Warsaw being obliterated, bleeding to death?' Calmly but not convincingly, he tried to explain that the troops on the frontline, had no orders to attack, no orders to move forward.

He claimed the reason was simply that in the Red Army, in contrast to other armies, all requests for changes in plans and for new orders had to travel up the ladder, all the way to headquarters in Moscow, and then back down again, and that these procedures were lengthy and slow. Thus, the order to enter Warsaw came, but too late. Facts on the ground confirmed that the Soviets were indeed slow in starting an offensive on this front. By 15 September they occupied only Grochow and Praga, where there was no fighting, and did not move into Warsaw until 17 January 1945 – five and a half months after the uprising had started.

During the first weeks of the Warsaw uprising, Grochow was relatively quiet, even dull. But the calm was shattered one afternoon by a startling incident. In a local tavern, not far from Szembeka Square, two Polish Blue policemen sat at the counter having a few drinks. Suddenly, two young men, one carrying a rolled paper under his arm, walked in and addressed one of the policemen: 'Are you so-and-so, born such-and-such date, son of so-and-so?' Upon confirming his identity, one of the young men opened his scroll and read, 'By order of the High Court of the Republic of Poland, for crimes committed by you on such-and-such date, you have been sentenced to death!' At that instant, the second man drew a pistol from his pocket and fired two shots. The policeman fell to the floor, dead. In less than three minutes, the two young men were gone.

I do not know the nature of this policeman's crime or what crimes were involved in similar incidents throughout Warsaw during the occupation. But I cannot help thinking that had the Underground court been equally effective in persecuting the crimes of blackmailers and denouncers of Jews, much pain and trauma would have been avoided, and many Jewish lives would have been spared. The Jewish Underground sent such requests periodically to both the Delegatura in Warsaw and to the authorities of the Polish government in London, but to no avail. Our pleas, with very few exceptions, fell on deaf ears.

The weeks of idle waiting in Grochow were extremely diffi- cult to take. The sounds of battles fought in Warsaw continued uninterrupted, day and night. Only the direction shifted, from one district to another. Then there was the smell, a terrible smell, and worst of all, the sight of Warsaw burning. Black, billowing smoke spread out against the sky, intertwined with columns of multicolored flames. In the midst of it was Warsaw's million-plus population, with all of its women and children, its old and sick people, and its national and cultural treasures. Warsaw was being systematically burned and leveled to the ground, destroyed street-by-street and block-by-block. Those remaining Jews who so laboriously and sometimes miraculously managed to escape, enduring first the camps and then the perils of a life in hiding, now faced a new threat of annihilation. Among them were also those few who had escaped the inferno of the Warsaw Ghetto uprising. They were now – individually and in small, organized units together with the Poles – fighting the common enemy.

My aunts Marysia and Mania, my cousin Marta, Maciej with his 8-year-old daughter Yola, Kuba, Roman, Wladek, and other friends were all trapped behind the ascending flames. The whole horizon was engulfed in a thick, black cloud of smoke. The shade of blackness varied; its height would sometimes shoot up or drop lower, but the tragedy that the smoke represented remained constant, day in, day out. Warsaw was ablaze, and just as before, in the ghettos and in the camps, a feeling of total powerlessness overwhelmed all of us who lived across the Vistula.

On the afternoon of 14 August Krysia came to my house on Kiprow Street to celebrate my birthday. She brought a flask of vodka, and I supplied some fruit and small sugar cubes. But our mood was grim, and it was not a happy celebration. We knew it was a real possibility that the uprising would end in defeat. We felt the noose tightening, that our very lives might be in danger and that we might be taken away any day now. We expected to be separated and perhaps never see each other again. Our work in the Underground, which had been a source of purpose and satisfaction, had already come to a halt. The contacts with those to whom we had provided subsidies were lost, and our own means of support had begun to vanish. Only one thing remained: a unique and incredibly strong bond between us.

Krysia was particularly worried because she had a sick mother and a fiancé in hiding. She was also short of funds. As a full-time, paid courier for the ZOB, her work had ended abruptly when the uprising started, and she had received only one month's pay in advance.

For food we had only provisions we had managed to purchase during the first days of the uprising. In the stores, food supplies disappeared quickly, without replenishment. One evening I ventured out to the nearby square, but all the stores were closed, and not only because it was evening. There was no merchandise to sell, and the shelves were empty. Small groups of people, mostly women, were gathered on street corners, wondering in whispers what would happen next. Men did not dare walk around for fear of being taken away. As I turned to walk home, my eye caught sight of something lying in the middle of the street – a dead horse. The next morning, by the time the police curfew ended, the carcass had been picked clean of its meat.

Father Sztuka's sermons, to which I listened carefully every Sunday, were long, dull and uninspiring. While I had no particular objections to that, I did object to, and could not forgive, the fact that he never, not even once, mentioned the terrible suffering to which his fellow human beings – his 'brothers and sisters' as he used to call us – were subjected. The continuing oppression of the entire population of Poland, marked almost daily by the summary executions of hundreds of Polish patriots, was ignored; indeed, the Church's pulpits were never used to defend the victims, Jewish or Polish, or to condemn the Nazi perpetrators and their crimes. Perhaps even more importantly, not once did he appeal to the population for help and sympathy for the victims. It wasn't much more than a year since half a million people in the Warsaw Ghetto had been murdered, starved to death, or sent to the death camps, not long since the ghetto had been burned to the ground. The tragic events were still very fresh in people's minds and hearts. Yet, about all these victims, there was only silence.

The great moral power held by the Church and the individual priests was not used to uphold its own moral values. The Church, with its elaborate infrastructure and communication channels, was the only institution that knew what was happening inside occupied Europe. It was also the only institution with the prestige and the moral power to speak out and make an impact, but it remained silent. It failed us, Poles and Jews, and so, too, it failed itself, terribly and without the potential for forgiveness.

The Russian front fell silent. 'If the Russian front lines are in the east, why are the German tanks moving west?' people were asking. They were moving west to fight the insurgents. Apart from military vehicles, the streets were empty. Increasingly, we were worried about our food situation: with no fresh supplies we wondered how long we could last. There were many children, sick people, and elderly among us. With each passing day, people looked more tired and more resigned to an unknown fate.

On the morning of 23 August I heard a commotion: German SS gendarmes were going from house to house, calling for all young and sometimes not-so-young men to come out and assemble in the street. At first, we thought this to be a precautionary measure: to prevent young people from Praga, Grochow, and the vicinities from reinforcing those fighting in Warsaw and to ensure no 'second front' east of the Vistula. We thought that we would be confined in some sort of camp. We were wrong. We were about to be taken away.

I immediately decided to hide and, if discovered, to resist. After all, I was armed: I had a revolver and two grenades. I went to the basement looking for a good spot but my thoughts were muddled and panic-stricken. If I tried to shoot, I might kill one or two of them but in the end I would be overpowered and killed. No one would ever know what had happened to me. Naturally, such an ending did not hold much appeal. Fully aware of how close we all were to the war's end, I abandoned any idea of resisting.

I was still mulling over what to do when a gendarme caught up with me. *'Raus! Raus!'* he shouted. 'Take your things and move out to the assembly point! *Schnell, schnell!'* I asked for and was granted a couple of minutes to get ready.

Upstairs in my room, I quickly packed a change of clothing and some food into a backpack and into my small briefcase, the one I brought from the Tomaszow camp. Interspersed among the clothing, I placed some tools: chisels, wood and metal blades from a handsaw, and wire cutters. If anyone asked, the tools were for electrical work, although a closer examination would have revealed that their purpose was quite different. These were tools much better suited to making an escape than to fixing electric circuits.

However, I still had one more thing to do before I left, and that was to hide my arms arsenal. Normally I kept it in its hideout under the wardrobe, but since the uprising I was keeping it at the ready, under the mattress. In the heat of the moment I thought of taking it with me. After all, these were the most precious possessions I had. On second consideration, I thought it was too risky; should the gendarmes find the weapons on me, I would be dead in an instant. So I did something considerably more stupid, something that worried me for many, many months to come. I packed the revolver and the two grenades into the wood-burning oven and, to hide them from view, covered them with lots of crumpled newspapers. Then I went to the assembly point. What I failed to consider was that come next winter, my landlady would try to light the oven without first cleaning it, and the house would blow up. She had a little daughter, and her sister lived just below our apartment. I certainly did not want to put them in any danger, and I often thought of the hazard I had created for my landlady at Kiprow Street. But it was a worry I could do nothing about.[20]

When I reached the assembly point, some 100 to 200 people were already gathered there. At ten o'clock sharp, in a column six abreast and guarded by the SS, we were marched to the east railway station in Praga. The column comprised mostly young men, along with a few young women: wives who had volunteered to join their husbands or women taken because they were suspected of belonging to the Underground. At the station, we were loaded into closed cattle cars, about 60 to a car. An hour or two later, the train started to move slowly westward, in the direction of Warsaw. Why were we taken, where we were going, and what they were going to do to us, we did not know.

From close up, the sight of Warsaw was even more gruesome than we had imagined. The skeletons of burned out, multistory buildings started to appear on the horizon. There was a bleak expression on everybody's face, reflecting our concern for our loved ones, relatives, and friends: we all wondered what had happened to the people inside those buildings. The city of Warsaw was decimated. This beautiful city, often referred to as the Paris of the East, now was lifeless and in ruins.

The train moved slowly westward, adding cattle cars at three other Warsaw stations. The sight of flames and smoke surrounded us completely. Shooting could still be heard, but not with the same intensity as earlier, since ammunition was running low and many fighters had already fallen. There were parachute drops from Allied planes, but most of them were too late – many of the designated areas were no longer in Polish hands. The uprising's offensive had begun to transform itself into defense, regrouping, aiding the wounded, putting out the fires, and organizing common kitchens; it became a battle for survival. The heroism and zeal of the young insurgents could not overcome the overwhelming might and the brutal determination of the Nazis.

Our own status and destination remained a mystery. As soon as we left Warsaw, I began preparing for a possible escape. With the blades that I brought with me, I started to saw at the car's wooden floorboard, but this did not last long. Several men, realizing what my plans were, decided that this would endanger all of them, including the women among us, and asked me to stop at once. Reluctantly, I obliged; I had no choice.

In the locked car we were packed like sardines, with standing room only. The only fresh air came through four openings, about 24 inches wide by six or eight inches high, each in an upper corner of the car. This trip in a cattle car was a new experience to most if not all of the prisoners. The experience was also new to me, but as a Jew I was bothered by it more than most, because I knew it was how Jews were deported from ghettos. After about two hours, we arrived at our destination: a gigantic train repair yard in Pruszkow, a small town about 20 kilometers southwest of Warsaw. It was established as a transit camp for the masses of Warsaw deportees, prisoners of all sorts, and insurgents. Warsaw was being evacuated. As we learned later, the Germans had ordered a complete displacement of Warsaw's inhabitants and the total destruction of the city.

Even surrounded by barbed wire and guarded by Nazi SS and German soldiers, the camp was a welcome relief. At least we were still in Poland. There was water and minimal daily rations of food, some sanitary facilities (or at least some bushes), and fresh air. But there was no accommodation; everyone was on his or her own. There were many large empty buildings about, but they were more like hangars, not very suitable as sleeping accommodation. The first night, I lay down next to a tree, with my briefcase and backpack rolled into my jacket to make a pillow. I fell asleep in no time, only to be awakened around midnight by ear-splitting thunder and the sky lit up by lightning. The storm was unlike anything I had ever experienced. Rain lashed down in buckets. When I woke up, there was water on the ground all around and underneath me. Soaked and chilled to the bone, I put my hat over my face, turned around, and fell right back to sleep. I am not sure what prevailed, my youth or my exhaustion.

The next couple of days were warm and sunny. I found a few pieces of office furniture and a place inside one of the hangers to protect myself from the elements in the future. The question that troubled all of us, though, was what the Germans were planning to do with us. When we arrived, there were tens of thousands of people there already; in addition, new transports were arriving every day, several times a day. But transports were also leaving. Many women, children, and elderly people were released and shipped to various parts of occupied Poland, while most middle-aged women and men were sent to labor camps in Germany. The most uncertain and dangerous situation was that of young people like myself. We were prime candidates for concentration camps. The Germans classified all young people as having fought in the uprising, as they were not able to distinguish between combatants and civilians; the insurgents did not wear uniforms – only easily discarded white and red armbands and light military hats – and by the time they got to Pruszkow they had no weapons on them. Also, because the Germans had so far refused to grant the insurgents the status of combatants, which would have provided them with the protection of the Geneva Convention, they referred to all of us as '*die polnische Banditen*' (Polish bandits). Thus, although I was not caught as a fighter, I was nonetheless classified as such because of my gender and my age. As time passed, it became clear that most of the transports containing young people were indeed going straight to concentration camps, including Auschwitz.[21]

In the distance, Warsaw continued to burn.

18 The Printers' Transport

Besides transports to concentration camps, many transports from Pruszkow were to labor camps in Germany; these carried various specialists who were to be employed in their particular crafts, in addition to plain manual labor. In one of these transports, a group of printers from the Warsaw Printing Office was being sent to a Vienna camp to work in the State Printing Office of Vienna. That sounded like a good opportunity for me. The German WIFO employees of the Warsaw *Baustelle* where I had worked, including Mrs Follman and Mr Miertsching, had all been transferred to WIFO's branch in Liebau, near Vienna. I knew also that Austria was a Catholic country, and I thought it might be kinder to Catholic Poles. Moreover, at the very least, a job in Vienna removed the risk of being sent to a concentration camp. My main concern now was how to get onto that particular transport. To start with, I moved closer to the group of real printers and quickly added the word '*Drucker*' (printer) to the 'occupation' line of my labor card that already said 'electrician'. I doubted that this simple addition would convince anyone to give me a free ride to Vienna – there must have been a list of the printers from the Warsaw Printing Office – but I had nothing to lose.

One morning, as I was milling around the camp, one of the guards, a *Wehrmacht* soldier on the other side of the barbed wire fence, called over to me, 'Hey! What are you doing here?' I did not recognize him, as soldiers in uniform often looked alike to me, but he explained that he knew me from the WIFO *Baustelle* in Warsaw and that, on occasion, he had even borrowed a few tools from me. We exchanged a few words, and then he asked, 'Can I do something for you?' I told him that I wanted to continue to work with the people from the Warsaw WIFO, now in Vienna, and that I knew a transport to Vienna was being readied. He said he would try to help me and, that same afternoon, came back to the spot where we had agreed to meet, to take me to the transit camp commander, an SS *Obersturmbahnführer*. The visit was short, but it yielded the desired result: the commander declared that since the *Feldwebel* (sergeant) had vouched for me, my transfer to the WIFO branch in the vicinity of Vienna was acceptable to him. Within minutes the order to put me on the Vienna transport was typed and signed. He gave it to me and, with a wave of his hand, dismissed me.

Luck was with me yet again. Now I was not only scheduled to be shipped to Vienna but also no longer part of the combatants or Polish bandits group. It also meant I was exempt from being shipped elsewhere, possibly to a death camp. I didn't know what the future had in store for me in Vienna, but this piece of paper had improved my prospects and my mood considerably. This anonymous Polish bandit, with an uncertain, life-threatening fate, had become a certified worker destined for a labor camp in Austria.

It seemed that extracting or falsifying documents and looking for ways to get around the rules had become second nature to me. As for the soldier who helped me, I never learned what his name was and never saw him again.

I now stuck really close to the group of printers on their way to Vienna, about 30 in all. Gradually, other stragglers, both men and women, joined us. By the time the transport was ready to depart, there were more than 40 of us, mostly young men and women, with four Catholic priests on their way to join a Polish, Catholic church in Austria.

One morning, after getting some bread and black coffee, we were loaded onto a freight car that was then attached to a row of other cars and a locomotive. German policemen were assigned to guard the transport, with an elderly police officer from Vienna guarding our group.

The odyssey from Pruszkow to Vienna started on a high

note. We were happy to have a destination and to know we were heading to a labor rather than a concentration camp. We were also glad to be out of the transit camp, where the situation was tenuous at best and any semblance of order and normalcy was quickly breaking down. Every day more and more people arrived from Warsaw, making the meager supplies and facilities painfully inadequate. Although the Germans were releasing great numbers of women, women with children and older men, thousands of newly arrived young people continued to crowd into the depot. The Germans continued to treat all Poles with scorn: we were the *Untermenschen* ('subhumans'), the despised rebels of Warsaw, whose comrades were fighting a life-and-death battle against Germany; all young men were considered former combatants and called the 'Polish bandits'. Thus, we were happy to leave Pruszkow and we were in good spirits. We also thought that the presence of four priests among us would give us some support.

When the train finally rolled out of the depot, our guard placed himself at the partly open door and sat on the floor with his gun on his lap. Not a word was exchanged between him and us. I settled on the floor near the corner, under one of the four small windows, each with vertical iron bars in the car. There seemed to be enough room for everyone to lie down, a distinct improvement on the trip from Praga to Pruszkow where there was standing room only.

The first two hours of the journey passed quietly. As the train accelerated we could hear the increasing frequency of the rhythmic clicks of wheels against the rail and, from time to time, the hissing of the steam locomotive. Then, the train slowed down and then stopped. Through the small window – right above the place where I had settled down – I saw the station's name: Koluszki, a well-known railroad junction, about 50 miles southwest of Warsaw. We were some distance past the station, on a siding, with numerous tracks in the side and parallel to our train. I sat down on the floor with my back leaning against the wall of the car and engaged in small talk with my travel companions.

Next, a most unbelievable coincidence happened when another transport of Nazi prisoners rolled into the Koluszki station. The Nazis' constant displacement of people led to many unusual coincidences, some were strange and unique, others banal or tragic. But this one, for me, was the most heart-wrenching and painful experience of the entire war.

We waited for our train to start moving again, when we heard screeching sounds on a track next to ours. Curious, I stood up on my toes to get a look through the window. What I saw was the oncoming cattle car train, full of people. It came to a stop. The cars were similar to ours, only this time the window openings had barbed wire in addition to bars. I continued to look out. No sooner did the train stop, when a middle-aged man's head appeared behind the window just opposite me. His face was pale and gaunt, his dark eyes bulging, his hair disheveled. Our eyes met.

'Where are you coming from?' I asked.

'We are from the Lódz Ghetto. We are Jews. Please, do you have some water?' the man answered.

'From Lódz?' I repeated, in disbelief at the coincidence. Lódz was my hometown and my parents and my sister were in the Lódz Ghetto. I was there, outside the Ghetto, a little over a month ago, trying to establish contact with the Ghetto.

My thoughts turned immediately to my family. Where were they? Perhaps in the car I was facing? How could I find out? Did I dare to ask the man facing me, with all the people around me within hearing range? I did dare.

'Do you know the Neumark family? Felek Neumark. They lived on Brzezinska Street?' I blurted out. 'Do you know them?'

'Neumark, yes, yes … I know them, the tall one [my father was over six feet tall], they are on this train somewhere, but not in this car. But, do you have water? Please, I need water,' he pleaded in an anguished voice.

'Are you sure that they are on this train?' I asked. (I disregarded his plea for water because I did not have any; besides it would be impossible to exchange any matter, especially any liquid.)

'Yes, yes, I'm sure,' he answered.

'But where are they?' I asked anxiously.

'Sorry, that I don't know, I don't know.' His voice was fading. 'I don't know,' he repeated. And then he disappeared.

I could hardly believe what I had just heard. I felt sick. I felt a dull pain in my stomach; my mind was blank. I felt as if my heart had stopped beating. I felt totally, utterly helpless, more than at any time before ...

I sank to the floor below, leaning against the wall, and covered my eyes and part of face with my palm, pretending to be dozing off. I did not want anyone to see my face, although I know that I did not cry. I cannot explain why, but I did not. I badly needed time to myself.

Shortly thereafter the journey resumed. The images of where the other transport might be going, my helplessness, the pleading for water by the man from the other train – all swirled in my head. After a while, I began also to think about my own danger: what if my travel companions heard my inquiries, sensed my anxiety and understood my involvement with the Neumarks, with those from the Ghetto? What if they understood that I might be Jewish?

But there was nothing I could do now. I had to return to my seat on the car's floor and to my status of a prisoner from the Warsaw Uprising on his way to a Nazi labor camp, and to pretend that this unbelievable encounter never happened.

The guard never saw or heard me talking to the people from the other train; he was not there at the time. Whenever the train would stop for any length of time, our guard would jump off, lock the door from the outside, and disappear. There was a separate car for the guards, where they ate their meals and spent the nights.

The trip to the camp in Vienna, which had started on a happy note and which we had expected to take one or two days, took three weeks and was anything but happy. In fact, it was horrible. During this time, we were cooped up in a dirty and bare cattle car, we were concerned as to our real destination, and most of the times, for days on end, we were without food or water. The four little windows in the upper corners were the only source of fresh air, and only during the day, some light. Facilities were available to us only occasionally, at the whim of the guard, when the train stopped for a longer period.

When from time to time we did stop at a railroad station, we were allowed to make purchases from the bar counter there. The problem was that the stations we stopped at were small and no food was available there; sometimes we could buy some drinks and fill our canteens with water. If a Red Cross office happened to be at a station, then the workers would provide us with some provisions, usually hot soup and milk with dark bread. Most of the time, though, the train would stop in the middle of nowhere, for no apparent reason and for an unspecified length of time. Sometimes we would be stationary for hours on end. On one occasion, we were allowed out, under the watchful eye of the guard, to search for nourishment in the immediate vicinity; we were successful and found three sacks of discarded, rotten pears. At times, when our train stopped at a railroad crossing and our door was open, people behind the barrier would throw edible items to us: a quarter-loaf of bread, apples, pieces of chicken, or a container with a homemade marmalade. Others just waved handkerchiefs at us, wishing us good luck.

Most of the time we were a three-car transport with an extra passenger car for the police guards. Occasionally, two or more cars with deportees like us and an additional guards' car would be attached to our convoy. As time went on, the periods when a locomotive pulled us forward became increasingly rare, while the times we sat in the middle of nowhere became more and more frequent. Sometimes we sat for days at a time. We were hungry and thirsty all the time, we were bored to tears, and we were very, very dirty. We had not washed in weeks. The time passed slowly; people just sat on the floor quietly, expressionless, half-dazed, half-numbed.

146

When I think back to the different times during the war –
in the ghetto, after the escape or in the cattle car on the way
to Vienna – I wonder if being in a daze, or feeling numbness
or no emotions, was not a blessing in disguise. I wonder if it
was not nature's way to wrap us with a protective shield, to
deaden our sensitivities to hunger pangs or to fear or despair;
to anesthetize us. I do not recall having ever had strong
feelings of either pain or despair.

I mostly kept to myself. I was polite to everybody but
friendly with no one. Being reserved was partly in my character, but it was also deliberate, as I did not want to be asked too
many questions. Someone may have known the house I lived
in, my family, or the school I attended. I was also afraid of
becoming too talkative; I wanted to avoid any slips of the
tongue. One young lady, who slept and sat next to me
throughout the journey and with whom I liked to talk, was
Lucyna. She was two or three years older than me and was a
student of chemistry at one of Warsaw's clandestine universities. No matter what subject we started discussing, she would
find a relationship between that topic and some law or principle in chemistry or science in general. She related the war, the
chaos in the world, and the mass displacement of populations
to the principle of entropy, defined as the steady increase in
disorder and disorganization in any closed system. I understood very little of her explanations, but I tried to be a good
listener.

Twice a day, in the morning and evening, the group would
intone traditional prayers: '*Kiedy ranne wstaja zorze*' ('When
The Dawn Comes') and '*Wszystkie nasze dzienne sprawy, Przyjm
litosnie Boze prawy*' ('All Our Daily Problems, Lord, Receive
Them With Mercy'), whose most words I still remember. And
that was when I would come to life: I sang the loudest. In fact,
often I would initiate the singing, even though I never had a
good voice. My enthusiastic singing, interpreted as piety, and
my general conduct throughout the trip, being generally
polite and helpful and never using curse words, made a
lasting impression on the four priests who shared our 'Orient

147

Express'. This came to light about three months later, when we were settled in Vienna, and the Printers' Transport group gathered for a traditional Polish Christmas Eve dinner in one of Vienna's restaurants, in Floridsdorf, close to where most of the printers made their home. The four priests had organized the evening and had conducted the services. The food was good and the festivities followed uneventfully, but when the time came for the traditional sharing of the wafer with his flock, the head priest, a middle-aged, thickset, friendly man, decided to preface the sharing with a little introduction. He rose and said, 'I wish to share my first wafer with Zenon, who is a shining example of a good Pole and a good Christian.'

Confused and in disbelief, I rose; he approached me and placed the wafer on my tongue. Little did the priest know how much I appreciated his words but, at the same time, how very much they were off the mark – at least with respect to the 'Christian'. After the dinner, a couple of men patted me on the back in a congratulatory manner. The young women in the group seemed to be more ambivalent: indeed, I might be upright and pious, but how much fun was I? And how come I did not chase them like the other men did? Overtly, I was thrilled with my performance. Inside, however, I was partly embarrassed and partly confused. There were times, albeit brief, when I was not so sure how much of a performance it really was.

During the third week of our journey towards our destination, emaciated and both mentally and physically exhausted, we reached Strasshof, a small town in Austria a few miles north of Vienna. At first we had no idea where we were or why we had stopped there. But we soon found out that it was a place for quarantine, a requirement for all prisoners entering the Third Reich. Since I had never been quarantined, I considered it routine and did not give it much thought.

But I was wrong. The quarantine called for both men and women to take off all their clothes, so that the prisoners could shower while their garments were sent to be disinfected. Both sexes were given soap and led to communal, but separated, shower facilities and then to two waiting rooms, separated by an open door. From the time I heard we would have to disrobe, I was filled with alarm. What if someone saw me and questioned my being circumcised? I was also constantly aware that 'a guilty person *looks* guilty'. Fortunately, I was in luck again – with the door open between the two waiting rooms, the women on the other side of the door became the focal point of the men's curiosity, not me. Except for the priests, who remained seated on benches located around the room, the men focused all their attention on the opposite sex. They had not the slightest interest in whether anyone in the waiting room was circumcised.

In the early afternoon, our clothing and our few worldly possessions were returned. We dressed and continued milling around, as there was absolutely nothing with which to occupy our time. Across the street from our facility was a small kiosk, which I was given permission to visit. It had mostly newspapers and magazines, some knickknacks, and postcards with printed stamps on them. With the few German marks I had on me, I quickly bought a couple.

The first people to whom I wrote were the Szokalski family in Tomaszow, telling them that I was alive and safe, and thanking them. But I did not give them my return address. Firstly, I did not have an address; secondly, I would not have revealed my address even if I had one, for safety reasons. Their daughter Lucja told me many years later how happy they were to hear from me, to know that I was still alive. The second card I wrote was to Mrs Follman, the secretary at WIFO in Warsaw, who had helped me get my permits to go to Lódz. I did not have her exact address, only the company's name and location. I wrote that I would like to work for WIFO once more and that I would be writing again as soon as I had a permanent address. I crossed the street back to the facility. I was a little surprised at the laxity of the place, since I was still considered a prisoner, but at the time I didn't give this matter much thought.

At the end of the day we were given two blankets each and

told to prepare for the night on the floor of the room we were in. We were also given five diamond-shaped patches of cloth, no bigger than two by three inches, with a white letter 'P' (for Polish) on a dark blue background, to be worn on all outside clothing, although no one bothered to put it on. The next morning we were to be transported by trucks to our final destination, a camp in Vienna.

19 A Bird Without Wings

In the morning, as scheduled, we were loaded onto three trucks and delivered to the camp, located on Landsmannstrasse–Hauptstrasse, in the Third District of Vienna. The camp was a complex of barracks and small buildings, surrounded by a six-foot wooden fence. One military sentry, in full gear, stood next to the main entry gate, guarding it. The security arrangements of this camp both struck and surprised us. What kind of camp was this? We were sent here as labourers, but we were also war prisoners, 'die Polnische Banditen' from the Warsaw Uprising. But this camp did not look like either a prisoner-of-war or a labor camp. It most certainly did not resemble the Tomaszow Labor Camp that I knew, which had been surrounded by barbed wire and guarded by armed SS men. Inside the camp there were already other prisoners milling around: men and women of different ages and of various nationalities.

The accommodation in the camp was extremely spartan. There were no bunks or cots, no chairs or tables – just a few simple wooden benches against the walls. At night, each of us settled on the bare floor with the two blankets we had received in Strasshof. The facilities, including those for washing, were all outdoors, but it was still summer, so we could live with that. As for food, the portions were meager and not very nutritious, but we were fed three times a day. All in all, it was an improvement over the difficult conditions to which we were subjected in Pruszkow and certainly better than the three-week semi-starvation journey to here. Our main problem was boredom; there was nothing to occupy our time. Mostly, we rested all day from our long and tiring journey, chatted with each other, or just milled aimlessly around the courtyard.

For the first few days nothing special happened. There was no daily roll call, as we had had in the Tomaszow camp, and there were no work assignments. Our major concern was that we didn't know what the future held for us. If this was just a transit camp, rather then a labor camp, then we wanted to know where we would be shipped next. The possibility that we might be taken to a concentration camp was never far from our minds.

Given the lax security in the camp, the daily idleness, and an uncertain future, once again my mind turned to the possibilities of escape. I thought that either I could seek my old job at WIFO, or blend into the local population and find a regular job as an electrician. I went to work on it. I scouted the perimeter of the camp for the least conspicuous places, both inside and outside, and determined that the best place would be the corner of the camp and the best time to leave would be after dark. My decision to escape was more a spontaneous impulse than a rational, well-thought-out plan. I did not know either the city, or the rules and regulations governing the city or anybody in it. I had only one contact: Mrs Follman. But although I had written to her again with my new address, I hadn't heard from her. If I did escape, I had no idea where I would spend the first night or where my first meal would come from. Yet not to escape, especially when it was so easy, seemed a missed opportunity. It was now an ingrained instinct in me that when I heard the word 'camp', I immediately thought, 'escape'.

It happened the next evening. Without telling anyone, I collected my backpack and my briefcase, and, ten minutes later, with a quick jump over the wooden fence at the farthest corner of the camp, I was on the other side of the fence. Free as a bird; but, unfortunately, as I soon found out, a bird without wings.

My emotions ran the gamut from euphoria to anxiety as for

the next two hours I zigzagged in the direction of the city center, savoring the fresh, free evening air and wondering where I would spend the night I was afraid that I might be caught and was worried sick about the uncertainty that awaited me in the days ahead. But then I thought of being in a Nazi camp, no matter how benign, and I was happy to be free.

The streets were very quiet, with few pedestrians, mainly women rushing home after working late. I was becoming increasingly tired, both emotionally and physically, when after two hours of walking I stumbled upon a park, the Stadtpark, a renowned Vienna garden. There was no problem finding a suitable place to sleep: between the bushes and shrubbery, with the bust of the famous composer Johann Strauss on a pedestal for company. There was even a place I could refresh myself under one of the several fountains. I fell asleep thinking about the things I wanted to do the next day.

The morning started on a promising note. I walked from the park into the city center, within the 'Ring' in the First District. What a sight lay before me! Vienna was beautiful! With its wide, tree-lined boulevards filled with beautiful monuments and splendid palaces: the Opera House, the Hoffburg Castle, the Parliament, the Burgtheatre, and many, many other wonders of art and architecture, all within a few blocks. I bought a newspaper, the *Völkische Beobachter*, then looked for a coffeehouse where I could get breakfast; my stomach was growling in anticipation.

As I entered the first coffee shop I encountered, an old waiter in a tuxedo opened the door, bowed and greeted me with a *'Grüss Gott'* (God bless you). He accompanied me to a plush booth and offered me a glass of water the minute I sat down, all before I had had a chance to utter a word. As he served me coffee, and with my hunger strengthened by the enticing aromas surrounding me, I started to order breakfast. But the waiter stopped me. He looked at me politely but puzzled. 'Where are your ration cards?' he asked.

'I don't have any,' I replied. 'I'm a traveler, in transit.'

'But travelers also get ration cards,' he argued. 'I'm sorry, but I can't serve you breakfast.' 'It is not allowed,' he added sternly, turned around and left.

Frustrated, I had three more cups of this bitter and strangely tasting coffee, and read my paper. The *Völkischer Beobachter* carried a front-page article about the Warsaw Uprising. The good news was that the Red Army not only had occupied the entire eastern part of Warsaw, including Praga and Grochow; but had also managed to establish a beachhead on the western shore of the Vistula. That was about the middle of September and it was a clear defeat for the Germans; most importantly, it would take some pressure off the fighting Warsaw insurgents. A second news item was also important: the Germans, after intervention by the Allies, had granted Polish fighters of *Armja Krajowa* the status of combatants, which now gave them protection and certain rights under the Geneva Convention. Did this mean that the rest of us in captivity would now be accorded the status of prisoners of war as well? That we would no longer be treated as the 'Polish bandits' I wondered? But, of course, the paper did not say.

The bad news was that according to other claims in the article, that the uprising was about to come to a tragic end. What had promised to be the glorious liberation of Poland's capital after five years of murderous occupation was about to end in catastrophe. Indeed, a couple of weeks later, on 2 October, after a valiant and courageous fight that lasted more than two months, Warsaw capitulated. Commander Bor-Komorowski and his men laid down their arms and were marched off to a prisoner-of-war camp. (I learned later 90 percent of Warsaw was destroyed, and 250,000 people had been killed, maimed, or wounded. Of the remaining inhabitants, hundreds of thousands were dispersed and tens of thousands – mostly young men and women – were taken prisoner and sent to Germany to either labor or concentration camps.) Still hungry, I paid for the coffee and left.

I went out into the streets again in my search for breakfast in one of the many coffeehouses. I tried side streets and smaller shops, hopeful that they might be less strict. But to my dismay, the answer was the same at half a dozen other establishments: no ration book, no breakfast. Next, I stopped at a bank, where I exchanged a small number of zlotys for an even smaller number of marks. I needed cash to be able to offer a bribe. But the first time I offered one to a waitress, she looked at me as though I was from Mars: 'We don't do such things here, this is a crime,' she answered with harshness in her voice. Finally, I realized that this problem was much more serious than I had imagined and that I had to find a solution for it immediately. I quickly found a telephone kiosk and made a call to Mrs Follman. I was wondering if, somehow, I could get a job with the old *Baustelle*. To my great surprise she answered the phone. I felt my spirits revive; I had found someone, perhaps the only person in Austria, who knew me and would help me if at all possible. She was pleasant, as always, and glad that I had reached Vienna. But my mood soon changed as she warned me, 'Don't come to Liebau. The British are bombing us by day and the Americans are doing the same every night. Many people you know have been killed or wounded. Don't come here.' Being cautious, I did not tell her that I had run away from a camp, that I was floundering in the city, and that I was desperate. I gave her the camp's address and told her that I would try to get an assignment as an electrician elsewhere in the city, promising to call her back.

I went to several food stores and tried to purchase something to eat. But there too the response was always the same: they could only sell food in exchange for ration cards. I couldn't even buy a slice of bread, an apple, or a carrot. Unsuccessful in my quest for a meal, I tried to find accommodation. I looked for a private room or even a bed, avoiding hotels or agencies where registration would be required. In the camp they had my name and my ID card number, and for all I knew the police might have issued an all-points bulletin for me. But I soon found out that finding lodging was as difficult as finding food. In every building, on the first night, the concierge was duty bound to report to the police any visitor, any stranger who spent more than 12 hours in his building. There were no exceptions. So I had to spend my second 'free in Vienna' night at the main railway station. It would have been all right – the station was full of people but had many empty chairs on which one could rest – if not for periodic document checks by the gendarmes, who were looking for *Wehrmacht* deserters or, perhaps, people like me. Their presence sent me back to the park for the following two nights.

With no way to obtain food in a restaurant or store, I became a scavenger, wandering around the backs of fruit and vegetable stores, picking up rotting goods the store was throwing out. I also took to loitering behind restaurants in order to pick up food the patrons had left on their plates and that the kitchen girls were about to throw out. Then, I found one place that offered one item without ration cards: I could not only get coffee with refills and load up on sugar cubes, but also order up to two portions of marinated herring! All without ration cards! To boot, the place was elegant and had ambiance. It was a well-known restaurant called Rathauskeller (so-called because it was located in the basement of the *Rathaus*, the City Hall). It was beautifully decorated, tables were covered with tablecloths, china, and shiny cutlery, and the service was impeccable – just what any camp inmate was accustomed to. So, for the next three days, for a special meal in a place with atmosphere, I was there for lunch and dinner. I became a regular customer.

In the meantime, I found and offered my services to a couple of local electrical companies. But I had no more luck here than I had previously had with food or lodging. The problem? I did not have a German labor card and here, my Polish card was worthless. Everyone I approached sent me away with typical Viennese politeness minus sympathy or concern. Unlike Poland, in Vienna people were extremely strict; they obeyed the laws meticulously.

As days, even hours, passed, I grew increasingly worried. I realized that this problem was extremely serious. How was I going to survive? Sooner or later someone would recognize my illegal status and denounce me. And that could end worse than the camp on Landsmannstrasse. What was the good of being free if I was unable to find food or lodging or a job?

On the fifth day I was desperate. I saw no way out of my dilemma but to return to the camp. No matter what the consequences, I had to return to the camp. It was ironic that when hundreds of thousands, perhaps millions of inmates yearned to be free of the confines of Nazi camps, I felt so desperate on the outside that I wanted to voluntarily return to the camp; ready to face the possibility of ending up in a concentration camp. But I saw no way out.

That evening, as soon as it got dark, with a heavy heart and empty stomach and my mind preoccupied with the potential consequences of my adventure, I scaled the six-foot fence, as I did a few days earlier, but this time into the camp. My fellow inmates were surprised to see me. I must have looked as haggard and exhausted as I felt, because even before hearing my story they insisted that I have something to eat and drink. When I told them what had happened, they too had a hard time believing that life could be so regimented. In Poland, and especially in Warsaw under occupation, laws were but challenges to be evaded.

But they too had a story to tell me, one that frightened me beyond words.

The day before, a German had come to the camp looking for me. He was tall and slim, in civilian clothing but with a Nazi insignia in his lapel. He wanted to know where I was and where could he find me, but since they could not help him, he left. They had no idea who he was or why he was looking for me. As I listened attentively, I felt the blood drain from my face. I feared the worst. This man could be from the Gestapo. He could also be from the camp authority, except that in this unusual camp, they didn't seem to have missed me after I had escaped and didn't seem to notice now that I had returned. Perhaps someone I had contacted in Vienna, someone at one of the electrical companies, had become suspicious and denounced me. I tried to remain calm, but that night I couldn't sleep, worried about who the German was, what he wanted, and if he would return for me. The image of a concentration camp flashed through my mind.

One morning, about a week later, the man with the Nazi emblem in his lapel did return, and we met face to face. He must have seen the fear in my eyes, because he immediately started to explain the purpose of his visit: a job opportunity. He explained that his company needed electricians and that Mrs Follman, an acquaintance of his, had given him my name as the man for the job. 'There is a problem, however,' he told me. 'The camp commander has no authority to release anyone to a private firm that is not producing war material,' letting me know that he had already tried to get me out, but had been unsuccessful.

What a relief! I could hardly keep calm.

Then, when he was just about to leave, I proposed to him a plan that would solve his (and my) problem.

'If you can give me a place to sleep and provide daily a minimum amount of food, I can be at your place of work tomorrow morning,' I said. 'You do not have to worry about the camp commander. I know how to get out of here.' I suggested that he could pick me up that very evening, outside the camp fence, on the corner. He readily agreed to the plan. In the evening, at nine o'clock sharp, I threw my backpack and my briefcase over the fence and joined him on the other side. We took the streetcar to the company: Büro für Elektrische Anlagen, Am Hof 2, Vienna I. In the streetcar, we chatted. I assumed that he was an employee of the firm, so I asked him a number of questions. What kind of work were they involved in? Who were the other electricians? What kind of man was the boss, the man who ran the company? In answer to this last question, he just mumbled something unintelligible.

Once more I was out of confinement. Mrs Follman may have arranged it, but the way I felt, this man from the Elektrische Anlagen was a godsend.

Once more I was free!

20 An Electrician in Vienna

The first three nights I slept in the office of the man who ran the company: sometimes on the floor, which was hard but spacious, and sometimes on his armchair, which was soft but terribly uncomfortable. After a few days I was given a small but neat room on the company's premises with a real bed and bedding. Gertrude, the big boss's very young and sweet secretary, was put in charge of my meals. She was blonde and pretty, a little plump, and particularly solicitous and concerned about my comfort. It soon became obvious that Gertrude was more than just a secretary, and she usually left the office with the big boss. It was also no secret why she was plump: she was pregnant. And who was the big boss? It was none other than the man who had looked for me in the camp, who had been my co-conspirator in the escape plan, and who had picked me up outside the camp, Edward F. Neubauer.

The new work caused me some apprehension, not because the actual tasks were difficult or complex, but because of my questionable qualifications. I have never had any formal training as an electrician. But, overall, the job appeared to be promising; the working conditions seemed good, the people were friendly, and the required skills were not too sophisticated. At first, a lot of time was spent on my training, to acquaint me with the local codes and the general business of the company. In the firm, there were about 25 of us. This included Gertrude and one other Austrian woman – an office clerk who was always sad, as her husband was missing in action on the Russian front – some Russians, some Ukrainians, and one other Pole. What pleased me most in those first few days, however, were the meals. They were sheer delight!

Courtesy of Gertrude (or her mother), I was presented each noon with home-cooked dishes, samples of the world-renowned Viennese cuisine! What a treat for someone who was starving for the last five days and hadn't had a home-cooked meal in years. Unfortunately, this lasted only for the first three weeks. After that, I got my own ration cards.

About two weeks after I started work, my boss told me that he was working on legitimizing my residence in the city as well as legalizing my labor status. He appeared to be an influential Nazi party member, so I had no doubt that he would accomplish this. I felt my job was fairly safe already, but his efforts were an additional indication that he was pleased with my work and that he had no plans to let me go. Obtaining the ration cards meant that I had gained legal status. It also meant a degree of job security.

A new stage of my survival had started. Once more, I felt lucky. Although Vienna was under the German heel, and the Allies were bombing us, blackmailers, like those ever present in Warsaw, did not threaten me here. In Vienna, I was one of tens of thousands of foreigners, all of us speaking different languages, all looking and acting differently. Somehow, I felt safer and more confident that I would survive the war, more so now than at any other time since my escape from the Tomaszow camp. After all, the war was coming to an end and, to the best of my knowledge, no one was looking for Jews hiding in Vienna. Or perhaps it was the beauty of Vienna and the blue Danube (which was never blue) that filled me with such hope and confidence.

But while feelings of security and contentment filled my days, images of suffering and death often disturbed my rest at night. How could I feel free and secure among the very people who had perpetrated such terrible crimes? How could I feel content among those who had caused so much death and suffering, not only to the Jews and the people of occupied Europe, but even to their own people? These questions without answers plagued my sleep, exhausting me night after night.

Even though I was not an expert electrician, I had the

advantage over the other workers of knowing German. I also found that I was comparatively more familiar with the modern tools and electrical appliances used in Vienna than were my Russian co-workers. When we had a difficult problem, I was also able to consult German technical handbooks. But often I was sent out to do repairs in private homes and that had major disadvantages: I was on my own; there was no one to consult with; no handbooks; and no one to help when an extra pair of hands was needed. I worried that my incompetence would sooner or later reveal itself and that that would send me back to the camp. On the other hand, there were some distinct advantages in working alone: I did not have my boss looking over my shoulder, and I was able to crisscross the city and in the process learn about and admire the masterpieces of the European Renaissance, which Vienna held in such abundance.

Several weeks after I arrived in Vienna, I saw Miertsching again. He had heard from Mrs Follman that I was in Vienna and had asked her to arrange a meeting with me. One Saturday, he and I met at a coffeehouse on one of the city squares, the Swedenplatz; we met for about fifteen minutes. We chatted mostly about the situation at his place of work, which was being bombarded every night by Allied planes, and about my work at Neubauer's company. But the subject of his offer to help the Polish Underground in Warsaw – a subject that was very much on my mind and I would guess also on his – was never brought up. I never figured out, then or later, if his attempt to join the Underground was sincere, nor did I know why he wanted to meet me in Vienna. My best guess is that he wanted to erase any discomfort that his request had caused me and that he wanted to reaffirm the sincerity of that offer.

Before parting, he took 200 Reichmarks (RM) out of his pocket and gave them to me, saying, 'I am sure you could use this.' He was certainly right on that account, and I accepted the money without hesitation. (RM200 was roughly equivalent to a month and a half of my salary; a typical dinner in a restaurant, with ration cards, cost about RM2 to RM3.) This was the last time I saw Mr Miertsching.

Besides its beauty, what struck me most about wartime Vienna was that its inhabitants were predominantly women. Only here and there did one encounter an old man, besides, of course, the foreign workers like the ones working for Mr Neubauer. But mostly one saw only women, in the shops, in offices, and in people's homes. Mr Neubauer, who was in his early forties, was an exception, and I always wondered on what grounds he had been exempted. Was it because he was a successful and rich businessman and had bought somebody off, or was it because he was such an ardent Nazi and knew people in high places? Or both? I never did find the answer.

One morning, I was sent to a construction site not far from our office where a large motor for a woodcutting machine was out of order. It was something of an emergency, as the carpenter's schedule was tight and several workers were idle, waiting for the motor to be repaired. My problem was that I had never seen a motor up close, much less repaired one. I had no clue what was wrong with it or how to fix it. This task required skills way beyond replacing a switch or splicing broken wires and there was no time to read the troubleshooting manual. I turned off the power to the motor and proceeded to strip layer after layer of components, carefully marking where each component came from and in what sequence. I was looking for a broken part or a loose wire, screw, or connection. But I had no luck, and the more I tried to fix the motor, the more hopeless it seemed. A sense of panic began to creep into my mind as I imagined the consequences of my incompetence. Finally, after a couple of hours, since I had no idea what to do, I gave up and put each part back where it belonged, prepared to face my boss's ire and a kick to the other side of the door. I was already at the exit when something moved me to go back and turn on the switch. Then, to my surprise, instantly I heard a loud brrrrrrrrrrrrrrrr!

as the motor started to rev up. The sound transformed panic into joy.

On my return to the office, my boss congratulated me. The supervisor on site must have already notified him. Little did he know how much this job had terrified me and how close I had come to throwing in the towel and confessing my lack of experience. Fortunately, he did not ask what was wrong with the motor or how it was repaired.

Although Mr Neubauer helped me escape the confinement of the camp and, by doing so, gave me the chance for a freer life, I neither liked nor trusted him. He was an angry and mean-spirited man. A fanatical Nazi, proudly displaying the party's insignia on his lapels, he still hoped for a Nazi victory, even at this late date. I realized that all his assistance was self-serving, motivated by his business's need for an electrician, especially one with some knowledge of German, and not by any humanitarian desire. He seemed to delight in his almost daily diatribes against the Russian workers, calling them low-life, lazy, and incapable of doing an honest day's work. A few times I saw him running toward the Russian quarters with a revolver in his hand, cursing them for some minor insubordination. A married man with a family, he was having an affair with his secretary, who was less than half his age. During the latter part of her pregnancy he kept her hidden and locked up in a separate apartment he owned. It was a beautiful apartment in an exclusive part of town, filled with famous paintings, crystals, rugs, and antiques; I couldn't help but wonder who the original owners of those items had been.

Although often I had to discuss with my boss matters pertaining to work or, on occasion, I would be asked to run some errands for him, I tried to stay away from him as much as I could.

21 A Burden Lifted

Although I had comfortable lodgings, enough food, a satisfactory job, and, above all, freedom and relative safety, I was lonely and alone. Even my false identity was a burden to me. In Warsaw I had quite a few friends, people knew who I was; but here no one knew. I longed for family and friends, for some measure of normalcy.

The majority of Austrians, just like the majority of Germans, were rabid Nazis – at least, that was my perception. Generally, the people I met in my work lamented the war shortages, cursed the bombing by the Allies, and worried that the war was lasting too long; many were in mourning for their fallen sons and brothers. But one thing was sure: no one wondered what had happened to their Jewish friends, neighbors, or colleagues. Or, for that matter, did I ever hear any expressions of concern or sympathy with the millions of people who had been overrun by the German war machine and were now brutally oppressed. They must have known that the tens of thousands of foreign workers in Vienna did not come here as tourists or guests; that we were forced to come and work here, more often than not under conditions of slavery. They did not protest, ever.

Typically, the Austrians refrained from expressing political views. Those who held anti-Nazi views did not speak, for fear of being sent to a concentration camp. Those who still supported the Nazis kept quiet too, fearing what might happen to them after the war was lost. Most by now had realized that no war was ever won by continuous 'victorious retreats', which was heralded by the government's press and radio and was exactly what was happening to Germany on all fronts.

One of the homes where I had worked for several days was the Kauschler residence, at 4 Heinrichgasse, near the Donau Canal. The Kauschler family was always friendly and hospitable to me, but what impressed me most was that in that house, anti-Nazi feelings were expressed not only openly but with unique force and conviction. When, one week after we had first met, Marianne, the Kauschlers' daughter, invited me for dinner at their home, I accepted gladly. Marianne was a pretty divorcée, about 30 years old, a stage actress who had performed in both Vienna and Berlin. Her parents owned a food market on nearby Rudolf Square. Their only son had been killed recently on the battlefield in Norway, and the family was in mourning. In fact, the family was down right angry. 'Why did he have to sacrifice his young life? For whom? And for what?' they kept repeating. 'We never voted for that madman!'

While both parents worked long hours, Marianne spent her time at home, cleaning, doing needlework, and reading. She sought out my company because she was lonely. Each week we spent two or three evenings together, listening to music or just chatting. I not only enjoyed the home atmosphere and home cooking, but was flattered that someone would care to exchange thoughts with me. One evening, after several weeks of meetings like this, and without warning, she sprang up from the table, quickly closed all the windows and curtains, and turned on the radio to a new station. Soon, the familiar 'tatata tam, tatata tam' of the BBC's wartime refrain filled the room. Listening to a foreign broadcast was strictly prohibited by the Nazis and could cost a person his or her life. We had known each other for only a few weeks, but Marianne had quickly realized that we both were on the same side of the political spectrum, we both longed to be connected to the outside world, and, even more, we both longed to hear the truth – that the Nazis' situation was much worse than their propaganda machine had people believe.

The trust that Marianne showed me that night and a few more times thereafter led to a dilemma for me. Increasingly, I felt uncomfortable in not returning that trust, telling her made-up stories about my family and my background. The emotional burden of lying, and pretending day after day, month after month, that I was someone other than who I really was, tormented me. A desire to tell someone about my life, my true identity, constantly lay just under the surface, but until now I did not dare. Lying or pretending to a policeman or an agent of authority was quite easy; it was done to save my life. But lying to a close friend, like Wladek in Warsaw or now Marianne, weighed on my conscience.

Thus, one evening, spurred on by Marianne's trust in me, I blurted it all out. Before I could stop myself, the words spilled out of me, like a torrent that couldn't be held back. At that moment I didn't care about the possible consequences or Marianne's reaction. I told her that I had been hiding under an assumed name for the past year and a half. I told her how my luck had had its ups and downs but how optimistic I felt now that the war was coming to an end and my chances for survival were improving already. I also told her what had been happening to the Jews in occupied Poland and what had happened to some of my family members and my fears for the remaining ones. I told her about my parents and sister in the Lódz Ghetto. I told her how brutal and inhuman the Germans were and how much so many people, all the people but especially the Jews, had had to suffer. I stopped, drained by my outburst, and held my breath. Her reaction, at first, was one of shock and sadness. She came close and embraced me, saying how glad she was that I had managed to survive and she thanked me for the trust I had shown her. She told me that she knew, that they all knew something bad had been happening to the Jews at the hands of the Germans, but they didn't know what, and they didn't know how bad it was. She lowered her head, visibly shaken by the things she had just heard, embarrassed by her ignorance of the horror being perpetrated, by her own people, in her name, in her own land, and in the world. When she lifted her head again, I saw that she was crying.

We turned the conversation to other things, talking about her and her loneliness, her failed marriage, the loss of her brother. Yet, as we talked she seemed more distant, and I sensed that something was bothering her. There were moments when she would become very quiet and pensive, and that in turn began to disturb me. Had I endangered myself by confessing to living a double life? Did I say too much and loose a friend? I began to worry, but at the same time I felt as if a heavy stone had been lifted from my shoulders. I felt relief for having shared my secret with someone, something I had wanted to do for a long time.

The next time I saw Marianne I discovered what had been troubling her. She didn't know it at the time, but during her sleepless hours that night she had realized what it was: she regretted that I had revealed my secret to her.

'Should something happen to you tomorrow, I would not want you to think, not even for it to cross your mind, that I might have had something to do with it,' she told me when we met a day or two later.

'But I would never think that of you,' I said.

'Still, it's wartime. You never know what might happen. One doesn't know how one would react under certain circumstances,' she said, referring to the Nazis' use of torture.

I tried to comfort her and assure her of my complete confidence in her but I understood her worry. It showed her sensitivity. Yet, I was at a loss as to whether I should feel glad that my burden had been lifted or sad that I had created a burden for Marianne.

In the months that followed, our friendly relationship continued as before, even strengthened. But the topic of my true identity never came up again. I also visited her house less frequently. Soon Marianne's loneliness and political interest in anti-Nazism were replaced by the romantic attention showered on her by a young Frenchman. Although still friends, we now saw each other only on special occasions.

In November 1944 I rented a private room from a local family of three, at 19 Lilienbrunngasse, close to the

Lilliputaner Kirche, in the Second District; it allowed me to move away from the communal quarters of the Neubauer firm. My landlords, a husband and his wife, both in their early fifties, were always gloomy and hardly ever talked to me, and if this wasn't bad enough, they wanted me to be quiet too. When they rented me the room they did it on one condition: no visitors. One day, when I was sick for a few days, a female friend came to visit me and brought a basket with some food and medicines. My landlords delivered the basket to me but turned my friend away. 'We have a young son and it would not be proper for him to see a female visiting you in your room,' they explained later. Their 16-year-old son, Heinz, seemed a nice boy but he was always quiet and I don't recall ever having a conversation with him before he disappeared altogether – about a month after I moved in. On the positive side, the place was always clean and orderly and, my comforter was exceptionally warm.

Except for my periodic bouts of loneliness and a constant, lingering concern for my parents and other close family and friends, I led a normal life, quite comparable to that of thousands of other foreign workers. My accommodation was modest but comfortable, I had a solid job, I had regular ration cards, and I even had a chance for some entertainment, going to the cinema or to cafés. My preferred evening entertainment was to visit a café at Am Hof Square, in the vicinity of my firm's office, where a young, blind piano player in his late twenties played. The place was semi-dark, quiet and serene, and the music, which he played from memory, was delightful. I knew some of the composers – Schumann, Liszt, and Chopin – although before the war, I had never been to a concert or any other live musical performance and had heard classical music only on the radio. It was a new and wonderful experience.

Other times, especially at weekends, I spent time in the old-style Viennese coffeehouses, where I sipped ersatz *Kaffee mit Schlagsahne* (artificial coffee with foamed cream). Despite the war, these places still offered a pleasant and comfortable environment. In winter, they were well heated and always offered a library of newspapers and magazines. What I enjoyed most was that I could sit there for hours, read the papers, and use their elegant and clean facilities – all for the price of a few cups of *Kaffee mit Schlagsahne*.

The food, in general, which one could buy only with ration cards, was not plentiful but it was more than sufficient. Each morning on my way to work, I would pick up eight little Viennese rolls, called *waeckerls*, at the bakery, intending to eat them for breakfast in the office, where the company was providing free Ersatz tea. Invariably, however, my appetite would get the better of these plans, and I would consume all of them long before I got to work. I ate lunch and dinner at various places; some workplaces offered cafeteria-style facilities. But more importantly, as I remember it in Vienna, I was never hungry nor did I feel in danger of being unmasked. I stayed in occasional contact with my companions who had accompanied me on the trip from Poland; but I made some new friends. My life, in stark contrast to Warsaw, seemed no longer threatened in any way. I led a life that was as normal as that of any foreign laborer.

In addition, there was now someone in Vienna who knew who I really was. That burden was lifted, and it made a difference.

22 *A Matter of Days*

In January 1945 the Red Army conquered Warsaw and most of Western Poland. It was also rapidly advancing on the central European front, and in March it surrounded the Hungarian capital Budapest, about one hundred miles east of Vienna, which was expected to be the next target. In the meantime, German forces were retreating everywhere, sometimes fighting only in isolated pockets. The news from all battlefields, including the Western Front, heralded Germany's defeat.

On the surface, the anticipated liberation would be the fulfillment of my dreams, culminating in all my efforts coming to a successful conclusion. In reality, however, it raised many concerns, even fears. I wondered what would follow the Red Army's entry into Vienna. What would I do next? How would I find out what had happened to my family? Would I stay here and if not, where would I go? For me, liberation was an abstract concept, and I had no idea what would follow for me. I had been a 15-year-old boy when the war had started. I was now a young man of 20 whose experiences for the past five years had revolved around self-preservation. How would the liberators treat me? With sympathy? With indifference? Perhaps they would be scornful because while they were fighting and risking their lives on the battlefront, I was living the life of a civilian in the hinterland.

Just in case, I quickly began to study Russian. I already knew conversational Russian, but now I set about learning how to read and write it, in Cyrillic. In the meantime, while the general mood in Vienna became increasingly depressed and somber, my job situation took a turn for the better. I became the chief maintenance electrician in a building located in Freyung Square at the corner of Rennweg Street, near the headquarters of the Neubauer firm. It was a gray, multistory, baroque-style palace with an imposing entrance. A wide marble staircase with dark mahogany balustrades led upstairs, at each floor, to corridors with heavy, dark wooden doors opening into offices and conference rooms. I had worked there before but now I was assigned as a house eletrician.

The work itself proved to be easier than I had anticipated. Most of my duties consisted of simple repairs and fell well within the range of my limited competence. Occasionally, this meant simply recommending that the office buy a new gadget or appliance. Although there was a lot of work, I could frequently delegate it to my three young Russian helpers, Natasha, Nadja, and Igor. The problem was that while they were pleasant and willing, they knew even less about electrical appliances than I did.

Over 90 percent of the office workers in the building were women, just as in the rest of Vienna, not taking into account, of course, the thousands of foreign workers. For the most part, these women were polite, considerate, educated, and cultured. It was difficult to reconcile the personae of these women here, as we drank our ersatz tea or ate lunch together, with the images I often carried of their husbands, brothers, and fathers in uniform, some of them committing unspeakable atrocities.

Ever since I had arrived in Vienna, in September 1944, the Allies bombed the city. As time passed, the bombing raids multiplied and so did the daily problems. Everyone appeared to be preoccupied and forever in a hurry, rushing off after work to do the shopping or to take care of a new emergency at home. Each day, after a bombing raid, some new area of daily activity was affected. There were days when the streetcars would not run; sometimes we returned home and found that the electricity was off or gas or water not available. Each interruption was temporary, lasting only a few hours, but every inconvenience had a ripple effect. If the streetcars were not running, for example, I got home late, and by then the grocery store was closed. To me, however, each new inconvenience was a good omen.

Often, while people hurried into the shelters, I went into the street when the sirens were wailing and the bombs were falling, just to see the sky blanketed with Allied planes. There were antiaircraft guns installed on almost every tall building, but by now they were manned by youngsters, literally schoolchildren, with little or no training, and less, if any, success in their task. Not once during these last weeks did I see or hear about an Allied plane being shot down. Sometimes, within my narrow field of vision, the sky was almost totally dark, with hundreds of planes flying overhead. The sight was exhilarating. It meant that an Allied victory was near, and that filled me with great hope – hope for the civilized world, hope for the victory of good over a terrible, terrible evil. It also meant the end of the war and salvation for many.

With the frequent bombings of the city, we all had to spend many hours a day in the underground shelter. Although generally an inconvenience and a waste of time, for me this circumstance led to a fortuitous event, an event that impacted the quality of my social life in Vienna: I met a new friend.

In the shelter, the space was cramped and there was nothing to do, so it was easy and common to strike up conversations with people. One day, in November, I became acquainted with a young lady named Friedl; she was usually reading a book, finishing office work that she brought with her, or helping some elderly person. The day we met, I noticed that she was reading *Ferien vom Ich* (Vacations from Myself) by Paul Keller, and in response to my questions she began to tell me the book's story. The essential argument of the book, as I remember it now, was that for a therapeutic holiday to be effective, it was not enough simply to change one's surroundings or just relax. One needed to do the opposite of whatever one was doing in daily life. For example, a medical doctor should peel potatoes in a field kitchen, or a factory worker should take up archeological studies. She was so enthusiastic about the book that I asked to borrow it. It was the first book I had ever tried to read in German and I was surprised at how well I managed; perhaps I was trying harder knowing that it would impress my new friend. When we both tired of reading, we chatted.

Friedl's family was of Czech origin and went by the name of Dworschak. She told me that she worked in the statistics department of the company and that she liked mathematics, even though she did not have a formal education in the field and had only a high-school diploma. We talked about books, operas, movies, and, of course, the war. She was well read and well informed. To my surprise, we seemed to think alike and we had similar likes and dislikes. I also liked her appearance – her smile, her high cheekbones, the expression of sincerity in her eyes – and her sunny disposition. I especially found her laugh attractive; it was open, genuine, and spontaneous. And it became contagious. Within a short time, my own smiles became more frequent and natural; soon I found myself also able to laugh, something I had not done in a long time.

Hardly noticeable at first, our attraction to each other was growing and in time led to flirting: little compliments, timid fleeting glances, and pleasant smiles upon eye contact. One day, when our duties interrupted our chatting, we decided to meet after work at a nearby café, even though under the Nazis' wartime rules it was against the law for Austrians (now Germans and members of the Third Reich) to fraternize with foreign workers. We knew neither the scope nor the letter of that law or whether it was enforced, but we did know that such social mixing was frowned upon by some Viennese. This, however, did not deter us and we began to meet regularly after work. Taking chances was my modus vivendi, so I quickly found a way to arrange these meetings without anyone knowing. During the day at work, we would exchange notes by leaving them in the electrical box next to Friedl's office. In the evenings, which were getting darker earlier with each passing day, we would then meet at a corner a couple of blocks away so people from the office would not see us leaving the building together. In general, we decided to disregard the law and were prepared to explain, if stopped, that we worked in the same firm and that the meeting was part of that work.

One wintry night stands out in my memory. As I walked Friedl home, after an air raid had disabled public transport, we came upon an elderly lady in front of us carrying a heavy suitcase. Friedl quickly caught up with the lady and offered to carry the suitcase for her, since we were going in the same direction. It was only a small gesture, but it was clear that helping others was in Friedl's character, and it made me care for her even more.

On the weekends that followed, we exchanged other books, went to the cinema, listened to music, and took long walks in the famous Vienna woods. We read poetry by the nineteenth-century Austrian poet Friedrich Halms. Friedl introduced him to me as her favorite poet. What I always liked best, and still like, about his poems is that they express profound truths in the simplest of terms. Halms wrote, for example:

> In misfortune, many will lament with you;
> When the rays of good luck embrace you,
> Some may bear it without envy,
> But rejoicing, will be only the one who loves you.

Or,

> End equals Beginning, often in life,
> But only seemingly, not in fact.
> How blissful it is to be a child
> But how sad, to become a child again:

And on happiness, Halms wrote:

> Happiness means different things to different people;
> But if I were asked to point the way, I would say:
> First love: someone, something of your choice and
>   pleasure.
> But love it with passion; engulf yourself with that love,
>   give totally of yourself.
> Then create: anything of your liking and inclination, in

any field or realm.
But do it with ardor and enthusiasm; with zeal and fervor;
To the limits of your strength and ability.
Then give: the more you give, the richer you will be, in the
eyes of others.
And then, die. For it is better never to reach the glory of
happiness, and experience only what we once were.

For New Year's Eve 1944, Friedl prepared a special dinner with all kinds of Viennese dishes and delicacies, including a Wiener schnitzel and the famous *Zwetschkenknoedl* (a plum cooked inside cake dough and sugared on the outside). At midnight, to Johann Strauss's waltzes, we danced. She had to teach me the steps, as this was the first time I had ever danced. Before the war I had attended a boys-only school, and social contact with the opposite sex, like mixed parties, were rare. And we never danced during the war. Friedl also introduced me to another experience: the opera. The first story she told me was that of *The Flying Dutchman* by Richard Wagner. Other stories followed. She knew the stories of all the great operas.

From that time, I became a frequent guest in her parents' home, almost part of the family, so much so that during the last two weeks before the liberation, when life in the inner city became chaotic and unsafe, I stayed in their home. Her family were social democrats, deeply nostalgic for the Austro-Hungarian empire of Franz Josef[22] and staunchly and openly anti-Nazi. They often lamented the disappearance and plight of their Jewish friends and neighbors and the sufferings of the millions upon millions of others across Europe whom they didn't know.

Soon Friedl and I became very close friends, spending time together and enjoying each other's company. And then, we were in love. She was charming, intelligent, and unusually wise. Her feminine grace, her strength of character, and her quiet goodness all had a considerable influence on my life; we remained special friends for the rest of the war, for the months that I remained in Vienna after the war, and for many, many years thereafter. It was an exceptional and unique friendship.

Friedl was only the second Christian during the war to whom I revealed, with complete confidence, my most closely guarded secret: that I was Jewish. Just as when I had divulged my true identity to Marianne, it was because I trusted her unconditionally and because I felt dishonest not telling her the truth about my family and my background, when she had been so open about herself. But, as with Marianne, I also needed to unburden myself. What I did not realize then or, to my shame, did not consider then was that my revelation had created a heavy responsibility for both Marianne and Friedl. It could have cost either woman her life. The Nazis had no mercy for those who knowingly harbored or helped in any way someone who, under their 'inhuman laws', was condemned to be annihilated.

In April 1945, two Russian armies, one under the command of Marshal Malinowski and the other under Marshal Tolbuchin, joined to encircle the city of Vienna. The fall of the city was only a matter of days.

Life in the city became even more disorganized than it was under bombardments, and a great number of people, myself included, stopped going to work. For the time being I continued to stay in Friedl's parents' house, which was in a residential area in the Fourteenth District, on the outskirts of the city. Although the outer districts were not subjected to daily bombardments the way the industrial and central parts of the city were, the alarms were citywide, so the entire population spent most of its time in shelters.

In the last days of the war, and in obvious anticipation of the Red Army's entry into Vienna, I noticed that several women were feverishly altering Nazi banners in our shelter, flags that had once been proudly displayed from the fifth-or sixth-floor windows of a building, reaching all the way down to the first floor. The women now stripped the swastikas and white circles from the banners, leaving solid red material that would be hung out to welcome the victors. Switching political allegiance seemed to have come rather easily.

The thirteenth day of April was a bright, sunny day. Around mid-morning, as I gazed idly out of a second-story window in Friedl's parents' apartment, I saw two Russian soldiers appear in the street. Instantly, a feeling of euphoria rose within my body and a feeling of joy and happiness came over me. After almost six long and tragic years, this was the moment of my liberation from the Nazi yoke!

The war had finally ended for me. I was free! I had survived!

I turned from the window and, without a word, ran down the staircase as if the building were on fire. I chased after the soldiers and embraced and kissed each of them. They stared at me, astonished and speechless. In my excitement I neither identified myself nor told them why I was so happy.

The next morning I got up very early to go to the Russian headquarters; I wanted to volunteer for service in the Red Army. Unconcerned that the war would end in another few weeks, despite my lack of any military training, I wanted to do my part. I packed a lunch in my backpack and, to the surprise of my hosts, left the house. On my way, I stopped every officer I met and told each the same story: that I was from the Allied country of Poland, that I was a Jew, that I was hiding in Vienna under a false name, and that I now wanted to volunteer to fight the Nazis. And the answer from each one was the same:

'Go to the headquarters,' they said.

'And where is that?' I asked.

'Oh, no! We cannot disclose that. That is a secret and you are a total stranger,' was the standard answer.

As I was on my own, I started walking in the direction the Russians were coming from. Then I followed the newly strung telephone lines, noticing that the bundles of wires thickened as I got closer to the command post. Finally, three hours later, I found myself explaining the purpose of my visit to a junior officer on the outside perimeter of the Red Army headquarters. Suspicious about who I was, he wouldn't allow me to come close to an officer with any kind of authority. Instead, and on his own, he determined that the Soviets did not need me, did not want me, and further, did not trust me. From the questions this junior officer asked, he insinuated that it would have been impossible for a Jew to survive in Nazi Vienna, much less to have lived in hiding through most of the war, and that therefore I must be a Nazi collaborator seeking to switch sides now that the war was lost.

'You cannot be a Jew. The Fascists killed all the Jews,' he stated flatly.

After examining my Polish documents he concluded, with remarkable perception, that he couldn't rely on them to establish my identity, since, by my own admission, they were false. Certainly his suspicion about people switching sides was not unfounded. Hundreds of thousands, perhaps even millions, of foreign laborers in Germany, including the 20-plus Russians and Ukrainians who had worked with me at the Neubauer firm, made such a switch, as had some German opportunists. Many nationals of the Soviet Union and eastern European countries, such as Hungarians and Slovaks, were Nazi collaborators who now wanted to hide their pasts, and they did so by volunteering to serve with the Red Army. In the early months of the German–Russian war, many Soviets, after being taken prisoners of war, declared themselves pro-Nazi and formed combat units. They then, fought together with the Germans against their country of origin. The most famous among these turncoats was General Vlasov, a Soviet general, who had been a prisoner of war, switched sides, and then formed the Russian National Liberation Army to fight on the German side against the Soviet Union and the Allies. During the last weeks of the war, Vlasov was captured by the Soviets on the Czechoslovakian front. He was tried as a traitor and quickly executed.

The crux of the matter was that the Russians did not want me. Tired and greatly disappointed I started the trek back. As I approached the center of the city, I noticed more people in the streets than usual and, within seconds, I realized that the stores were being looted. While the Russian soldiers had initiated it, the looting was enthusiastically taken up by the local population and stores were being rapidly and completely emptied. Seeing the number of people involved in this activity, I impulsively decided that one more looter would not make much difference. I crossed the street, walked into one of the department stores, and joined in the looting. I needed many things, as I had not purchased a new piece of clothing for a very long time. After filling up my little backpack with shirts and underwear, I noticed the shoe section. Discarding the shirts and underwear, I replaced them with three pairs of boots. Then I saw a roll of wool fabric and took out two pairs of boots to make room for that. After many more cases of such indecision, I finally ended up with a Tyrolean hat that was too large, a suit that did not fit me, and a pair of boots that was not a pair. My misconduct was not a great success.

In the meantime, the Red Army was inching its way toward the center of the city and the Danube Canal from the northwest and the south. The army looked surprisingly primitive and undisciplined. The infantry was non-motorized, only foot soldiers, each one wearing a folded blanket placed diagonally across his chest and a Kalashnikov rifle hung over his shoulder. They walked singly or in small groups but never marched in a column. The supplies were loaded on horse-drawn peasant wagons with solid rubber wheels. Tanks, armored vehicles, and heavy artillery were nowhere to be seen. When night fell, the soldiers sat down on the pavement and, leaning against a house, fell asleep. They carried modest food provisions, usually dry rations or a quarter-loaf of dark bread, in knapsacks or coat pockets. Occasionally, the field kitchen would pass by to distribute coffee or soup and some cooked vegetables.

There was little, if any, underground resistance by the Austrians. I had heard of many desertions from the German Army (one of the women employees in Neubauer's office confided in me that the Nazis were looking for her soldier husband but assured me that they would never find him) and there were antiwar, anti-Nazi graffiti on walls and bombed-out buildings. I remember one such verse verbatim:

Wir wollen kein Maler von Gottesgnaden,
Wir wollen kein Führer von Berchtesgaden,
Wir wollen kein Eintopfgericht mit Herring,
Wir wollen so fressen wie Feldmarschall Goering!
(We don't want a painter from God's mercy,
We don't want a leader from Berchtesgaden,
We don't want one-course dinners with herring,
We want to eat like Field Marshal Goering!)

Many voices were clamoring to declare Vienna an 'open city' in order to avoid damage or destruction of its many artistic and cultural treasures. The SS *Leibstandarte* division stationed nearby had other plans, however. Under the command of the notorious Nazi stalwart Sepp Dietrich, the division, came up with a plan to let the Russians take the north- and southwestern parts of town, almost without a fight, and then to ambush them as they tried to cross the Danube Canal. Of course, I was completely unaware of this planned ambush. I only knew that I could no longer gain access to my rented room on the German-held side, which was just one block behind the SS lines.

The area that the Russians occupied lay southwest of the Danube Canal, included the inner city's First District, and extended all the way to the banks of the canal. The Germans in the meantime formed a strong line of resistance on the other side of the canal in the Second District, in the northeastern quadrant of the city. The canal itself was a man-made waterway, bypassing an elbow in the Danube River. It was more than 100 feet wide, including the embankments, and at least 20 feet deep. Within the city's center, about eight bridges crossed the canal.

The SS first blew up all the canal bridges. Then, quietly, they requisitioned all the buildings, each about six stories high, that faced the canal and the inner city. They positioned themselves behind the windows, which were now packed with sandbags that camouflaged a machine gun at every casement. They were concentrated particularly in buildings facing the bridges and the streets leading toward the bridges.

Unaware of this SS line of defense on the opposite side of the canal, the Russians sent in an engineering battalion to build pontoon bridges over three or four of the ones that had been blown up. When the bridges were almost complete, a large number of troops assembled on the embankment ready to move across. Since the occupation of the western and southern parts of the city had been uneventful, with the Germans offering no resistance, it looked as if the occupation of this section would be just as easy. But this was not to be the case. The *Waffen* SS lured the Russians and now were lying in wait.

As soon as the troops started to cross the canal, a concerted barrage of gunfire began. It was a barrage full of fury and the resulting carnage was incredible. From upper windows across the canal, the machine gun fire did not cease until every Russian soldier on a bridge or ready to cross it was dead or had fled and all the new bridges were again destroyed. Then silence fell. But in a couple of hours, new battalions of Russian engineers and soldiers had been sent in, this time under cover: first to remove the bodies of the dead and then to reconstruct the bridges. Initially, it appeared that the German defense had subsided; there was intermittent firing, but only a few casualties. But as soon as the freshly assembled soldiers prepared to cross the new bridges again, the barrage started anew, and the new massacre was as deadly as the previous one. What surprised me most was that the Russian military did not seem to draw the obvious, logical conclusion: that the German defense was overwhelming and they needed to change their strategy. The odds were unequal, yet the Russians continued sending one wave of troops after another against the entrenched positions of the *Waffen* SS, with a total disregard for the great loss of life among their own soldiers.

Abruptly, one afternoon, after the Russians had finally brought in heavy artillery, the fierce fighting stopped. The SS men abandoned the buildings and withdrew. I could observe these events from up close as I was standing about a block away from the canal, on a side street, Heinrichgasse, where

Marianne's parents lived. I was there because I was waiting to cross the canal so I could get to my rented room and retrieve the few possessions I had left there. I started to walk in the direction of the new bridge. But as I reached the end of the street, a grotesque sight beyond anyone's imagination met me. The pavement, the road, the tree-lined walkway, and the concrete embankment – a strip about 70 foot wide – were covered with the bloodied bodies of Russian soldiers. At first, I found small spaces in which to step between the bodies, but as I got closer to the bridge the number of corpses increased. Finally, it was impossible to avoid stepping on the dead as they lay in pools of their own blood, in layers two to three deep. Soon after, a new column of soldiers arrived. Their task was to remove and bury the dead.

I managed to cross the canal and reach the house and the safety of my rented room. When I entered, I was surprised to find my landlords unusually excited and cheerful, because they were generally sullen and never friendly toward me. We had never exchanged information about one another and certainly never discussed war or politics. My dislike of them was primarily motivated by their mysterious, unfriendly behavior, which always made me wonder whether they were Nazis or Nazi sympathizers and whether they disliked foreigners, Poles or just me. I also wondered why my landlord was not in the army, since he looked fit and healthy and was only in his early fifties. But now they had good news for me. They told me that they were planning to move to a nicer apartment in a better section of town and wanted to know if I would like to move with them. (There was probably a city law that required that landlords take their renters with them when changing apartments.) Despite my misgivings about them, I needed a place to live, so I accepted this unexpected offer immediately.

A few months before the Russians had arrived, my landlords' son Heinz had joined a *Waffen* SS unit (*Wehrwolf*), a guerrilla unit that in the last months of the war became the Germans' last resort, their cannon fodder. I didn't know if he had volunteered or had been drafted as the Nazis, in their desperation at losing the war, conscripted boys as young as 14 and 15 into the SS. Whenever he visited his home, he, the SS man, and I, the Jew, slept in adjacent rooms. The idea of sharing an apartment with an SS man and having to see that hated uniform up close, however occasionally, filled me always with disgust.

As for the parents, not long after Vienna fell, the mystery of their gloominess – and political affiliation – was solved: my landlords revealed that they had always been and still were communists and that he had just rejoined the re-emerging Austrian Communist Party. That affiliation was the reason he was receiving now all kinds of privileges, among them a better apartment. After a few weeks we had all moved to the ground floor of 9 Donaustrasse, an elegantly furnished apartment abandoned by a Nazi official who had fled the city.

In the first weeks following the Russian takeover of Vienna, a number of events took place in rapid succession. The first day after it was officially announced that Vienna was now under a new authority, the 'Russian Komandatura', I went in search of other Jews, to seek out others who had survived. Although I often thought that I was the only Jewish survivor in Vienna, some inner voice told me that I might be wrong and that I should find out. I walked to the place in the First District where Vienna's main synagogue had once stood, in the area of Judengasse and Judenplatz.

When I reached the site of the synagogue, which was now a pile of rubble with twisted steel beams sticking out in all directions, I found at least 20 other Jews roaming around who had endured in one way or another and now, just like me, were looking for other Jews. Most were natives of Vienna who had managed to survive the entire war, some even with the tacit approval of the authorities. One of them claimed to be a rabbi; another happened to be from Warsaw. The latter had been captured during the Warsaw uprising and brought here the same way I had been. He was quite a few years older than I, around 40, but we were drawn to each other, perhaps because of the great similarity of our experiences. Quickly, we became friends. To the best of my knowledge he and I were the only two Polish Jews who survived the war, at least a part of it, hiding in Nazi Vienna.

Ivo Vesby was a former musician with the Warsaw Philharmonic Orchestra. I visited him many times in Vienna and frequently spent the night in his apartment near the opera house when it was late and I didn't want to walk to my distant home. Later, I met him in Lódz on one of my brief postwar trips to Poland and, in the 1950s, we met a couple of times in New York, where he had settled after reuniting with his Polish wife and teenage daughter.

Ivo was not only musically talented and intelligent but also had a dry and biting wit. When we met in Lódz, we found ourselves with a group of his friends, some of whom were discussing and exalting the virtues of the newly installed communist regime. After one of the regime's fanatical adherents sat down, Ivo took the floor. He asked the speaker if, under the new regime, one would be free to express one's wishes.

'Of course, of course!' the speaker responded.

'In that case, my wish is to be wherever, anywhere, that you are not!'

There was sound applause, and I wholeheartedly shared Ivo's sentiments.

A few days after the liberation, the Viennese *Israelitische Kultusgemeinde* (Jewish Community Office), opened its doors. I rushed in to register; I wanted to join the Jewish community officially, and, more than anything else, I wanted to establish my true identity as Zenon Neumark, no longer did I wish to be known as Zenon Matysiak. In the next few weeks, I made a point of informing my friends, associates, neighbors, and anyone else I met of my true name and heritage. This seemingly trivial gesture restored my self and reconnected me to my roots: I felt free at last. At the *Kultusgemeinde*, I was registrant number 28.

Among the things I witnessed during the first days after liberation was a horrific lack of discipline among the ordinary

Russian soldiers. They looted both homes and stores and raped women young and old, indiscriminately. It appeared that the primary goal in life of the Russian soldier was to rape, plunder, and drink a lot of vodka. It was rumored, and reports later confirmed, that for the first few days the Russian commanders granted the victorious front-line soldiers total freedom to behave as they liked, to compensate them for their great sacrifices and as a reward for their final success in conquering the city.

My friend Marianne was among the many women who suffered at Russian hands. It had happened in the shelter of the house where they lived, on Heinrichgasse, in the presence of many of her neighbors while the battle for the city was still raging. When a few days later the fighting ended, the Kauschlers asked me to accompany Marianne from their home in the inner city to stay in a relative's home in the suburbs. I agreed, of course. While we managed to reach our destination, several kilometers away, by foot, the trip was not without incident. On the way, we were stopped several times by soldiers and lower-ranking officers demanding that Marianne go with them. Only my insistence that I was a Pole, as proven by my Polish documents, that I was an ally and not an enemy, and my plea that Marianne was my girlfriend (she looked much younger than her age), helped me manage each time to dissuade the soldiers from taking her.

A few days after the liberation I stopped by my old firm. There I found that most of the Russian employees who lodged there were continuously drunk. The younger women proudly showed off gifts that their new Russian boyfriends had stolen. Watches seemed to have been their preferred booty. Even Natasha, one of the prettier and better-educated girls, pulled up both her sleeves to display a row of watches on each arm.

Bombed-out tram equipment and tracks and the lack of electrical power made a mess of Vienna's usually well-function-ing public transport system. Fortunately, on a narrow, quiet street near my house, I found a black military bicycle that a retreating German soldier must have abandoned, and, repeating an earlier escapade, I took it. In the absence of public transport, bicycles became a precious commodity and I felt fortunate to have one. But I didn't have it for long. One day, I was riding on the Kaertnerstrasse, in the center of town, when a Russian soldier stopped me and asked for the bicycle. I refused, in Russian, on the grounds that I was a Pole, an ally of Russia and, hence, not subject to freelance requisitioning (a euphemism for plundering), as any Austrian might be. We argued for a while until he became impatient and pointed to an officer walking along the pavement, about 50 feet away. 'Argue with him,' he said, explaining that it was that officer who had ordered my bicycle to be taken from me. I ran over to the officer to get him to change his mind, but he had no idea what I was talking about; he had never given such an order. When I turned around to reclaim my prize, I saw the soldier riding it off in the opposite direction, and I was unable to catch up with him.

The common joke in Vienna at the time was that Stalin had made two major mistakes: first, to show Europe to the Russian soldiers; and second, to show the Russian soldiers to Europe!

Despite the chaos of liberation, life in Vienna became more bearable and normal day by day. I tried to return to work, but Mr Neubauer was nowhere to be found, and the firm closed its doors. Luckily, my limited knowledge of Russian came in handy, and I got a temporary job with a unit of the Red Army as a German–Russian translator. As I continued to obtain jobs for which I was utterly unqualified, I began to feel as if I were becoming a specialist in incompetence.

Then, after a few days, the looting stopped, utilities began functioning again, and life began to get back to normal. Within a week or so, there were concerts, chorales, folkloric dance performances, and plays, mostly presented by the Viennese, but also by the Russian occupying forces and their recreation groups. All sorts of cultural events were revived.

Several times I saw three performances in one day and took part in spontaneous street singing and dancing between each event. The street events usually started with Russian soldiers performing some folk dance, like the hopak, or singing and clapping to tunes played on an accordion or a balalaika. I liked the old Russian folk tunes and even knew some of the lyrics; I had grown up with similar music and it took me back to my happy youth. Throughout Vienna, there was music in the air!

The street scenes invariably ended with spontaneous dancing, especially when Strauss waltzes were played. At first only soldiers danced, but slowly the local girls and women accepted invitations, and soon everybody participated. This reflected both the love of art and music for which Vienna was so well known and a tremendous pent-up hunger for entertainment and recreation. This freedom of expression confirmed that, indeed, we were free at last and hopefully free forever. I don't know how it happened, but only a few days after the Russians took over the city, all the theaters, concert halls, and cinemas opened their doors and were immediately filled. One of the more outstanding performances I remember was the opera *Elektra*, with a libretto by Hugo von Hofmannstahl and music by Richard Strauss. Soon thereafter, I saw my first American film, *It Happened Tomorrow*. Unfortunately, it was in English and I understood very little of it; but I could not pass up a film with such an intriguing title. Each day was filled with new and different experiences, experiences that I was deprived of for over five long years. And what made these entertainment escapades even more enjoyable was the fact that Friedl was my constant companion.

While the end of the war was a dream come true for most people, many, including myself, were ill prepared for it. The prospect of having to face the reality of the terrible losses, both human and material, suffered during the war years was an emotional shock. Now that I was no longer preoccupied with survival, feelings of grief, loneliness, and uncertainty surfaced. The instinctive desire to survive, which had guided and driven me until now, was suddenly no longer central to my life. And there was nothing to take its place.

I was now faced with starting a new life with no education, no money, no home or country and, perhaps, entirely alone. Where were my parents, my sister, and my other relatives? Where were my friends and the world of happiness and security I had grown up in? Where to go and what to do? How to catch up on lost education? How to start building a normal life? I was still strong and healthy, and at least I had places where I could stay and be fed: both Friedl's and Marianne's families offered me places in their homes. Also, there were several organizations, such as the Red Cross and the United Nations Relief and Rehabilitation Administration (UNRRA) that dispensed free meals and provided other assistance if needed. But although my immediate needs were not a problem, I felt numb, confused, and very uncertain about my future.

The fact that in Austria I had revealed my identity to two women, Marianne and Friedl, was first and foremost a sign that I trusted these two individuals. But it was also more: it was a sign of the sense of safety that I felt in Vienna, in contrast to the constant fear I had felt in Poland. It was ironic that in the city where, only a few years earlier, the population had voted a resounding 'Yes' to the union with Nazi Germany, the city where the Nazi party had been the second strongest party before the *Anschluss*, the city that had been home to many war criminals, I had acquired a sense of safety that had eluded me in my native Poland.

As it turned out, Vienna, and perhaps all of Austria, was one of the safest places in central and eastern Europe for a Jew to hide. Because so few Jews chose to hide there (probably fewer than 100) and because tens of thousands of foreign workers of diverse ethnicity lived there, the Vienna Nazis neither expected nor looked for Jews among them.

If only this had been known! Many other escapees, perhaps thousands, could have hidden and survived there. But unfortunately, this is the kind of knowledge gained only through the benefit of hindsight. We did not know it. We could not have known it.

23 Return to Reality

The time to face the postwar reality came sooner than I had expected. My first thought was not to go back to Poland, at least not yet, but to stay in Vienna a while longer in order to regain my bearings. The prospect of facing the truth was frightening. But I quickly realized I had no choice; I had to go back, at least for a week or two. The preparations were simple: I filled my backpack and briefcase with clothing, food for the road, and, for bartering purposes, a bottle of vodka. The more difficult problem was finding transport. The only method available at that time was hitchhiking, either with peasants or on Russian military trucks. The peasants could provide transport for only short distances, and their vehicles were slow. The Russian truck drivers knew only the general direction in which they traveled; their time of departure, the route to be taken, and their destination were left undetermined. These details were either unknown to them or secret.

One Sunday morning in late May, accompanied by Friedl, I set out for my point of departure: Sweden Square in the Third District of Vienna. We said a brief good-bye, she wished me a good trip, and left. As she walked away, I noticed her wiping her eyes with a handkerchief.

The road that branched off Sweden Square led to the northeast, the direction of Poland, and was a general assembly area for Russians who were leaving Vienna. Many trucks made temporary stops there, and I set about trying to find a truck driver going in my direction who would give me a ride. My semi-fluent Russian came in handy, but the bottle of vodka I had purchased the day before was even more helpful.

The covered truck's bed had benches on each side, and I joined the soldiers in the back of the truck, so as not to be visible from the outside. The soldiers were a friendly bunch. They were in good spirits because the war was over, they were alive, and they were going east toward their homeland. They offered to share with me what little they had, from cigarettes to bread to American chocolate bars. For better digestion, a bottle of vodka was being constantly passed around.

The truck I was on was part of a long convoy, each truck full of soldiers. There was a great deal of confusion organizing the departure, so it was early evening by the time we finally started moving. We were only about two or three hours out of the city when the convoy stopped in a lightly wooded area. The soldiers were ordered to get off the trucks and set up camp for the night. As far as I could tell, I was the only civilian in the camp, but that did not seem to concern anyone. I followed my companions, trying to be both helpful – clearing an area, collecting branches for a fire – and inconspicuous. Some food provisions were distributed, including a sort of soup, which each group had to heat up.

About the time everyone was getting ready to retire for the night, a senior Russian officer casually wandered into our compound. He was quite jovial as he exchanged pleasantries and backslapping with other soldiers and junior officers. Suddenly his eyes focused on me, and his face grew serious. He turned to me and asked sharply, 'And who are you?' His voice had a menacing undertone that unnerved me, but I managed to answer, giving him my name, nationality, and religious background. '*Ja Neumark, Jewrei z Polszy*,' I answered. I told him the circumstances that had brought me to Vienna and told him I was trying to go back to my home country, Poland.

He listened, ominously silent, and then asked to see my documents. I pulled out my wallet and laid all the relevant papers before him. I did not think about it at the time, but he noticed immediately that I had two sets of documents. One was my Polish ID card under the name Matysiak. The other one was from the Jewish Community Office in Vienna, with my original family name, Neumark. My attempt to explain the two names was cut short. Instead, he wanted to see the rest of the contents of my wallet. Most of it was insignificant except for one piece of paper, which he carefully unfolded. It was a hand-drawn map featuring a winding road, a few localities, a railroad crossing, a wooded area, and a dashed line denoting the front line. The last little circle on the map had the name Rembertow next to it. I quickly explained that it was an old map of an area near Warsaw, drawn before the Warsaw Uprising when I was considering crossing the front lines to the Russian side. But my explanation did not satisfy the officer. He studied my papers, including the map, and then asked if I had worked for the Germans.

'Yes,' I answered, 'I was an electrician at the Neubauer's electrical firm in Vienna.'

'No, no. Did you collaborate with the Germans?' he said.

Finally, I understood what he was getting at. It struck me as preposterous that he would think that I had served the Nazis in the war or that I was now a spy. I restated my background and added proudly that during the war I had been in the Polish Resistance, neither of which impressed him. Only later did I realize that the Russians viewed belonging to the Polish Resistance negatively because part of the Polish Resistance was ultranationalistic and considered Russia an archenemy.

The officer returned my documents, said something to the effect that civilians were not allowed in a military camp area, and then walked away. By that time it was past ten o'clock, and most of the soldiers were already asleep. I too went to sleep.

Soon after I fell asleep I was awakened by a commotion, and a flashlight beam shone directly on me. Someone called out my name. When I opened my eyes there were two soldiers in front of me, rifles mounted with bayonets hanging over their shoulders. 'Come with us,' they ordered. I quickly collected my things and was soon being escorted through the forest. An image of me tied to a tree and blindfolded, facing a firing squad, crossed my mind. Surely they would not kill me, I thought. After all I have been through, and now, with the war at an end, why would they kill me? I panicked that I might die there in the forest without anyone ever knowing why or what had happened to me. With a soldier on each side of me, we walked in silence. When I asked the soldiers what was going to happen to me, the only answer I received was 'Keep going.' After what seemed like an eternity but was probably only about 30 minutes, we reached a country road and stopped. The night seemed strangely still, and very, very dark. I looked at the soldiers, my executioners, and waited for them to reach for their weapons. But, instead, they pointed in the direction that I should go and told me not to show myself again.

Without hesitation, I started to run in the direction they pointed, away from the encampment, not sure if this was some sort of trick or another lucky escape. When I was certain that they were no longer in sight, I stopped to catch my breath. I continued on, although I slackened my pace, and, after about an hour, I noticed a flickering light through the trees, then several lights. I walked faster and soon reached a village. Knocking at a few doors and confronting a few sleepy residents, I encountered a new problem: I was in a place where the residents spoke a language that I could not understand. It was Hungarian, a Finno-Ugric language, not related to any of the three main families of languages, Anglo-Saxon, Romance and Slavic, spoken in Europe. Then, one woman remembered an old man in the village who had served in the Austro-Hungarian army during the First World War and spoke German. She took me to him. He gave me a glass of milk, lodging for the rest of the night, and a promise to have me taken the next morning, by horse and buggy, to the nearest rail station in Bratislava, Slovakia.

A few hours after arriving in Bratislava I boarded a freight train that had a long line of open cars, each loaded with wide, thick boards, pulled by a steam locomotive. Its destination was Katowice, Poland. I was the only 'passenger' with empty space all around me, so I stretched myself out flat on my stomach on top of the boards. It was almost summer and it was a sunny day; I actually enjoyed basking myself in the warm, breezy air. But as the sun started to set and the train accelerated, the cold winds made me shiver. I sought protection from the wind chill but there was none. I decided to move to the front of the train, closer to the engine, so I crawled forward to the edge of the car, crossed to the next car, then to the car in front of it. I continued traversing the cars until the white, warm steam from the locomotive engulfed my cold body. I congratulated myself on having such a brilliant idea. Content, I bathed in the moist, warm air until we arrived at our destination. When I reached the station I noticed that people were looking at me strangely. Ignoring the stares, I went to the bathroom to freshen up after the journey. As I casually turned toward the mirror, I could hardly believe my eyes: I was pitch black! I looked like a chimney sweep.

I spent the night in a Red Cross shelter for homebound repatriates and the next morning set out to reach my goals: Lódz, Warsaw, and Tomaszow. When I arrived in my hometown of Lódz, I realized that at last I would have to confront the reality of learning the fate of my family. The overwhelming feeling of pain in facing this reality could not be lessened by the faint but pleasant memories of my childhood there.

The first place I went to was the Jewish Community Center. The place swarmed with distraught, dazed people who, like myself, were looking for others whom they knew would not be found. The walls were plastered with little notes, scribbled on light and dark pieces of odd-shaped paper, each in different languages, in cursive and print, but all with a common denominator: names in large, bold letters with a plea for news, any news, about their loved ones. The notes gave details of the persons being sought such as their physical description and places where they had last been seen. Some notes had pictures of children, wives, husbands, sometimes an entire family. The saddest notes were those without pictures that ended with 'last seen ...' and a place and a date. It struck me also that many of the notes had signatures and a plea to be contacted, but with no return address or location, just a name. Most people here were just passing through. They had no mailing address, no home, belonged to no community, no city; often they no longer even had a home country.

Through the center I found that Marysia was alive and living in Łódz. When I located her, we embraced warmly. From Marysia I learned that my Aunt Mania had perished in the Warsaw Ghetto and that while Marta survived her encounter with the Gestapo, she died a few months later during the Warsaw uprising under unknown circumstances. But my Uncle Jozef had survived the Łódz Ghetto and was also in Łódz, reunited with his wife, Stenia; I found both of them without difficulty. Wladek, I learned much later, had also died during the Warsaw uprising. As a soldier of the *Miecz i Plug*, he had died in an attack on the German police headquarters in Malachowskiego Square in the first few days of the rebellion. He had proven himself, yet again, a dedicated patriot, a brave warrior, and a hero in the fight against the Nazis. Many years later, Wladek was posthumously awarded several medals for his bravery.

During my stay in Łódz, I learned that my sister Rena may have survived the war. Some concentration camp inmates who knew her in the Łódz Ghetto and were now back in their hometown provided sketchy but encouraging information. The problem now was to find her.

I did not visit the house where I had lived, or my gymnasium, or the park nearby where I used to play with my friends. I was not strong enough.

I decided to spend the next two days in Warsaw. I had become very fond of this city where, in a short 15 months, I had lived through the most momentous and extraordinary experiences of my entire life. I remembered Warsaw as a beautiful city, but for me the attraction of the city was more than its physical beauty; I also felt an emotional attachment. When I stepped out of the main railway station onto the familiar Marszalkowska Street, I felt anguish and sorrow at the sight of the city in ruins. The devastation was absolute. When I had left it a year ago in the very midst of the uprising, it was ablaze and engulfed in a sea of dark smoke, being bombed from the air and systematically burned, block by block, by Feuerwerfer cannons on the ground. I didn't expect that much would be left, yet now, seeing nothing but rows and rows of skeleton walls and piles of rubble several stories high, I could not believe my eyes. The destruction was beyond imagination.

Rebuilding had already begun, however; in fact, it was in full swing. Restoring the transportation system, including clearing the roads and restoring the bridges across the Vistula, had the highest priority. That's why the railway station was functioning and why buses and private cars were offering their services. Thus I was able to get to Praga on the east side of the Vistula, relatively untouched by the uprising, where the Jewish Committee was operating.

As I was standing in line at the information desk, out of the corner of my eye I saw a young woman suddenly jump over a couple of chairs and then I heard my name called out. It was Krysia. We embraced and kissed and held each other for a long, long time, excited and happy to see each other and, above all, overjoyed to know that the other had survived the war. We exchanged a few personal titbits about our current status and whereabouts. She told me that her mother and Henryk, now Krysia's husband, were with her in Warsaw. She also told me apologetically that she had stolen my bicycle, the one I had appropriated from the *Baustelle* and which I had left at my apartment on Kiprow Street in Grochow. She had presented herself to the landlady as my cousin, with a mandate from me to retrieve the bicycle, and the landlady had let her have it. I told Krysia that I now lived in Vienna, and that I had no plans to stay in Poland or, for that matter, any plans for the future, except to find my sister. After a while Krysia was called back to work and we left each other without a proper good-bye, without arranging another meeting, and without exchanging addresses. We both assumed that we'd see each other in a day or two, or a week at most. But that did not happen, because in the excitement of the moment, we forgot to exchange our current last names. I returned to Lódz.

After spending a few more days in Lódz looking, without success, for news about Rena, I went back to Vienna, the only place where I had an address. A few weeks later I left Vienna again to return to Lódz with the hope of finding more information about Rena or at least of gaining some clues on how to continue my search. Before leaving, I sent a letter to my Uncle Enrico in Milan, telling him that I was alone and searching for family members; that I had no plans for the future but wanted to continue my education. I sent the letter to his prewar address not knowing if he was even alive, as during the latter part of the war the Nazis had also occupied most of Italy, including his hometown.

On my return to Lódz a surprise awaited me: while I was back in Vienna, my sister had visited Lódz in search of me. Not finding me there, she went back to her temporary home in a displaced persons camp in northern Germany. No one knew where exactly in Germany she was, but I was now eager to track her down as soon as possible.

I did not intend to go back to Tomaszow. It offered nothing to me now except sad memories and a city without family or friends, dilapidated remnants of the ghetto and the camp. Yet, like a criminal drawn to the scene of his crime, I was pulled back for a last look, perhaps the last one ever. After all, not all the memories were sad: I remembered the many family gatherings for holidays and occasionally for winter or summer breaks and I remembered them as happy times amid warm and loving grandparents, aunts, uncles, and cousins.

From the railway station I went straight to Piekarska Street, the main street of the small Tomaszow Labor Camp, the place where I had planned my escape, where my odyssey into the unknown had started. The area looked like a ghost town. It had almost the same contours as when I had left it, except for the high weeds sprouting from every patch of soil and creeping out of nooks and cracks between the rocks. Everything was still, empty – not a soul in sight. But then I noticed the silhouette of someone sitting on a rock, bent over, his forearm under his chin, motionless, like Rodin's *Thinker*.

As I moved closer I could hardly believe my eyes: it was Ignac! Drawn back to Tomaszow by the same inner need that compelled me to return, we had both arrived at the same place, the cradle of our escape conspiracy, at the very same time. The last time I had heard from Ignac, he was in Riga, almost a year earlier. With tears in our eyes, we embraced. We remained silent for a long, long time, each buried in our own thoughts and memories. In silence, we embraced again. We were both alive!

With our mission to survive accomplished, we pondered what to do next. To start with, we decided that together we would head back to Lódz, now the temporary capital of the country and a center for refugees and survivors. Each of us was hoping against hope to encounter a family member, a lost friend, or a neighbor.

With each passing day we stayed together, Ignac and I began to realize the losses we had both suffered, the ruin that the war had brought about: it not only ruined our past, but also created problems for a new future. The depth of each loss was beyond anyone's ability to comprehend. In the preface to the Polish poet Adam Mickiewicz's epic *Pan Tadeusz*, he wrote, 'Motherland, you are like health, how to prize you only one who has lost you can tell.'

Yet there was no alternative but to face the challenges ahead of us, to start life anew. The question was how. How does one mend something that has been broken into a thousand pieces and where the main, the key, elements have been irretrievably lost? Where does one learn to do this? How does one begin life anew?

I didn't have any idea how to start or what to do next. But two notions for the future began to crystallize. One was to pursue my education as soon as possible, in spite of the almost six-year gap. The second decision was to leave Poland and search for a new homeland. Ignac had arrived at similar conclusions, so once again we joined forces on the road to a new adventure, to a new life, and into a new world.

Before we could start, there were immediate difficulties at hand. In my case it was the task of finding my sister. Similarly, Ignac was looking for his brother Heniek, who, he found out, had settled in Poland in order to finish studying in medicine. After settling some odds and ends in Poland, we embarked on a journey that would keep us together for the next two years, through several countries and many new experiences.

Before leaving Lódz, we were joined by Hela, a young Jewish woman from Germany. She was Roman's friend, and I had known her in wartime Warsaw. She wanted to leave Poland to reach her two sisters in the western hemisphere: one was living in Cuba and the other in South America. She asked us to take her with us, so the three of us went from Poland back to Vienna for a few days' stay. I wanted to say a few good-byes: to Friedl, Marianne, their parents, some neighbors, and a few new friends, such as Ivo Vesby. I also wanted to collect and pack my few worldly possessions, including some that had sentimental value for me: a few photographs, some letters, and remnants of a diary I started writing during the last weeks in Warsaw.

In Vienna I found mail: a letter from my Uncle Enrico. Back at his old home in Milan, he invited me to come and stay with him and offered to help me any way he could but especially with my education. I immediately accepted the offer but explained that first I had to search for Rena, disregarding for now the problems crossing the border into Italy. 'But we'll be there!' I told him in my letter. In my excitement, however, I neglected to mention who or how many 'we' represented.

The three of us spent a few pleasant days in Vienna, mostly resting and visiting the sights of this beautiful city.

Friedl had accompanied us, acting as our guide, whenever she could take time off from work. Then came the last day before moving on and it was time for me to say good-bye. In a way I was sorry to leave Vienna; so little was left of my past and my future was so uncertain.

Now, good-byes are never easy, but there was no good-bye that I can recall, during the war or since, that was more difficult for me than the parting with Friedl. She was a wonderful person and our youthful relationship in this wartorn city was so very special. There were tears, embraces, and kisses, and then more embraces. In silence, we hoped against hope that some day we might see each other again.

Then we were off to Germany. I found Rena in Belsen-Bergen, her last concentration camp and now a displaced persons' (DP) camp. After five years of separation, we almost did not recognize each other. Our meeting was tearful but silent. Later, I found out that of the 20 letters I had thrown into the Lódz Ghetto, 2 were delivered to my parents' home by kind passersby. Rena told me about the excitement and the joy my family had felt and the tears they had cried at the news that I was alive. It was with my sister that I realized the fate of my parents, as Rena was the last one to see them, in Auschwitz.

The four of us, Rena, Hela, Ignac, and I, traveled back to Austria on the way to our final destination, Italy. Slowly and by different means of transport we reached the main passage between the two countries, the Brenner Pass. There we settled in a little hotel and began to develop a strategy on how to cross the border. We made several attempts, which included making an unsuccessful illegal crossing on foot; trying to bribe Italian prisoners of war on their way home to take us along as family; attempting to hide in Allied military trucks but being quickly discovered and put on the ground in the middle of nowhere, in the midst of winter, at an altitude of 5,000 feet; and paying professional Austrian smugglers in advance to help us cross, who then never showed up. In the end, a group of immigrants making an *aliyah*[23] to Palestine brought us to Milan.

It was on a cold February evening at about seven o'clock when the four of us, each loaded with a backpack and with a suitcase in each hand, trotted the short distance between Milan's Stazione Centrale and 27 Via Scarlatti. My uncle's place was in an imposing multistory building, dark gray, with a large entrance gate. The concierge, peeking from behind a glass window on the side of the gate, seemed amazed at the sight of us. I don't think he had ever seen such a ragged group of travelers visiting any of his tenants in this upmarket apartment building, especially not Signor Enrico, a well-to-do bachelor and tenant of some 20 years. But the concierge's bewilderment paled compared to my uncle's expression when he saw the four of us appearing at his door. Four stragglers! Four unexpected guests – two of them total strangers – for an indefinite stay! 'Didn't I invite just *one* nephew?' he seemed to mutter to himself. Nonetheless, he welcomed us warmly.

Exhausted and starving, we got there just in time for a sumptuous, warm, homemade supper. And our appetites were never more ready for it.

After five turbulent years of war, I had reached the calm waters of postwar Italy and a safe haven at my uncle's home. No longer did I need to hide behind someone else's identity. No longer did I need to look over my shoulder in fear of being recognized or ask myself when waking in the morning if I would survive the coming day. The words 'home' and 'security' took on new meanings. For the first time in many years I could begin to think of more than mere survival.

It was here in Italy that I had finally and fully realized that the war had ended, that I had survived, and that I could look to the future.

Epilogue

> The secret city of the 'Aryan' Jews of Warsaw, in 1940–45, was in short a remarkable achievement, made possible by the initiative, courage, and perseverance of the Jews, and the heroic altruism of some Poles ... It casts an unfamiliar light on the Holocaust as a whole and as an excursion into the uncharted continent of evasion as a response to the Holocaust, it is a phenomenon well worth further reflection and study.[24]

In the spring of 1993 I flew to Warsaw to attend the events marking the fiftieth anniversary of the Warsaw Ghetto Uprising. I hoped to reunite with some old wartime friends and comrades; 50 years had passed, and if I didn't see them now it was unlikely that I would ever see them. After I had settled comfortably in my seat in the half-empty plane, however, I realized that there was more on my agenda. For the past few years I had been searching for something else, something whose exact nature had eluded me. But, as I closed my eyes, it finally came to me: I wanted to revisit my past.

Ludwik, my friend from the Tomaszow Ghetto and the Aryan side of Warsaw, awaited me at Okiecie Airport. Older, a little haggard and disoriented, but also, as always, brilliant and warm, he showered me with words of welcome. He had already written to say that, as happy as he would be to see me, he wouldn't invite me to his house.

'I live in the slums,' he wrote. A lawyer by education, a lecturer in history at the Polish Military Academy with the rank of colonel, and now a freelance journalist, he was in poor health and lonely. 'I feel no longer needed by anyone, anywhere,' he said when we reunited. I was saddened and felt as if I was about to lose another old friend. But I insisted on going to his apartment. It was, indeed, very small and modest but neat and cozy. Three of the four walls of his living room were covered with shelves, from the floor to the ceiling, all filled with books; Ludwik was a voracious reader. But, at least in my eyes, the place was no slum; it was Ludwik who saw it through the dark glasses of a sad old man.

In the Victoria Hotel, located in the center of town, where many of the anniversary activities were to be held, hundreds of people milled about in the large, elegant lobby. Outside, Polish and Israeli flags fluttered in the light spring breeze in front of the hotel and around adjoining buildings. I rushed to the tourist desk to see the program. It was packed, morning till evening, for three solid days. Didn't they have lunch breaks in today's Poland, I wondered?

The ceremonies of the next few days were unbelievable: beautiful, well organized, and deeply moving. It was a truly unique experience. A parade of Polish, Israeli, and other dignitaries, including the prime minister and the primate of the Catholic Church of Poland, laid wreaths at the foot of the imposing, 36-foot-high monument to the heroes of the Warsaw Ghetto uprising. A military honor guard stood at each side of the granite monument. There were ceremonies at the Jewish cemetery; a play titled *We, Polish Jews* by Julian Tuwim and Yitzhak Kacenelson was performed by the Kaminska Jewish State Theater of Warsaw; a popular Polish Catholic singer, Slawa Przybylska, presented a program of Yiddish songs at a small 'Hybryd' theatre, near the city center; and there were many other interesting activities. But all these paled in comparison with the culminating event, which was held on the evening of 19 April the anniversary of the start of the uprising in 1943. After sunset, as darkness fell and total silence engulfed Anielewicz Square,[25] hundreds of boy scouts distributed lighted candles to the throng of tens of thousands. We waited in anticipation. The square was then filled with the sound of the Polish army band playing the Polish national

Epilogue

anthem 'Jeszcze Polska Nie Zginela', and then 'Hatikvah', Israel's anthem. City and government officials welcomed us, Prime Minister Yitzhak Rabin spoke in Hebrew, translated into Polish, and Polish President Lech Walesa's words were translated into Hebrew. A choir sang Jewish partisan songs in Yiddish, and finally, the chief rabbi of Israel chanted 'El Malei Rachamim', the prayer for the dead. In the midst of darkness, illuminated by a sea of lit candles held by thousands of people around the ghetto heroes' monument, six columns glowed brightly. It was an unforgettable evening.

In the days that followed, I spent a lot of time by myself, thinking about my youth in wartime Warsaw as a Catholic Pole. I visited the places where I had lived or worked, traveled on trams I used to take, sat at the window in the familiar corner coffee shop at the Polonia Hotel. And then, with plenty of time to spare, I thought of my life after the war: about the places that became my new home, about the many people who had influenced me, and about the major events that had shaped my life.

Once the war was over, reunited with my sister Rena and joined by my friends Ignac and Hela, I settled in Milan, Italy, where Uncle Enrico had been living for a long time. It was February 1946. Determined to continue my education, I enrolled in the electrical engineering department at the renowned Politecnico di Milano. It was a challenging undertaking. Major gaps in my secondary education, language barriers, and constant harassment by the Politecnico's administrators – who demanded that I produce a high-school diploma – were all serious problems. But gradually, with a few sympathetic staff members and generous financial help from Uncle Enrico, the problems were resolved.

About five years later, as I was just one year short of earning an engineering degree, I was offered an opportunity to migrate to the United States and a scholarship to the University of Oklahoma. At first I declined, but I really had no choice: the United Nations Relief and Rehabilitation Administration (the UN's organization aiding refugees) had

203

an agreement with the Italian government that all refugees would find permanent homes elsewhere within five years.

With some trepidation about facing yet another new language and other unknowns, I packed my bags and moved to the United States. I adjusted quickly, though. After all, for me, unknowns were always expected.

After obtaining a B.Sc. degree in electrical engineering from the University of Oklahoma in Norman and a Master of Science degree in physics from the University of California in Los Angeles, I pursued an interesting, productive, and rewarding career in the aerospace industry, working with a variety of advanced technologies and on a number of major defense and space programs. With my wife Irene and our two young daughters, Arianne and Karin, I settled in southern California, where I have lived for more than 50 years.

My sister, Rena, remained in Italy and married. She died in 1998 aged 76. Ignac and Hela, after staying in Italy for about a year, emigrated to Australia.

In the years following the war, I had a persistent desire to reconnect with people who were my old friends, people who had helped me, or people with whom I had crossed paths during the difficult times of the conflict. I felt a special bond with them. I was particularly interested in finding those who had helped me survive – to thank them face to face and, if I could, offer help. Over the years I made an effort to locate them, finding some but not others. I remained in touch with some, such as Ignac, Ludwik, and Krysia, until their deaths, and I am in contact with others, such as Yola, Roman, Stasiek, and Heniek, to this day. My search efforts were not always successful. By the time I located the addresses of some of the people who had helped me, such as Stefan and Zofja Szokalski, it was too late.

Only after the war did I find out from Heniek what happened to the leader of our Akiba group, Yitzhak Rosenblat, the person who had inspired me to take action and thus was instrumental in my survival. Heniek told me that after their arrival at Auschwitz, an SS officer ordered the newly arrived Blizyn men to take off their clothing and began selecting those able to work. All inmates quickly obeyed, except one: Yitzhak. He hesitated, afraid to expose his thinner and shorter left leg, the consequence of the polio he had suffered in his childhood. That hesitation sealed his fate. He was immediately ordered to stand with the condemned. Fully aware of what this meant, he turned briefly to Heniek and said, 'If by chance you see my brother, tell him what happened to me,' and then calmly went to his death.

On my first trip to Vienna after the war, in 1957, I visited Mr Neubauer's electrical firm, now smaller and in a new location. I wanted to tell him my true identity and to inquire about Mrs Follman. While Mr Neubauer pretended to be friendly, it was clear that he felt very uncomfortable, probably wondering what the real purpose of my visit was. In response to my revelation that I was Jewish, he lied shamelessly, saying, 'These questions never mattered to me.' And no, he did not know the whereabouts of Mrs Follman.

To my great regret I never saw Mrs Szewczykowa again. In the mid-1970s, during a trip to Poland with Rena, I sought her out. I had hoped to embrace her and thank her for being such a trusted friend, but it was too late; she had passed on. I still feel guilty for not finding her in time to say thank you. Even though I knew how to find her house, I had never memorized her address, so I could not write to her.

Going on to Warsaw, I looked up all the places where I once had lived and other spots that had special meaning for me. Among others, I went to 37 Osowska Street to visit my old landlords, Helena and Zbig. They and their little house were no longer there, but a neighbor suggested that I check with a lady living nearby who had been their friend. A woman of about 50 answered my knock at the door. She invited me in and was pleasant but informed me that she didn't know what had happened to my former landlords; they had moved away many years earlier. Then I inquired if she knew, by chance, any of their wartime friends, specifically a young and pretty girl, a niece of the local priest. The lady looked at me, opened her mouth, and froze. She almost fell off the chair. 'But this must be me!' Zosia exclaimed.

Slowly, the images of a long lost past came to life. She remembered me; she remembered our furtive rendezvous in the park; she remembered the Easter dinner party at our little home and the breakfast the following morning at the parish, after I took her home. We tried to catch up on each other's lives during the past 30-plus years. During our conversation, one question did not leave my mind: Did the landlords, or she or other neighbors, know that I was a Jew in hiding? 'Did you talk about the Jews?' I asked. 'Did you wonder about me or anyone else who was new to the neighborhood, who he or she might be?' Zosia thought for a while and then answered, 'I think that we had a suspicion, but we were not sure. We were young and did not much think about it; it did not concern us and besides, we had so many worries of our own. As to the Jews, we did not fully realize what was happening to them,' she added apologetically.

Rena and I also visited my other home in Grochow, on Kiprow Street, where we found the husband of my former landlady at home. He knew all about the story of the grenades and the revolver in the oven; in fact, he told us, 'The whole neighborhood knew about it!' The one thing he did not know was that while he had been in a prisoner-of-war camp, his wife, unbeknown to her, had been harboring a Jew.

My worries about leaving the grenades in the oven were somewhat mitigated by knowing that good housekeepers like my landlady always clear an oven before lighting it.

During one of my trips to Europe, I traveled to Germany to find Paul Biebow, the German who had befriended me in Ujazd, on my first job outside the Tomaszow Ghetto. All I knew was his full name and that he had lived somewhere near Lübeck, a northern port city. I had remembered this from the sender address on the food package he had courageously brought to me one Christmas when I was in the ghetto. I went to Lübeck and for several days looked up the name 'Biebow'

in telephone directories for every town near Lübeck; I made a
list during each day and in the evenings I made phone calls.
The responses varied from a polite 'No, you've got the wrong
party,' to an angry and suspicious 'The war is over. There are
no more Nazis here!'

But one day, all that tedious work paid off. A young man
thought I might be looking for his grandfather. He referred
me to his father, Heinrich Biebow, living on the family farm
about 50 kilometers south of Lübeck. I reached Heinrich that
same evening. For Paul, I had come too late; he had died a few
years earlier. Heinrich, a man of my own age, was indeed the
one who had served as a soldier on the Russian front and was
the son Paul had told me about in Ujazd, on the construction
site where we had met. I invited Heinrich and his wife to
lunch at the Stella Hotel, where I stayed, and offered them
some small gifts I had brought from Italy as a token of appre-
ciation for his father's kindness. But I also wanted to find out
more about this gentle, humane man. I wanted to understand
what had motivated him to be so kind to a young stranger, in
such contrast to his comrades; I wanted to learn what his
attitude had been toward Jews, toward the Nazis, and toward
the war.

First the son gave me his father's picture, taken in Ujazd.
Then we talked about our families and our present lives.
Finally we turned to his father. He told me that Paul had never
wanted to work with the Nazis; in fact his political convictions
were such that he had ended up in jail a couple of times. He
had not volunteered for the paramilitary service in Org. Todt
but was drafted. The son also told me that he and his father
had never agreed politically. What he did not tell me, but
what was easy to guess, was that he, Heinrich, was still an
unrepentant Nazi. Later we exchanged a couple of Christmas
cards. I attached a gift check to one card; it was cashed but I
never received any acknowledgment. Then our brief correspondence stopped. I suppose neither of us felt comfortable
keeping in contact.

Ignac and I continued to be good friends until his passing

in 2000. After a year of engineering studies in Italy, Ignac continued his education in this and other fields, in Australia. There he embarked on several remarkable careers. First he became an engineer, then a physicist, then a university lecturer, and finally a practicing medical doctor. In 1993 Ignac wrote his memoir, in which he describes our joint planning and preparation for escape from the Tomaszow Labor Camp, his and Stasiek's escape from the Blizyn concentration camp, and their struggles for survival in Warsaw and Riga.[26] The book credits my trailblazing escape and help in Warsaw as the key to his and Stasiek's survival. In his book as well as on several occasions before, Ignac told me that the letter I sent to him from Warsaw, while he was still in Blizyn, was absolutely critical to his survival. The letter said, 'in Warsaw, one CAN survive' and implored him 'to come immediately' with the word 'immediately' underlined. He said that the letter had given him the necessary encouragement and the final impulse to escape from the camp. Perhaps most importantly, it provided him with an address on the Aryan side.

Ignac wrote his book in a great hurry because he was aware of his deteriorating health: he died in Australia after suffering for several years from Lou Gehrig's disease.

Krysia and I lost track of each other during the Warsaw uprising: because she was a woman, she had been allowed to remain in occupied Poland, while I and all other young males were taken to camps in Germany. After the war, we accidentally found each other at the Jewish Committee headquarters in the Warsaw suburb of Praga, and our joy at finding each other alive and whole was beyond description. To find a loved one alive and well in this topsy-turvy, confused situation was a miracle. But after our encounter in Praga, I lost track of Krysia, because in the excitement of having found each other we forgot to exchange our new names and addresses. In the Underground I knew only her first name, Krysia; she in turn, knew my last name as Matysiak, a name I had shed the day the war ended. Thus we lost each other.

Then one day, at a gathering of survivors in Los Angeles, I

mentioned Krysia's name to some people, and one of them said, 'I know her; her last name is Mucznik.' He had heard that she now lived in Switzerland. I tracked her down, and in the late 1980s I flew to Zurich to meet with her again. Several visits and contacts by correspondence and telephone followed.

I wish I could tell Krysia's story here – her many heroic deeds during the war and her postwar life – but I don't know it. She wouldn't tell it to me. Only now and then would she drop a few titbits. But I do know that the years after the war were sad ones for her. She and her husband stayed in Poland till the early 1970s, while most of their friends had already left during the first years after the war. When they finally arrived in the West, most of their friends were already well settled and had become professionals or achieved success in various endeavors. Krysia and her husband felt as though they had missed the boat.

Krysia wanted to be remembered the way she was during the war years: young, pretty, and full of vitality; those were her happy years. Her past was made up of heroic deeds but her present consisted only of images of that past, with little hope for a better future; at least, that was how she felt. During my visits I found her sad and depressed, with little will to live. Although she had received the Partisan Cross from the Polish government, she felt abandoned and forgotten by her comrades from the Underground, the organization she had served so faithfully and courageously.

Krysia and I remained close friends, joined by that special bond, until her death in Zurich in 1999.

I searched for the Szokalski family from the time the war ended, but it was not easy to find them. Because they had signed the *Volksdeutsche* list, they chose to – or had to – leave their hometown of Tomaszow and left no forwarding address. I wrote to the old address but the owners did not answer my letters. On my trip to Poland in the mid-1970s, I visited several neighbors and former neighbors – but no one knew what had happened to them or their whereabouts. When finally I did discover their new home, in 1993, I found only Lucja, the daughter.

It was while on a visit to Warsaw. I remembered that the Szokalski family had been Protestants, and that gave me a clue to tracking them down. The next morning I took the first train to Tomaszow and went straight to the only Protestant church in town. The bishop was a young man, new to the parish, and he had no information about the Szokalskis but he gave me the names of the few remaining 'old-timers' in the church who might remember them. I visited each one on the list. At my fifth contact I had a stroke of luck; I found a man who knew that Lucja had moved to Bytom. I went straight to the post/telephone office and found her telephone number. Lucja herself answered the phone.

'Do you remember a young boy whom you and your parents harbored in your garden in 1943?' I asked.

'Of course I remember! Pan Zenon!' she exclaimed. 'We often wondered what happened to you. We did get a couple of postcards, but then we lost track of you.' I told her I was coming to visit her today, 'right now', but she objected.

'Oh, my God! No, not today! No! No! My hair is in such a mess. I have to go to the beauty parlor first. You can come tomorrow at the earliest,' she responded. But I would not hear of it. Half an hour later I was on a bus to Bytom. The trip took four and a half hours and it was dark when I arrived. With my heart pounding and a bouquet of 12 red roses in my hand, I reached her ground-floor, one-bedroom apartment. When we saw each other we both had tears in our eyes. We embraced. Her hair looked just fine!

After a modest dinner, we chatted and reminisced. It was not easy. We had to revisit the most difficult events of our lives and cover half a century's worth of events. She told me of her family's dilemma at the war's end: the Poles considered them traitors because they had signed the *Volksdeutsche* list, and they feared retribution, especially by their neighbors. On the other hand, they did not want to follow the defeated German Army into Germany, for they felt Poland was their homeland.

Without a clear destination they abandoned their city of birth, leaving behind their home, their business and most of their possessions. Finally, they settled in Bytom, a mining city in southeast Poland, near where the German border had been before the war and where many other German nationals and ethnic Germans lived.

Happy, finally, to have reunited with Lucja, I started a friendly correspondence with her and offered her financial help. In one of her first letters to me, Lucja wrote that she was surprised when she received the first check: 'I did not think that you really meant it,' showing also some embarrassment.

'But it was my mother who helped you, not me,' she protested. In another letter, with a touch of shyness and a bit of coyness, she wanted to know, 'Does your wife know about the checks you are sending me?'

Shortly after my return home I applied to Yad Vashem, via the local Israeli consulate, to list the Szokalski family as 'Righteous Among the Nations'. When I wrote to Lucja about it, she first sidestepped the issue and then subtly indicated opposition to it. This was not necessarily out of modesty. I don't know for sure, but my guess is that she did not want her friends and neighbors to know that her family had hidden a Jew during the war and she did not want the expected publicity. This need to hide one's help and kindness to Jews during the war was not a common one, but neither was it unique. I have heard of several similar cases. It's a sad commentary on the times we live in.

Although during my trip to Poland in 1993 I did not meet up with any of my comrades from the wartime Underground, this visit was nonetheless crowned by my witnessing the spectacular commemoration of the Warsaw Ghetto uprising and, more importantly, my locating Lucja Szokalska.

After a 12-day stay in Poland my journey came to an end and I departed for home. Ludwik accompanied me to Okecie Airport, where we had lunch, wrote a couple of postcards to people we knew, and said several good-byes. Then, with his

211

head bowed, Ludwik turned around and left. But a few minutes later Ludwik, a bit out of breath, caught up with me while I was standing in the departure line.

'One last good-bye, Zenek. One last embrace,' and he kissed me on both cheeks. Sadly, it was our last good-bye. Ludwik died in 1998, before I had a chance to visit him again.

Friedl passed away in Vienna on 1 October 2002. Her daughter Gabi notifying me of her passing in a brief note. Anticipating her demise, Friedl must have given her daughter my address with the request that she notify me. Her note ended with 'In my Mother's name …'

I lost contact with Marianne in the late 1990s. One day my phone calls were no longer answered, and even our traditional exchange of letters before Christmas stopped.

I often find myself thinking about the human bonds that I formed during the war years: with Lucja and Ludwik, with Krysia and Paul, with Roman and Wladek, and with Ignac, Stasiek, Kuba, and Friedl. There were many others, some whose names I no longer remember. These bonds were truly unique – timeless and unbreakable. They were unlike any friendships or relationships I had had before the war or have experienced since. Even those based on occasional or brief association were as solid as the Rock of Gibraltar.

Escape from Nazi confinement in ghettos or camps was a viable option for only a few, but those who did escape had a much better chance of survival than those who remained in confinement. Of my own family and friends who escaped to the Aryan side of Warsaw – a group of about 20 – 17 succeeded in surviving the war. Of the three who did not, Aunt Mania, pursued by blackmailers, returned to the ghetto where she had perished; Adas, tired of a life in hiding, joined the Hotel Polski 'exchange' trap and went on a journey from which he did not return; and my cousin Marta died during the Warsaw Uprising in August 1944.

This eyewitness account is written to share the story of my escape from a Nazi Labor Camp and life with false Aryan papers, first in Nazi-occupied Warsaw and later in Vienna. In the main, it describes the unique challenges and perils faced by those who chose the path of escape and became fugitives, under conditions where both the fugitives and those helping them faced the punishment of death.

Above all, this memoir is meant to honor the unparalleled courage and sacrifice of several young men and women I met in the Polish and Jewish Resistance, and to pay tribute to the many decent and courageous individuals – Jews, Poles, and even some Germans – who at a great risk to their own lives and the lives of their families, helped others and me to survive.

Jerusalem, 29 December 1993

Mr. Zenon Neumark
1953 Westridge Ter.
Los Angeles, CA. 90049
U.S.A.

Dear Mr. Neumark,

RE: Szokalska, Lucja & parents - (8291)
===

We acknowledge with thanks the receipt of your letter, dated
15.10.1993.

This file will be placed on the agenda of the Commission for
the Designation of the Righteous. Please take into consideration
that there is quite a number of files waiting in line to be
examined by the Commission, but we shall do our best to expedite
this matter.

Thanking you for your cooperation.

Sincerely yours,

Dept. for the Righteous

Case-3/m.p./s.o./

1

Letter from Yad Vashem in response to author's request to designate Lucja Szokalska and her parents as Righteous Among Nations

Notes

1. Originally, the term Aryan was one of the Nazi 'racial' definitions to distinguish the Germans from the Jews. During the war, it connoted all non-Jews (e.g. Poles) and all non-Jewish objects (e.g., city districts, appearance, documents). It is used here, and throughout the text, in the latter sense.
2. Gunnar S. Paulsson, *Secret City: The Hidden Jews of Warsaw, 1940–1945* (New Haven, CT: Yale University Press, 2002).
3. Leo Cooper, *In the Shadow of the Polish Eagle* (New York: Palgrave Publishers, 2000).
4. *Volksdeutsche* were Polish by birth and citizenship but were of German descent; predominantly Protestant. Often, at home, they spoke German.
5. Organization Todt was the largest construction and armament company in Germany; part of the Ministry of Armament. It was responsible for providing construction labor and supplies for the German Army.
6. They remained in Russia for part of the war, later spending some time in Japan, Burma, and India. Finally, towards the end of the war, they migrated to Palestine.
7. The group was named after a Rabbi and a spiritual leader during the Bar Kochba revolt in the second century CE. Akiba was also the name of a Zionist organization.
8. This was the Polish name for someone from the Slesien, a region in central Europe which, before the war, extended across both Polish and German territory.
9. I ran into Felek in Warsaw; he successfully escaped using this certificate.
10. Vladka Meed, *On Both Sides of the Wall. Memoirs from the Warsaw Ghetto* (New York: Holocaust Library, 1979).
11. Jacob Celemenski, *Elegy for My People* (Melbourne, Australia: The Jacob Celemenski Memorial Trust 2000; original, in Yiddish, published in 1963.
12. Yitzhak Zuckerman, *A Surplus of Memory: Chronicle of the Warsaw Ghetto Uprising* (Oxford: University of California Press, 1993).
13. At the time, such pills were easily obtainable and most of us carried them in the event we were captured by the Germans.
14. After the war, Ignacy Loga-Sowinski became the president of all labor unions in Poland.
15. Mr Wrona was supposed to deliver the vaccines by throwing the package over the barbed wire fence at night to his confidant inside the camp. Whether he did it or not or whether the right man received it or not, I never knew. I know only that Tetka never received them and died shortly afterwards.
16. I learned later that the information regarding my sister was incorrect. Rena ran a lending library in her home, a perfect occupation for her as she had always loved books.
17. I learned later that one of the sisters was a professional nurse and was jailed for performing an illegal abortion.
18. It was from my Aunt Stenia that I later found out that the Ukrainian was indeed

my former teacher at Schwajcera. When we met, he was using false ID papers, just as I was, because the Nazis were persecuting him for not signing a pro-Nazi Ukrainian list and because he too was a member of the Polish Underground. She also told me that all three, my former teacher and the two sisters, knew that I was a Jew and that they genuinely wanted to help me.

19. The former Soviet Officer and I exchanged arguments in a long and animated discussion, all in Russian. In spite of disagreements, I was pleased with myself. I was pleasantly surprised at how quickly and conveniently the Russian language came back to me. I almost wanted to pat myself on the back. But it would have been premature because that feeling of contentment was quickly crushed. Before saying good-bye to each other, my Russian friend looked at me with a twinkle of satisfaction in his eyes and said 'I never realized how much Polish I understand!'

20. When, in 1945, I did return to Warsaw, I rushed to Kiprow Street to check on my landlady and her house, to see if there had been an explosion. My landlady was not home but the house, luckily, was still there.

21. According to Paulsson, *Secret City*, 60,000 of Warsaw's residents, both combatants and young civilians like myself who passed through Pruszkow, ended up in Auschwitz and similar camps.

22. Popular ruler of the dual monarchy of Austria-Hungary from 1848–1916.

23. Denotes immigration of Jews to the Holy Land.

24. Paulsson, *Secret City*.

25. Named after Mordechai Anielewicz, the 23-year-old head of the ZOB and commander of the Warsaw Ghetto Uprising.

26. Ignatius Bierzynski Burnett, *In the Footsteps of Memory* (Camberwell, Victoria, Australia: Morescope Publishing, 1993).

The Library of Holocaust Testimonies

Through Blood and Tears:
Surviving Hitler and Stalin
Henry Skorr

Henry Skorr has told his story, in a series of interviews conducted by Ivan Sokolov, in an effort to preserve the memory of those he loved, and a world that no longer exists. Henry takes the reader from his childhood in Kalisz, Poland, through the horrors of the Nazi occupation, the insanity and brutality of the Soviet system, the corruption of the newly re-formed Poland, and finally to the shores of Israel. The main part of the story deals with his time in the Soviet Union, providing the reader with a rare insight into the plight of Polish-Jewish refugees, as well as native Russians, during the war years. The memoir adds an important voice to the catalogue of survivors' tales; with courage and honesty, Henry Skorr articulately presents us with the Soviet experience, giving voice to the thousands who fled east and the millions he found there.

February 2006, 384 pages
ISBN 0 85303 477 X £14.95/$24.00

The Library of Holocaust Testimonies

Trust and Deceit: A Tale of Survival in Slovakia and Hungary, 1939–1945
Gerta Vrbová

This autobiography describes the dramatic events in Slovakia and Hungary between 1939 and 1945 seen through the eyes of a Jewish child/teenager, Gerti. The rise of fascism in Slovakia destroyed the peaceful co-existence of the Jews with their Slovak neighbours and demoralized both groups. The threat of deportation of Jews from Slovakia to Auschwitz forced Gerti and her parents to flee to Hungary, where deportations of Jews to Auschwitz had not yet begun. There the family lived under an assumed identity. The dangers and isolation associated with this existence plunged Gerti into depression and forced her to learn skills of deception to survive. As Hitler's grip on Hungary tightened and the dangers for Jews in Hungary increased, Gerti's father was arrested. Gerti and her mother had to flee to Slovakia in the spring of 1944, where they assumed yet further false identities. During the summer of 1944 Gerti met her childhood friend Walter (Rudi Vrba), who had escaped from Auschwitz and told Gerti about his first-hand experience of witnessing the mass murders there. With time the remaining few Jews in Slovakia were rounded up. Gerti and her mother were denounced and taken to the Gestapo. The knowledge of the death factories waiting for them encouraged Gerti to take a serious risk and escape. Her mother, however, gave up hope and stayed to perish in a concentration camp. Gerti, then on her own, returned to Budapest and lived through the round up of Jews and the siege, assuming the identity of a Hungarian refugee from Russian-occupied Hungary. To survive she had to use her hard-learned skills in assessing who she could trust and whom she had to deceive.

April 2006, 182 pages
ISBN 0 85303 630 6   £14.50/$20.00

The Library of Holocaust Testimonies

A Village Named Dowgalishok:
The Massacre at Radun and Eishishok
Avraham Aviel

This is the unique and true story of a young boy, skilfully describing the small Jewish agricultural village of Dowgalishok in eastern Poland (modern-day Belarus) and its neighbouring towns of Radun and Eishishok. With a loving eye for detail the Jewish atmosphere is brought to life along with the village inhabitants, from the pastoral days before the Second World War to its sudden destruction by the Nazi regime.

The first part of the book is a vivid description of Yiddish-kite that has vanished forever. The second part is a bleak testimony of a survivor of the ghetto and the slaughter beside the terrible death pit outside Radun. The third and last part of the book is the story of twenty-six months of escape and struggle for life, first in the woods among farmers and later on as a partisan in the nearby ancient forest.

The author tells his story in a simple and fluent style, creating both a personal testimony and a historical document. The Hebrew edition of the book was well received by many critics, both in Israel and around the world, for its deeply moving quality as well as for its documental value as a record of one of the darkest chapters of mankind.

June 2006, 300 pages
ISBN 0 85303 583 0 £14.50/$19.50

The Library of Holocaust Testimonies

Scorched
Irit Amiel
Translated from the Hebrew by Riva Rubin

The heroes of the stories in this book are people who in the hell of the Holocaust were doomed for life, people who speak only with reluctance about their past, about the heavy baggage of their life's experiences. Being a witness, Irit Amiel uses the memories of her childhood friends and translates the long silences of people living in the Israeli melting pot into testimony. The stories are written in a simple and restrained way, but the voices coming out touch the most profound human feelings. Each story is powerful and often painful, but is imbued with a sense of hope.

'There is immediacy and a strength to each of these stories that makes it clear just how much they derive from real experience. The emphasis is on individuals, and on their characters. Each person whose story Irit Amiel tells lives again in these pages.'
From the Foreword by Sir Martin Gilbert

September 2006, 94 pages
ISBN 0 85303 634 9 £12.50/$19.50

The Library of Holocaust Testimonies

My Own Vineyard:
A Jewish Family in Krakow
Between the Wars

Miriam Akavia

This rich novel, in the best tradition of family sagas, tells the story of three generations of a Jewish family in Krakow, from the beginning of the twentieth century to the eve of the German occupation of Poland in September 1939. The story of this large, middle-class Jewish family is also the story of a deeply-rooted Jewish community and its considerable cultural and material achievements, until disaster strikes and it is wiped off the face of the earth.

At the beginning of the century, Krakow was under Austrian rule. The mother of the family died, leaving a husband and eight children. A different destiny awaited each of the children, each story reflecting the options which faced Polish Jews at that time. With the outbreak of the First World War, the eldest son joined the army and was sent to the Italian front. He returned a broken man, and died shortly afterwards. The second son married happily, became a successful lumber merchant and a paterfamilias. He veered between Jewish and European culture and regarded Poland as his homeland. One of the sisters, a natural rebel, fell in love with a Polish non-Jew. When he abandoned her, she became a Zionist and emigrated to Eretz Israel. Her older sister was happily married to an old-style religious Jew. Another sister married an assimilated Jew and was uncertain as to her national identity, while the fourth fell in love with a communist. Their prosperous brother had three children – two daughters and a son – who enjoyed life in independent Poland between the wars. When the Germans invaded Poland, the family missed the last train out and with it the chance to be saved. Most of the family perished in the Holocaust.

September 2006, 340 pages
ISBN 0 85303 519 9 £14.50/$23.50

The Library of Holocaust Testimonies

In the Shadow of Destruction: Recollections of Transnistria and Illegal Immigration to Eretz Israel, 1941–1947
Josef Govrin

Translated from the Hebrew original, *Be-Tzel ha-Avadon*, published by Beit Lohamei Haghetaot Press, 1999, in collaboration with Yad Vashem, Jerusalem, and the Center of Research of Romanian Jewry, the Hebrew University of Jerusalem.

This book is a personal account of a young boy's struggle to survive the Holocaust in Transnistria. The descriptions are presented against the background of contemporary events, combining personal recollections with an historic overview, before, during and after the Holocaust.

November 2006, 116 pages
ISBN 0 85303 643 8 £16.50/$25.00

The Library of Holocaust Testimonies

Sentenced to Life: The Story of a Survivor of the Lahwah Ghetto
Kopel Kolpanitzky
Translated from the Hebrew by Zvi Shulman

Kopel Kolpanitzky grew up in Lahwah, Byelorussia. His entire family was murdered in the Lahwah ghetto uprising against the Nazis, except for his father, who had previously been imprisoned by the Soviets. Living in the forests, he joined a partisan unit and then fought as a soldier in the Red Army. After the war he left the army and in trying to reach Eretz Yisrael almost reached the shores of Palestine before the ship he was on was stopped by the British and its passengers sent to a camp in Cyprus. A year later he finally arrived in Eretz Yisrael just before Israel's independence. He served in the Israel Defence Forces and later entered into business with his father, who had joined him in Israel in the early 1950s.

November 2006, 288 pages
ISBN 0 85303 695 0   £14.50/$23.50

The Library of Holocaust Testimonies

In Hiding
Benno Benninga with Bill Halstead

In Hiding relates the story of a Jewish family of four when a
Dutch couple offered to hide them from Nazi atrocities
during the Second World War. The couple agreed that they
would conceal this family for a large sum of money, thinking that the war would soon end. When it appeared that
the war would last much longer than first anticipated, the
hostess grudgingly kept the foursome hidden, but threatened and physically and mentally abused them. Using his
father's detailed journal and his own vivid memories,
Benno Benninga relates the cruelty that this family had to
endure, not from the Nazis directly, but from their own
neighbors during more than two years of persecution.

November 2006, 180 pages
ISBN 0 85303 632 2 £14.50/$23.50

Hiding in the Open

228

Notes

229

Hiding in the Open

Notes